# APPLYING PSYCHOLOGY

## to early child development

### CARA FLANAGAN

Series Editor: ROB McILVEEN

## Hodder & Stoughton

A MEMBER OF THE HODDER HEADLINE GROUP

# DEDICATION

This book is dedicated to those who matter most: Rob, Pip, Jack and Rosie.

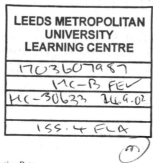

British Library Cataloguing in Publication Data

Flanagan, Cara
  Applying Psychology to Early Child
  Development. – (Applying Psychology
  to... Series)
  I. Title II. Series
  155.4

ISBN 0 340 64392 7

First published 1996
Impression number    10  9  8  7  6  5  4  3  2
Year                 1999 1998 1997

Typeset by Transet Ltd, Coventry, England.
Printed in Great Britain for Hodder & Stoughton Educational, a division of Hodder Headline Plc, 338 Euston Road, London NW1 3BH by Redwood Books, Trowbridge, Wilts

# CONTENTS

Starting from the beginning; pre-natal influences; low birth-weight babies and SIDS; avoiding negative outcomes; temperament; birth and bonding; choosing a name
**Focus on...** smoking; 'hothouse' babies; breastfeeding. **Psychological perspectives:** nature and nurture

What can newborn infants sense and perceive? why do infants roll off sofas? some other innate abilities; critical or sensitive periods; theories of perceptual development: Piaget's theory, nature versus nurture, enrichment versus differentiation
**Focus on...** squint eyesight. **Psychological perspectives:** the cognitive perspective. **Research techniques:** conducting research with infants

Bonding; separation anxiety; cognitive maturity; the ethological view; other functions of attachment; early theories of attachment: behaviourist and Freudian views; Bowlby's theory of attachment; criticisms of Bowlby's views
**Focus on...** transitional objects. **Psychological perspectives:** the ethological perspective; the psychodynamic perspective. **Research techniques:** measuring attachment

Stages of language acquisition: first words, two-word utterances (grammatical speech); theories of language: learning theory, nativist theory, functional theories, interactionist theories, conclusion; cognitive and linguistic development
**Focus on...** language acquisition in deaf children. **Psychological perspectives:** the behaviourist perspective

Nature versus nurture; speeding up cognitive development: the evidence;

increasing intelligence: the evidence; Piaget's theory of cognitive development; Vygotsky's theory of cognitive development; Bruner's theory of cognitive development

**Focus on...** compensatory programmes. **Research techniques:** comparing nature and nurture; assessing intelligence in early childhood; interviewing children

Enculturation; gender development; learning sex-appropriate behaviours; healthy gender stereotypes; the self-concept: self-development; self-recognition; other self-concepts

**Focus on...** homosexuality; a cross-cultural view of the self-concept. **Psychological perspectives:** the sociocultural perspective; the biological perspective; the humanist perspective

Parenting style; reward and punishment; teaching moral behaviour; parents and prejudice; parents and aggressiveness; parents and cognitive development; parents and personality; learning to become a parent

**Psychological theories:** prosocial or moral development; the development of aggression

Attachment and loss; the effects of separation; different kinds of separation; long-term effects; other childhood experiences of separation: hospitalisation, fostering, divorce, parental death, adoption, neo-natal special care

**Focus on...** childcare provision for parents who work. **Research techniques:** studying children over time

Siblings and ordinal position effects; grandparents; friends: stages of friendship, popularity; play: the value of play, encouraging play

**Focus on...** only children (singletons). **Psychological theories:** play

What are the 'media'? how the media exert their influence; stereotypes; counter-stereotypes; displacement effect; social deprivation; stimulation hypothesis; is television a good or bad thing?

**Focus on...** television violence and aggression

Causes of disability; sensory impairment: hearing impairment and deafness, visual impairment and blindness; genetic conditions: Down's syndrome, Fragile-X, Duchenne muscular dystrophy (DMD), other inherited disorders, phenylketonuria (PKU) and hyperthroidism; disabilities which develop pre- or perinatally: spina bifida, cerebral palsy; chronic problems with onset during childhood: diabetes, asthma, eczema and epilepsy; childhood illness and injury

**Focus on...** a personal success story; genetic counselling; coping with disability

Particular psychological disabilities: mental retardation; specific learning difficulties: autism, attention-deficit hyperactivity disorder, conduct disorder (delinquency), bullying; emotional disorders; habit and eating disorders: bedwetting, stuttering, obesity, anorexia and bulimia; mental illness; special talents

**Focus on...** labelling; therapeutic techniques

Deprivation and privation; institutional care; managing institutional care; children reared in isolation; physical under-development

**Focus on...** effects of privation - attachment disorder; effects of privation - child abuse

# PREFACE

The aim of this book is to examine some of the ways in which the discipline of psychology can be applied to an understanding of early child development. The book consists of three main parts, each of which represents a way of approaching this area of psychological concern.

One approach that psychologists have taken is to divide life into stages or phases. In the first part of this book (**Stages of Development**), we will look at some of the things psychological theory and research have told us about the stages through which a child passes on its way to adolescence.

Another way to look at development is in terms of different experiential rather than maturational factors which influence a child's development. Unlike the first part, the second part of this book (**Influences on Development**) is not concerned with identifying changes which occur at particular ages. Instead, Part 2 will attempt to describe the ways in which psychological theory and research have contributed to our understanding of how certain social factors, such as parents and the media, can influence a child's development.

Parts 1 and 2 are concerned with what might be described as 'typical' early child development. In the final part of this book (**Atypical Development**) we will look at early child development and describe how we can apply a knowledge of psychology to both the understanding of atypical development and the ways in which parents and others can be helped to cope with a child that has developed atypically.

# ACKNOWLEDGEMENTS

I would like to thank Rob McIlveen for his excellent advice and guidance throughout the project.

# Stages of Development

## STAGE THEORIES

One way to approach the study of development is to divide life into stages or phases. There are four critical features of such stage theories:

1 They are based on qualitative changes in behaviour over time and age.
2 They describe an invariant sequence of development. The rate may differ between individuals, but the order is always the same.
3 Each stage has structural cohesiveness; in other words, the description of behaviour within each stage should be consistent and coherent.
4 Stages form a hierarchy because each subsequent stage in some way builds upon earlier ones.

The best-known examples of stage theories are Freud's psychosexual stages (see page 39) and Piaget's stages of cognitive development (see page 67). All stage theories rely on the concept of maturation, a biological process which is modified by experience. Stage theories are useful for identifying developmental delays and thus locating the cause of such a delay, such as deafness or mental retardation. However, it is important not to regard stages as too fixed, and a more recent development has been to use the term 'levels' because it has a less definite connotation.

The first five chapters of this book look at the key events during each of the early stages. In Chapter 1, we look at pregnancy and, most importantly, at what parents can do to maximise their infant's potential. Chapter 2, on early infancy, focuses on perceptual development as the most outstanding aspect of development in this stage. The infant is also forming emotional bonds during this period, but the process becomes most marked in the second half of the first year. Chapter 3 explores this stage of attachment and separation anxiety.

During the whole of the first year, the infant has been absorbing linguistic information and practising sounds and, finally, first words are produced around the child's first birthday. The process of language acquisition is described in Chapter 4. Finally, Chapter 5 looks at cognitive development, another process which has been on-going since the moment of conception but which is most accessible for study in the pre-school period.

**Box 1.1** A generalised stage theory of childhood

| STAGE/AGE (APPROX.) | KEY CHANGES |
|---|---|
| **Pre-natal**<br>Conception to 280 days | Development is governed largely by biological processes, though the infant's interaction with the environment is also significant. |
| **Early infancy**<br>0 to 6 months | Infants are born with some abilities. However, what they can do and understand is small in comparison to what they learn during this period. They must begin to make sense of the vast amount of incoming sensory data and learn to co-ordinate their bodies. Emotional development also begins with early bonding and somewhat indiscriminate attachments; they show no separation anxiety. |
| **Late infancy**<br>6 months to 1/1½ years | During the second half of the first year, infants make some important cognitive leaps. They understand object permanence and form specific attachments, both of which are associated with developing cognitive schema, which allow predictions to be made about the world. Infants can sit up and therefore manipulate things more easily; they become mobile and make various pre-linguistic vocalisations, such as babbling and echolalia. |
| **The end of infancy**<br>1 to 2 years | Infancy 'officially' ends with the onset of speech. The ability to use language changes the way children interact with the world, socially and cognitively. Children also start to walk, to enter into fantasy and role-related play, to recognise themselves and develop fine motor control for things like drawing, jigsaw puzzles and building towers from bricks. |
| **Pre- school**<br>2 to 5 years | Cognitively, children begin to think symbolically rather than in terms of physical representations. This might be either a cause or an effect of having language. Socially, children form their first friendships; and play is initially 'parallel' with increasing amounts of interaction. During this period, they develop a sense of a separate self and gender and increase their linguistic and cognitive competence in areas such as counting, learning songs and rhymes, and asking questions about the world around them. |
| **Middle childhood**<br>5 to 7 years | Children will have started school and will be learning to read and write. The school experience is also a social one, and children are much influenced by peer norms. Their thinking is still rather self-centred (egocentric), and their moral sense is tied to simple notions of right and wrong rather than more complex considerations. |

*Early Childhood* (bracket spanning Pre-natal through Pre-school)

**Box 1.1**   A generalised stage theory of childhood *(continued)*

| | |
|---|---|
| **Late childhood**<br>7 to 13/14 years<br>(adolescence) | During the primary school period, children's thinking becomes more logical and adult-like. This means they can go beyond simple arithmetic and they may learn    the basics of scientific reasoning. Their play now often involves rules, and they are beginning to understand other's feelings. They are still more concerned with what the peer group and adults regard as appropriate, rather than making self-determined choices. |

*chapter one*

# THE PREGNANT PARENTS

## CHAPTER OVERVIEW

In the past, it was thought that the foetus resided in a relatively impregnable fortress and that the foetal nervous system was insufficiently developed to register experience. Recent research has shown that the opposite is a more accurate picture: virtually everything a pregnant woman experiences will in some way be passed on to her highly sensitive infant. This chapter outlines the short- and long-term effects of such influences as drugs, nutrition, hormones and smoking. Possible outcomes include complications of pregnancy, low birth-weight, physical and cognitive impairment, and sudden infant death syndrome (SIDS). In this chapter, we will also discuss issues related to birth, breastfeeding and 'hothousing'.

## STARTING FROM THE BEGINNING

When we consider the effects of experience, as opposed to 'nature', we should include events before birth and even before the moment of conception. For example, sperm cells may have been damaged by radiation, or ova may be in a poor condition because the mother's own mother had a poor diet. This latter possibility is called the *transgenerational link*. All a woman's eggs are present at birth. Therefore, if a woman's mother had a poor diet when pregnant with her, this will affect her ova, and her mother's poor diet will be apparent in her children.

Other matters are more within the control of prospective parents, such as checking their own health and diet. This might include checking for immunity to German measles, giving up smoking, reducing alcohol intake and increasing folic acid. Such changes mainly affect the prospective mother, but fathers are involved as well, since lifestyle changes usually involve both partners. Pre-pregnancy genetic screening may involve either parent if their family is a known carrier of certain diseases (see page 144).

# PSYCHOLOGICAL PERSPECTIVES:
## *Nature and nurture*

The debate over nature versus nurture runs through all of psychology. Many theories seek to explain human behaviour either in terms of inherited factors or life experiences. In truth, all organisms are a product of their genetic endowment *and* their nurture. We cannot ever hope to separate one from the other. An organism's *genotype* is its particular set of genes, whereas its *phenotype* is its actual manifested behaviour. One way to visualise this is to think of two identical seedlings, one raised in rich soil with plenty of water and sun, the other given adverse growing conditions. What we observe is their phenotype, a product of nature and nurture.

Genotype predisposes an organism to certain developmental outcomes. We might think in terms of a *reaction range*. Genes set upper and lower limits for, say, height, and the environment determines the actual outcome.

The *canalisation principle* suggests that genes channel development along predetermined pathways that are sometimes difficult for the environment to alter. Alternatively, it may be that genotypes have a significant influence on an organism's environment, and in this way genotype shapes phenotype.

# PRE-NATAL INFLUENCES

The influence of external agents, such as drugs, nutrition, chemical additives and hormones (collectively called *teratogens*), is not simple to predict. It is often thought, for example, that all pregnant women who took the drug thalidomide gave birth to deformed babies. In fact, mothers who took the drug after the fortieth day of pregnancy usually had normal babies, and only some mothers (perhaps as low as twenty per cent) who took the drug earlier had deformed babies. The infant's particular deformity could also be related to the time when the drug was taken. If it was around day twenty-six, it led to abnormalities of the arms, whereas around day twenty-one, infants were born without ears. The effect of any teratogen depends on such things as the developmental stage of the infant, the genetic susceptibility of the foetus, the length of exposure and the physiological state of the mother. Therefore, we cannot say that one cause invariably leads to a certain detrimental effect, but that certain influences during pregnancy are associated with certain outcomes. In fact, it is more often than not the case that poor outcomes are associated with parents with a cluster of interrelated risk factors, including smoking, alcohol, pollution, poor diet and living conditions. It is these multiple risk factors which are of the greatest concern to health care professionals and prospective parents.

# LOW BIRTH-WEIGHT BABIES AND SIDS

Almost all teratogens result in two major immediate effects. The first is the restriction of oxygen (*anoxia*), which causes cell damage especially in the brain. The second is the lack of sufficient nutrients which results in a lack of cell growth, again most importantly in the brain. The consequence of this is an infant whose vital organs have fewer cells and, in extreme cases, who has suffered significant brain damage.

These immediate effects of teratogens have two important outcomes. First, babies are born with lower birth-weight than they would have had. Second, there is an increased incidence of certain complications of pregnancy and birth, such as miscarriage, difficult delivery and neo-natal death. The long-term prognosis for low birth-weight babies is very dependent on their diet and care after birth. For the first few years of life, such babies are often below normal on developmental tests. If malnutrition continues, the child is likely to suffer intellectual retardation and have more emotional problems than other children. If the infant's diet is good, these ill-effects disappear within a few years. Resnick et al. (1990) followed nearly 500 children who had been placed in special care units at birth. Those who had birth-weights of less than 1000 grams later had poorer cognitive development scores, but overall sociodemographic factors had the greatest influence on outcome: disadvantaged parents are less able to compensate for developmental delays and they are also more likely to have special care babies in the first place.

There may be hidden effects both for those who appear to recover and those who don't. Infants born with, for example, fewer brain, lung and kidney cells will be more susceptible throughout their lives to retarded development or to infection. One illustration of this comes from a study by Barker (1992), who found that underweight babies are more likely to develop heart disease and late-onset diabetes as adults. This poor development is referred to as *intra-uterine growth retardation* (IUGR) and may be one explanations for SIDS ('cot' or sudden infant death syndrome). Hinchcliffe et al. (1992) have discovered that some SIDS infants are growth retarded, so that they appear perfectly well, but have no reserves of strength for coping with infection and are easily overwhelmed. Risk factors for SIDS, such as sleeping position, overheating or parental smoking, will place extra physiological stress on such susceptible infants leading to sudden and apparently inexplicable death.

# FOCUS ON...
# *Smoking*

EEC Council Directive (89/622/EEC)

## PROTECT CHILDREN: DON'T MAKE THEM BREATHE YOUR SMOKE

FIGURE 1.1 *Legislation now requires cigarette companies to warn parents of the dangers of passive smoking for their children*

## What are the effects on the foetus?

1 Irreversible cognitive and physical deficiencies from lack of oxygen leading to brain damage.
2 Unsuccessful pregnancies because of increased incidence of prematurity, spontaneous abortion, stillbirth and neo-natal death. Pregnant women who smoke are twice as likely to have stillborn infants, and there is a relationship between the number of cigarettes smoked and the percentage of stillbirths (Julien, 1992).
3 Retarded foetal growth resulting in low birth-weight and cell deficiencies in vital organs such as the kidneys. This may led to decreased immune responses and has been associated with SIDS. Even though a baby is born with an average birth-weight, this does not mean they have not been affected. They might have been heavier, and their internal organs may be under-developed.

## Why is smoking associated with these effects?

1 The carbon monoxide contained in cigarette smoke affects the oxygen-carrying capacity of the mother's blood, therefore reducing the amount of oxygen delivered to the foetus. This means that the baby grows more slowly. Some cells will not develop, leading to irreversible damage to biological systems.
2 Tars cause cancer (they are carcinogenic) and act as tumour promoters.
3 Other chemicals, such as ammonia, cyanide and butane, are also present in smoke. All of these are poisonous.
4 Mothers who smoke eat less because nicotine suppresses the desire for sweeter-tasting food.
5 Nicotine is a stimulant and leads to increased energy expenditure through higher levels of arousal. This causes the mother to burn up more of her food intake.

## Other considerations

1 Passive smoking will also affect the pregnant mother and her infant. The same toxic chemicals are produced at both ends of a cigarette. Therefore a pregnant mother should avoid being in the presence of smokers.
2 Smoking after birth, especially when a

mother breastfeeds, turns the infant into a passive smoker. Children who live with smokers have increased respiratory infections and decreased lung capacity (US Surgeon General's Report, 1986).

3 Mothers who smoke are also more likely to come from a low socio-economic class, which means they will have a cluster of other at-risk factors, such as poor housing, poor education, and have had mothers who smoke, an example of a trans-generational link. Government statistics show that babies of unskilled manual workers are fifty per cent more likely to die than those of professionals (OPCS, 1995).

## Why do some parents continue to smoke?

1 The effects of smoking are subtle, for example low birth-weight babies. In the case of thalidomide, no mother would consider taking this risk.

2 It is possible to believe that the effects are not that serious. For example, there are many examples around of women who smoked during pregnancy and yet appear to have produced quite normal children.

3 The effects are delayed rather than immediate.

4 Many of the effects are, or appear to be, reversible, unlike the effects of thalidomide.

5 Giving up smoking involves a change of lifestyle, and even personality, probably for both parents.

6 Giving up smoking when you know you're pregnant is already too late. Therefore some mothers don't bother.

7 Simply reducing smoking is not effective and may in fact increase stress and irritability because of nicotine craving. Therefore some people do not even try to give up.

# AVOIDING NEGATIVE OUTCOMES

The question of why people don't comply with medical advice concerns health care workers, as does the issue of how to promote health care. Health psychologists offer various suggestions. It is possible that parents fail to understand what they are told. For this reason, antenatal clinics have many easy-to-read leaflets (see Figure 1.3, page 12). Good communication between parents and their doctor or other health care workers is important, and it may be that professionals need better training in passing on information and forming supportive relationships. These issues are examined in detail in another book in this series, *Applying Psychology to Health* (Banyard, 1996).

Parents may intend to take a course of action but simply forget. Such forgetting could be due to unconscious repression of information as a means of coping. Some parents may not take medical advice because it runs counter to their personal beliefs. They may, for example, be Scientologists or practise homeopathy.

Parents have to weigh up costs and benefits if a suggested treatment has unpleasant or undesirable side-effects, such as having to give up smoking or discovering that they are a carrier for Huntington's chorea. Equally, the seriousness or reversibility of the outcome will affect their decision about what to do. The health belief model (Rosenstock, 1966) attempts to explain health behaviour in this way, suggesting that there are three factors which can be used to predict what a person will do in any situation (see Figure 1.2). The first is the perceived threat of a disease. The second is the perceived benefits of treatment and the barriers to action. The third is personal variables such as sex, age and personality. This is a cognitive approach which emphasises rational behaviour; however, human behaviour is often irrational and therefore the model does not predict behaviour very well.

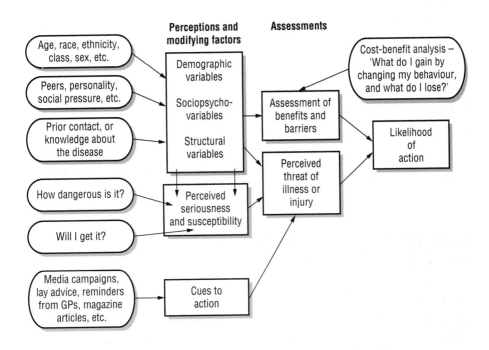

FIGURE 1.2 *The health belief model*

Janis (1984) suggests that attempts to persuade people to change their behaviour must shake complacency and that minimal appeals to fear are the most effective means of promoting health behaviour. The Yale Model of Communication (based on Hovland et al., 1953) suggests the following to induce successful persuasion: the source of the message should be credible, the argument should be one-sided, conclusions should be stated rather than left to be worked out, the message should be short, clear, direct and colourful, and the receiver should actively participate in the communication (Banyard, 1996).

**Box 1.2**   Some adverse pre-natal factors and their effects

| FACTOR | DIRECT EFFECTS | LEADS TO |
|---|---|---|
| **Age, maternal** | | |
| • under 20 | Physically immature, may not receive good antenatal care. | Perinatal complications. |
| • over 35 | Chromosomal abnormalities, poor maternal health. | Increased risk of Down's syndrome and other genetic abnormalities, perinatal complications. |
| **Alcohol** | | |
| • alcoholic mothers | Inhibits development of nervous system. | Foetal alcohol syndrome (FAS) : low birth-weight, hyperactivity, facial malformations, heart defects, mental retardation. |
| • 'social drinking' (over two units per day) | Inhibits development of nervous system. | Retarded growth, sluggish or placid behaviour, depressed IQ scores. |
| **Birth-weight** | | |
| • low, e.g. mother smoked, or multiple/premature birth | Poor cell growth, physical immaturity at birth. | Intellectual impairment, infant death, heart problems later in life. |
| • high, e.g. because mother diabetic or overdue birth | Abnormal development in diabetic mothers because of glucose levels. | Birth complications due to large head size. |
| **Diseases** | | |
| • sexually transmitted, e.g. AIDS or genital herpes | Infection. | Disease may be transmitted to the infant prenatally or at the time of birth. |
| • other diseases, e.g. rubella | Infection. | Major malformations in about twenty per cent of infants exposed during first three months |
| **Drugs** | | |
| • prescribed drugs, e.g. antibiotics, barbiturates, aspirin | Anoxia. | Malformations, lethargy. |
| • illegal drugs, e.g. crack | Physiological dependence, poor cell growth. | Miscarriage, birth complications, infant may be born addicted. |

**Box 1.2** Some adverse pre-natal factors and their effects (*continued*)

| FACTOR | DIRECT EFFECTS | LEADS TO |
|---|---|---|
| **Emotional distress** | High levels of hormones such as adrenalin. | 'Difficult' temperament, disturbed bonding between mother and infant. |
| **Hormones, male** | Masculinisation of female brain and body parts. | Adrenogenital syndrome, heart malformations, increased cancer risk later in life. |
| **Length of gestation** | Oxygen deficit, poor nutrition at end because placenta is beginning to fail. | Birth complications. |
| **Noisy environment** | Increases foetal movements. | Hyperactivity. |
| **Malnutrition** • during first three months (embryonic phase) | Lack of cell growth during critical phase of development. | Complications of pregnancy, low birth-weight, low intelligence, poorly developed immune systems, possibly associated with sudden infant death syndrome (SIDS) or later poor health. |
| • during last three months | Restricted cell growth during period of rapid growth. | Small babies with small brains. |
| **Radiation** | Cell mutations. | Poor motor performance, emotionality, deformities. |
| **Season of birth** | Mild dietary deficiencies in third month for children born in winter. | Higher infant mortality, schizophrenia (possibly), mental retardation. |
| **Sleep** | Increased amounts of growth hormone during REM sleep. | Foetal movements increased, higher intelligence. |
| **Social class** | Poor nutrition, lack of antenatal care. | Complications of pregnancy, intellectual deficit. |
| **Vitamins and trace minerals** • too much, e.g. vitamin A | | Cleft palate , heart malformation. |
| • too little, e.g. folic acid | | Associated with spina bifida. |

• • • • • • • • • • • • • • • •

***What is spina bifida?***

Spina bifida is a disability affecting the spine. It occurs very early in pregnancy and can result in a baby being totally or partially paralysed. In the UK around 400 babies a year are born severely disabled by spina bifida (and other similar conditions) – but you can help to reduce the risk if you follow the advice in this leaflet.

• • • • • • • • • • • • • • • • • • •

***What can I do to reduce the risk to my baby?***

• Make sure you eat more of a B vitamin called folic acid from your diet.
  **AND**

• If you think you may become pregnant take a folic acid tablet every day.

• • • • • • • • • • • • • • • •

***Eat foods to help beat spina bifida***

A baby's spine is most at risk from spina bifida during the first twelve weeks of pregnancy. This is why it is important to eat more foods rich in folic acid **before** you are planning a pregnancy. The foods which contain folates or folic acid are those recommended to everyone as part of a well balanced diet. They are vegetables such as potatoes, spinach, spring greens and other green leafy vegetables, fresh or frozen Brussels sprouts, green beans or peas and cauliflower or okra, and fruit such as bananas, grapefruit or oranges. Savoury yeast or beef extracts, bread and cereals, pitta bread, nan, and chapattis also contain folic acid. Some breads and many breakfast cereals have folic acid specially added to them. You can tell by looking at the label. Most beans and pulses such as lentils, red kidney beans and soya beans (and their products) contain good amounts, as do baked beans. There is also folic acid in milk and other dairy products such as yoghurt, and in rice and pasta.

FIGURE 1.3 *Doctor's surgeries are full of useful advice for pregnant mothers in the form of posters and easy-to-read leaflets. The information aims to educate prospective parents about certain pre-natal factors and their positive or negative effects*

# TEMPERAMENT

Factors other than teratogens, such as age or a mother's emotional state, may also affect the developing foetus. A state of distress or anxiety produces certain hormones, principally adrenalin, which can affect the foetus. It seems reasonable to assume that hormones might have a negative effect on the baby, and research confirms this. Mothers who are distressed during pregnancy are more likely to have babies who have a 'difficult' temperamental profile exhibiting hyperactivity, irritability and irregular feeding and sleeping habits.

However, Field et al. (1985) argue that mothers who are stressed before the child's birth, perhaps because of marital problems, poor housing, or an unplanned pregnancy, usually continue to be anxious, depressed or resentful. This kind of mother tends to be emotionally more distant and more punitive and controlling. This alone would account for difficult infant behaviour. We will look further at the child's developing temperament and personality in Chapter 7.

# FOCUS ON...
## *'Hothouse' babies*

When parents follow nutritional advice, their baby should be born more healthy and have a larger brain. There are some people who believe that if you stimulate an infant in the womb, you may increase their intelligence. Logan (1987) claims that programmes of prenatal stimulation have produced a children whose *average* IQs are 160.

There is no doubt that the developing foetus is capable of learning. At a simple level, research has shown that, where an infant is exposed to certain prenatal sounds such as the theme tune from *Neighbours* (Hepper, 1991) or passages from *The Cat in the Hat* (DeCasper and Spence, 1986), they show recognition of these after birth. This ties in with the infant's familiarity with his or her mother's voice, and those of other family members, and no doubt assists in early bonding. Such evidence essentially demonstrates that the foetus can be conditioned, which is not the same as showing that permanent changes in intelligence have occurred. In addition, the effects that have been claimed are *larger* than are found in any *post-natal* programmes of intervention. According to Gyte (1995), the advantages claimed for BabyPlus actually have very little basis in 'creditable' research.

Howe (1990) rejects the wilder claims of hot-

housing, but accepts that accelerated development is possible when parents stimulate their children. A remarkable example of this has been documented by Kunkel (1985). In seventeenth-century Venice, a number of orphanages gave their girls musical training, including instruction by the composer Vivaldi. The girls reportedly dazzled visitors with their extraordinary musical talents. Since Venetian children were placed arbitrarily in orphanages, and children not receiving instruction did not display any special musical talent, the girls' talents must have been caused by experience rather than innate abilities. There were benefits for the girls. They had a more interesting life and were more marriageable. Therefore they had opportunity *and* incentive.

A distinction should be made between genius and extraordinary talents. Genius is exceedingly rare and may in large part be genetically determined, as in the case of the uneducated Indian mathematician, Srinivasa Ramanujan. As a young boy, he found an old mathematics text book at his school and proceeded to work out much of modern mathematics for himself. The fact that such abilities developed with very little environmental stimulus suggests a genetic basis and calls for the label 'genius'. Special talents, however, owe much more to environmental stimulation. Feldman (1986) has studied many child prodigies in such areas as chess, music and mathematics, and considers that the distinguishing factor is the passion these children have to succeed. Howe considers that no exceptional abilities are displayed without a great deal of continued practice or effort. It may appear that some people spontaneously exhibit exceptional talents, but a look at the individual's early background shows that they were given an environment which was continuously 'rich in opportunities for learning'. This is the basis of the Suzuki method of training violinists. They are exposed to constant music from before birth, given toy violins in infancy and inspired to develop an intense desire to succeed. This approach probably underlies the achievements of hothouse babies.

# *A gift for a Lifetime*

*A*s a parent you want to give your new baby the best possible start in life. **BabyPlus** is a unique way to stimulate your baby's mind in the womb. Using sequences of rhythmic sounds **BabyPlus** exercises the developing brain so that your newborn baby will be better prepared to learn and understand from very early on in life. Experts worldwide are excited by the

FIGURE 1.4   *Advocates of pre-natal 'hothousing', such as Logan, have marketed products to improve an unborn baby's emotional, social and cognitive development. Reproduced Courtesy of BabyPlus UK Ltd*

# BIRTH AND BONDING

Birth marks the end of the pre-natal period, but events surrounding birth, the perinatal period, should also be considered. Again, we must consider permanent, physical damage (such as anoxia) and potentially reversible, psychological damage (such as disruption of early bonding).

The critical or sensitive period hypothesis suggests that there are certain periods in development when the neonate is maximally sensitive to learn certain things. At birth, this is to imprint upon or form a bond with their caretaker(s). Klaus and Kennell (1976) found that the amount of contact and the timing of the contact was important. They arranged for one group of fourteen randomly selected mothers to follow a 'traditional pattern of contact' after birth: they saw their babies briefly after delivery, visited them six to twelve hours later and fed them at four-hourly intervals. A second group had 'extended contact': they cuddled their babies for an extra five hours per day, including skin-to-skin contact. One month later, the extended contact group of mothers were physically closer to their infants and more soothing. A year later, this same group still did more cuddling and nurturing. Moreover, their infants scored better on tests of mental and physical development. However, Goldberg (1983) reviewed a number of similar studies and concluded that the effects of early bonding are not as large or long-lasting as Klaus and Kennell's results suggested. Nevertheless, such studies have had important effects in terms of policy in maternity hospitals and special care baby units, and for adopted children.

The emotional state of the new mother and her child at the time of birth may be profoundly affected by drugs used during labour. In the United States, some ninety-five per cent of women receive at least one form of medication during the birth process, such as drugs to reduce pain and those to increase uterine contractions. Brackbill et al. (1985) reviewed over fifty studies of babies whose mothers had received relatively large doses of medication. Not only are such mothers in a drugged state when they first interact with their baby, but the baby is also drugged due to its share of the mother's blood up to the moment of separation. Brackbill et al. concluded that these infants were generally more inattentive and irritable, difficult to feed and smiled less. The mothers often developed poor emotional attachments, possibly because their babies gave them negative feedback. Some deficits in physical and mental development appeared to persist as long as one year after birth. However, like low birth-weight, subsequent experience may more than compensate for this poor start.

What is a baby's experience of birth? Some people regard birth as a traumatic period when the baby is ejected from a warm, cushioned world into a bright, foreign and noisy environment in which the infant experiences the pain of taking its initial breath and the first experience of hunger. On the other hand, it may be that the baby is relieved to be out of its cramped environment and cognitively hungry for new experiences. MacFarlane (1977) has carefully observed newborn babies and noted that most of them settle down quickly and that there is little evidence to support the view that the delivery environment makes much difference to the infant. It may, however, make the mother and father feel more relaxed.

Home births are one means of improving the degree of relaxation experienced by the immediate family, though some health care workers feel that this threatens the physical well-being of the mother and infant. In fact, the infant mortality rate is lower for home births than for hospital births, but this may be because the women who have babies at home are a special sample. Mothers who are identified, through antenatal care, of being at risk for birth complications will be sent to hospital for the birth. Those women who choose to be at home are often more educated and have more positive expectations about the birth process, which also makes it more likely that they will have fewer problems. The benefits of home birth may extend beyond the birth period. For example, MacFarlane found that sixty per cent of women who gave birth in hospital experienced post-partum depression compared with only sixteen per cent of home deliveries.

Perhaps a key aspect of a home birth is the degree of control which the mother feels, since stress and pain are reduced by having a sense of control. For example, Girodo and Wood (1979) showed that participants who were trained to make positive self-statements ('I can cope') and understood why enhancing their sense of personal control was an effective technique, experienced less pain.

# FOCUS ON...
# *breastfeeding*

Breastfeeding offers a sensual physical relationship between mother and infant. It might be thought that this could promote early bonding. However, bottle-fed babies also receive close contact with their caretaker, and psychological research has not been able to distinguish between breast- and bottle-feeding in terms of a child's emotional development.

Breastfeeding has been found to confer significant health advantages. Research indicates a negative association between breastfeeding and infections of the ear, lower respiratory tract and intestine, as well as reduced risks of neo-natal death and some diseases like eczema and diabetes (Warren, 1995). Breastfed babies have increased immunities because the mother's milk contains her antibodies. Mothers who breastfeed also gain personal advantage because they are less likely to develop pre-menopausal breast cancer and ovarian cancer.

In part, such associations may be due to the fact that women from lower socio-economic classes are only half as likely to try to breastfeed their babies (OPCS, 1992). Such babies are more likely to have ill-health anyway because of the parents' lower standards of living. Some infections in bottle-fed babies are due to inadequate sterilisation of equipment. The nutritional aspects of breastmilk are particularly critical in Third World countries where substitutes are expensive and there is no sterile water available to make up the formula milk. For this reason, some health professionals boycott all products made by companies who sell powdered milk to the Third World.

In this country, parents might be concerned by findings that breastfeeding is linked with higher intelligence. Rogan and Gladen (1993) followed a group of about 700 children from birth. Those who had been breastfed performed slightly but significantly better on developmental scales at age two, and this effect was still detectable at school age. The slight advantage has been confirmed by other studies, even when maternal intelligence, education, training in child-rearing, childhood experiences, family socio-economic status, birth-weight and gestational age are controlled for (Fergusson et al., 1982). Farquharson et al. (1992) found neuroanatomical differences between breast- and bottle-fed babies examined in cot death post-mortems: the grey matter of breastfed babies appeared to develop better and more rapidly, probably due to the presence of long chain fatty acids in breast milk. Such fatty acids could be added to bottle formulas.

Despite the apparent advantages of breastfeeding recent statistics show that only forty-one per cent of UK mothers are still exclusively breastfeeding at four weeks (Beddard, 1995). Campaigns have tried to improve this, but the problem may be that some mothers do not have suitable role models, such as their female friends or mothers, and that there needs to be better support post-natally (such as greater acceptance of breastfeeding in public). Finally, there is the issue of convenience. Some mothers regard breastfeeding as a tie because it means that no one else can feed their baby. Bottle-fed babies, however, can be cared for by the father, giving the mother more independence.

# CHOOSING A NAME

On a lighter note, there is evidence to suggest that a child's name may well have some effect on their future success or problems in life. Harari and McDavid (1973) found that school essays written by children with 'attractive' names, such as David, Michael, Karen and Lisa, were given a better mark than those written by children with less attractive names, such as Elmer, Hubert, Bertha and Albert. A name may also communicate greater or lesser femininity/masculinity. Petrie and Johnson (cited in McIlveen et al.,1994) asked 255 students to rate a list of eighty-six names for femininity or masculinity and to answer a questionnaire which indicated how masculine or feminine they were themselves. This meant the researchers could produce a list of the most feminine names and the most masculine ones, and were able to show that feminine names had more feminine personalities. Such a correlation may be because parents who choose feminine-type names are also likely to encourage feminine-type behaviour. It could also be that people expect girls with feminine-type names to be more feminine.

Other evidence for the importance of a name came from a survey of some African police records, which showed that there were twice as many delinquent Ashanti boys born on a Wednesday than a Monday. Jahoda (1954) suggests this is a result of the Ashanti's practice of naming their children according to their day of birth and their belief that this determines their personality. A Kwadwo (Monday) is supposed to be quiet, retiring and peaceful, whereas a Kwaku (Wednesday) is held to be aggressive, quick-tempered and a trouble-maker. However, in both Jahoda's and Petrie and Johnson's studies, the names may act as a self-fulfilling prophecy, so beware the connotations of your child's name!

# SUMMARY

The value of the information presented in this chapter lies in the opportunity it affords parents to make informed choices. Throughout the whole of a child's life, parents are faced with decisions about how to act in the best interests of their offspring – pregnancy is just the beginning.

# *chapter two*

## CHAPTER OVERVIEW

The neonates' world has been described as 'one unanalysed bloom of confusion' (James, 1890). During the first months of life, the infant must learn to organise the mass of incoming sensory data so that it has meaning. This chapter looks at the twin contributions of nature and nurture to the development of visual, auditory, olfactory and cross-modal perception. We will also examine the critical period hypothesis as well as 'enrichment' and 'differentiation' theories of perception.

## WHAT CAN NEWBORN INFANTS SENSE AND PERCEIVE?

The visual sensory system in humans is not fully mature at birth. For example, although the lens of the eye will eventually be able to change shape (permitting it to focus on objects at different distances), at birth it cannot expand and contract. Therefore, infant vision is generally blurry with a fixed focal length of about eight inches (nineteen centimetres), approximately the distance between the infant and its caregiver when feeding. The infant's eye also lacks the ability to discriminate all colours, such as blues from greys. However, there are many things the infant's eye does detect, including movement, changes in brightness, some colours, and visual patterns which are not too detailed and have sufficient light/dark contrast.

Some perceptual processes appear to be present from the beginning. Pattern recognition is an example of this. Research by Fantz (1961) showed that neonates could easily discriminate certain visual forms and they preferred certain patterns, such as faces or concentric circles to plain disks. In a later experiment, Fantz showed that two-week-old infants marginally preferred a 'real' face to a scrambled version and both were preferable to a control which contained the same amount of light and dark (see Figure 2.1).

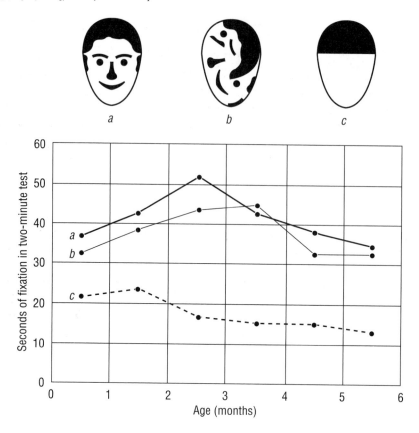

FIGURE 2.1    *Stimulus figures and results from research by Fantz (1961)*

The ability to distinguish faces is biologically adaptive. A newborn or neonate who can recognise and respond to its own species will better elicit attachment and caring. However, this perceptual ability can also be understood in other ways. The human face may be interesting as it is a good example of something a baby can see well because it is within its focal range. Also, it is a moderately complex pattern which is often in motion and therefore captivating. Infants very quickly learn to recognise the pattern of a human face. Although they are not innately programmed to prefer faces, they are programmed to select and scan moderately complex patterns, which are important in promoting the visual development of the brain.

# WHY DO INFANTS ROLL OFF SOFAS?

Other perceptual processes are also a combination of innate abilities and the effects of experience. All parents are familiar with the problems that begin when their infants become mobile. Most particularly, they seem to have no sense of depth and will happily sit back into thin air or roll off the edge of the sofa. Is this because they have to learn depth perception through painful trial and error or can they perceive depth but lack sensorimotor control?

Adults perceive three-dimensional depth using a range of cues. There are monocular cues, such as shadow and relative size, and binocular cues such as disparity. Depth discrimination is important for survival, therefore we might again expect it to be biologically controlled. This does not mean that it is present at birth, but that it should develop as a result of maturation and appear before an infant is mobile. Experiments conducted by Gibson and Walk (1960) tested the relationship between mobility and depth perception using the 'visual cliff', a glass top covering a drop of several feet (see Figure 2.2). Infants older than six months refused to cross the 'cliff' indicating the ability to perceive depth. Various animals, such as goats and kittens, demonstrated depth perception at a much younger age (one day old and four weeks old respectively).

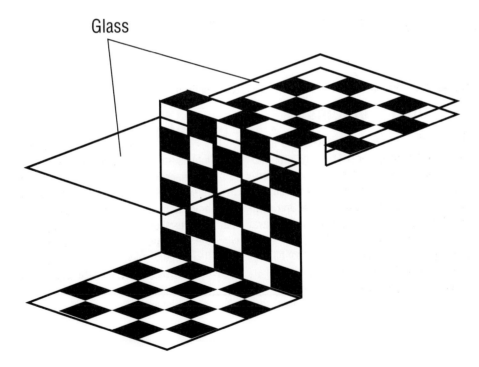

Glass

FIGURE 2.2 *The Visual Cliff*

Bower and his associates (1970) examined depth perception in infants aged six to twenty days old by observing their response to an approaching object. The infants signalled awareness by opening their eyes, moving their head back and putting their hands in front of their face. If the infant had no depth perception, their response to a large disk stopping further away should be the same as their response to a smaller, closer one because they both create the same retinal image. In fact, the infants were so upset by the smaller, closer one that Bower et al. abandoned the experiment and concluded that the infants could perceive depth from birth. Therefore, it seems clear that neonates have some ability to perceive depth from birth but have to learn sensorimotor co-ordination.

# RESEARCH TECHNIQUES
## *Conducting research with infants*

The same practical and ethical constraints apply when conducting research with infants as with all other human beings. Over and above this, other issues need to be considered.

## Practical problems

1  Testing a somewhat immobile and unresponsive subject is difficult and prone to subjective interpretation and experimenter bias. Researchers have developed many ingenious techniques, but the conclusions about behaviour are always based on inference.

2  Research tends to be laboratory-based. The way an infant reacts in unfamiliar surroundings and with strangers will be atypical. We cannot assume that the same principles apply in 'real life'.

3  It is impossible to test an infant who has had no experience, since activity in the womb has a major impact. Therefore we can never conclude that a particular behaviour is wholly innate.

## Ethical problems

1  Infants are especially affected by any experience. Therefore it must be questioned whether they should be exposed to *any* treatment.

2  Parents should never be deceived as to the true nature of the research involving their child, though such knowledge might bias the research, because parents will have expectations that they communicate to their infant.

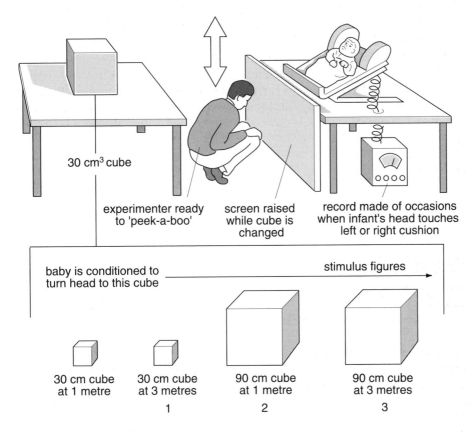

30 cm³ cube

experimenter ready to 'peek-a-boo'

screen raised while cube is changed

record made of occasions when infant's head touches left or right cushion

baby is conditioned to turn head to this cube

stimulus figures

| 30 cm cube at 1 metre | 30 cm cube at 3 metres | 90 cm cube at 1 metre | 90 cm cube at 3 metres |
|---|---|---|---|
| 1 | 2 | 3 | |

FIGURE 2.3 *Experimenters have to develop ingenious techinques when investigating infant behaviour. For example, in Bower's (1966) study of depth perception, infants were trained to respond positively, by turning their head, to rectangles of certain sizes. To do this, an assistant popped up and said 'peek-a-boo' when the infant looked at the object. Later the infant was tested to see if objects at different distances but the same retinal size would elicit the same responses.*

# SOME OTHER INNATE ABILITIES

Hearing and smell in infants have also been extensively researched. Auditory acuity is much better developed in human newborns than visual acuity. In fact, infants can hear sufficiently well inside the womb to be able, at birth, to recognise familiar voices and even passages from books (see page 13). Smell is also well developed at birth, probably also in order to promote attachment and safety. Very young infants seem to be able to distinguish the smell of their mother's milk from that of a stranger. MacFarlane (1975) found that six-day-old neonates responded differently to the two smells. In another study, Porter et al. (1983) demonstrated differential responses in infants from twelve to eighteen days to underarm odours. Mothers wore an underarm pad for eight hours. The infant was then exposed to two pads, one from their mother and one from a stranger, placed on either side of the infant's head. Porter et al. found that the breastfed babies showed a preference for their own mother's odour, but bottle-fed babies did not. This may be because they experience less close contact with their mother or because lactating mothers have a stronger smell, but in either case it shows a well-developed sense of smell.

There is ample evidence that infants enjoy music from birth. Butterfield and Siperstein (1972) found that babies increased their rate of sucking on a dummy when played folk music, but decreased it when the sound was non-rythmical. By the age of five months, infants show abilities to discriminate between tunes and recognise familiar ones, even when the pitch and tempo have been changed (Trehub, 1985). There is also a universal tendency for humans to associate major chords with pleasure and minor chords with dissonant feelings and darker moods. This suggests some innate auditory predispositions.

Cross-modal perception is the ability to co-ordinate different senses. If you close your eyes and can recognise an object with which you are visually but not tactually familiar, you are using cross-modal perception. It is possible that such abilities have to be learned, but to some extent they appear to be present at birth. Research has shown that one- and two-month-old infants show distress when they see their talking mother behind a screen and hear her voice coming from a speaker located elsewhere. This suggests that hearing and vision are already integrated (Aronson and Rosenbloom, 1971). A similar link between vision and touch has been demonstrated in one-month-old infants by Gibson and Walker (1984). They gave infants a flexible or rigid cylinder to suck on. Later the two objects were visually displayed and manipulated so that the infants could see that one would bend and the other would not. The infants gazed longer at the object which was unfamiliar through touch. Apparently they could 'visualise' the object they had sucked and this was now less interesting, therefore demonstrating their cross-modal perception.

# CRITICAL OR SENSITIVE PERIODS

If certain abilities are regarded as innate, then it might be suspected that they will appear only during some critical period. The concept of critical periods comes from embryology. During pre-natal development, there are specific periods for each phase of development. If something affects development during this 'window', the embryo can never recover. There may be similar critical periods in the development of behaviour, though perhaps *sensitive* is a better word – if learning does not occur at a particular time, this does not mean it can never happen, as in embryology, but that it will be less likely or more difficult for it to happen.

It can be argued that sensitive periods for learning are advantageous. Any behaviour which is important in ensuring survival is likely to be biologically determined because those individuals who exhibit such behaviour survive to reproduce. However, an individual who does not need a particular behaviour in its repertoire, such as the ability to perceive distances in people who live in a dense forest environment, might be using up valuable resources by 'maintaining' this potential. It would therefore be more adaptive for a species to only develop necessary abilities at the expense of those which are unused, and biologically determined systems would be likely to degenerate. This does, in fact, appear to be the case.

FIGURE 2.4 *Blakemore and Cooper (1970) demonstrated that kittens who spent their early weeks in a drum where they could only see vertical stripes were later unable to respond to any horizontal contours such as a rope stretched between two chairs. This supports the idea of a sensitive period in visual development after which some capabilities disappear.*

The classic research that demonstrates that biological systems do degenerate involves depriving or restricting the visual experience of newborn non-human animals. One such study, by, Blakemore and Cooper (1970), involved placing kittens in a drum with only vertical stripes (see Figure 2.4 above). Later, the kittens were found to be blind to horizontal contours. For example, whilst they avoided table legs (a vertical stimulus), they tripped over a rope stretched in front of them (a horizontal stimulus). When the kittens' visual cortex was examined, Blakemore and Cooper found an absence of any cells which responded to horizontal orientation. This suggests that there were actual changes in the brain.

Held and Hein (1963) showed that it is not just visual experience which matters, but physical experience as well. Two kittens were placed in a carousel (see Figure 2.5). One walked round in a circle wearing a harness which moved a basket containing the other, passive kitten. They both ended up seeing the same things, but only the active kitten experienced the associated motor experience. The active kitten developed normal vision, whereas the passive one had no functional vision (for example, it was unable to avoid obstacles). Therefore it seems that sensorimotor experiences are necessary to maintain innate aspects of perception as well as a variety of visual experiences.

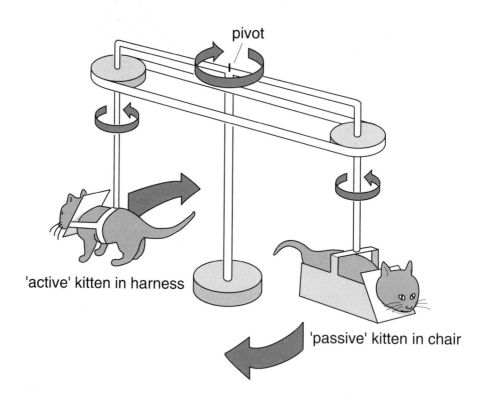

FIGURE 2.5 *Held and Hein's 'Kitten Carrousel'*

# FOCUS ON ...
## *squint eyesight*

## Deprivation

Some children are born with squint eyesight, or *early strabismus*. Their eyes do not line up properly. This affects their binocular vision because the input to each eye does not correspond, and the result is a kind of human visual deprivation. Banks et al. (1975) found that if such children are operated on before the age of three, they subsequently develop normal vision, but if the operation is left any later, the deprivation appears to result in some degree of abnormal binocular vision. Banks et al. demonstrated this using a method called the 'interocular transfer of the tilt after-effect'. This involves showing the subject a set of parallel lines which are tilted from the vertical and then showing them a set of perpendicular lines which should now appear tilted in the opposite direction. This effect should transfer to the opposite eye when a person has normal binocular vision, though the magnitude of the effect is smaller. Those who had their strabismus operated on before the age of three showed substantial transfer. Those operated on after age four had practically none at all. Banks et al. concluded that the plasticity of the human visual system was maximally sensitive around age two with a gradual decline thereafter.

The same results are found in studies of people with *astigmatism*, where the lens of the eye produces a biased input because it does not image all orientations equally sharply. Mitchell et al. (1973) found that when adult astigmatics have their vision corrected, many of them are still unable to see parallel lines in all orientations equally. Therefore the damage must be central and there must have been permanent changes in the visual cortical cells, as was found in Blakemore and Cooper's research with kittens.

Gregory and Wallace (1963) documented the case history of S.B., a man born with cataracts whose sight was restored when he was fifty-two. His first visual experiences were a blur of colours, but he gradually learned to match what he heard and felt with what he saw (cross-modal transfer). By and large, S.B. continued to rely on his other senses, and it is doubtful whether his visual perception was ever properly developed. This case study suggests that not only do parts of the visual cortex atrophy, but higher cortical centres which integrate perception also deteriorate.

## Enrichment

The inverse of the deprivation issue is whether *enrichment* can increase perceptual development. The effects of enrichment can be studied in institutionalised infants who spend a significant amount of time in their cribs receiving very limited emotional and cognitive stimulation. For example, White and Held (1966) placed red and white mitts on such infants when they were aged less than one month, and also provided them with multicoloured sheets. After a period of several months, this resulted in much earlier 'hand regard' (prolonged visual regard of the hands) than in a control group of infants who received no visual enrichment. Again, this demonstrates that visual development is *plastic*, in other words, it is modifiable by experience. It is worth noting that early perceptual deprivation is also cognitive deprivation because perceptual development is the beginning of cognitive development. Therefore perceptual deprivation should have a significant effect on intellectual development.

# THEORIES OF PERCEPTUAL DEVELOPMENT

## Piaget's theory

Piaget (1950) called the first stage of cognitive development the sensorimotor period, a time when infants are learning to understand what they sense and to take control of the world both cognitively and physically. Piaget suggested that infants are born with innate reflexes, such as sucking and grasping. These are innate *schema* which progressively develop in response to sensorimotor experiences, leading to the formation of new schemas. This process is called *accommodation*. When a schema does match experience, new information is *assimilated* into the child's knowledge.

Infants can only learn through these twin processes of assimilation and accommodation, and they rely on environmental interactions to drive this. Up to the age of four months, Piaget suggested that infants' behaviour can best be described as *primary circular reactions*, that is, certain simple repetitive acts which can be controlled and give satisfaction. Such acts include playing with their toes or smiling. Piaget called them 'circular' because the pleasure they produce encourages their repetition. These reactions are centred on the infant's own body. After the age of four months, however, infants move beyond themselves and discover, again by chance, that they can make interesting things happen to external objects, such as shaking a rattle. These new schemas, called *secondary circular reactions*, mark the beginning of differentiating the self from the rest of the world. (Piaget's theories are discussed further in Chapter 5.)

## Nature versus nurture

What can we conclude about the extent to which perception is innate or learned? Some aspects of perception are clearly biological, such as the eye itself or the visual cortex. However, even this biological system can be altered by experience, as shown by Blakemore and Cooper's research with kittens. Other aspects of perception are clearly learned. For example, much of what our eyes register is incomplete and/or ambiguous data. We use expectations, context, emotion and other cues to determine what we actually 'see' which is referred to as *perceptual set*. Piaget (1954) explained this in terms of *enrichment theory*: a person must add to or enrich their sensory input using available cognitive schemas.

The attempt to separate nature from nurture is further confused by maturation; abilities which appear after birth such as the eye's ability to focus, may not be due to learning, but to a maturing nervous system. In addition, abilities which appear to be innate because they are present at birth may be due to learning before birth in the mother's womb. Current research is giving us a clearer picture of what the infant is doing in the womb, and we are becoming more aware of the critical events which take place before birth in terms of sensorimotor development. Flanagan (1996) points out that regular exercise is vital in maintaining muscular tone and therefore the foetus is constantly moving around its weightless world. The eyes only open at seven months, so until then, foetal experience is limited to the co-ordination of touch and movement. Thus, the foetus strokes its face and umbilical cord and learns to suck its thumb. After birth, infants may find thumb-sucking harder than in their weightless, pre-natal environment, partly because of the effects of gravity, but also because infants may find the *sight* of their own hands confounds their pre-existing knowledge of the *sensation* of thumb-sucking.

# PSYCHOLOGICAL PERSPECTIVES:
## *The cognitive perspective*

In this chapter, we have approached early experience in terms of cognitive changes, that is, we have taken a cognitive approach to describing human behaviour. 'Cognitive' refers specifically to mental processes. Such explanations are often contrasted with the behaviourist approach (see page 49), which focuses entirely on external factors and regards internal mental processes as unnecessary concepts. In general, cognitive explanations of development focus on the child's formation of internal schema which generate expectations and thus shape behaviour. Cognitive theories lend themselves well to research, but the research tends to be laboratory-based and therefore not always applicable to real human behaviour. Also, until recently, cognitive explanations have tended to omit such factors as emotional influences and family conditions.

## Enrichment versus differentiation

Piaget's view of enrichment suggests that we impose meaning on our sensory data, either by making it fit in with pre-existing schemas or by generating new ones. Bower (1982) and Gibson's (1987) differentiation theory proposes that sensory stimulation is all we need. Bower's belief is that newborns can register all the information that an adult can, but are not able to handle it. What experience therefore offers is the opportunity to develop the necessary information processing strategies, whereas perceptual skills are innate and not reliant on experience.

Differentiation theory sees perceptual development as a question of learning to differentiate between the distinctive features of different classes of objects and the invariant properties that transfer from situation to situation. Perceptual development also involves learning to ignore irrelevant information and learning to pay attention efficiently.

Certainly, children *are* born with abilities to make discriminations, and these abilities improve with experience (cross-modal perception is a good example). However, it is also true that children soon learn to go beyond the actual data presented to their senses and impose their own meaning on it (the enrichment view). Research shows that people generate expectations about what they are likely to see and that such expectations are based on past experience. These influence what we perceive (rather than what we sense). Visual illusions are good examples of this. In the Ponzo illusion (see Figure 2.6), the oblique lines suggest perspective, and therefore the higher line appears to be more distant. We have learned to make mental size calculations for retinal images – those which appear to be nearer are perceived as shorter than the same retinal image which appears to be farther away.

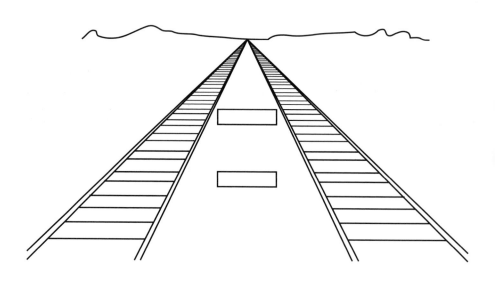

FIGURE 2.6 *Visual illusions such as this one, the Ponzo illusion, demonstrate how past experience affects our perceptions. This is support for the enrichment theory of perception and for top-down processing*

This distinction between enrichment and differentiation as theories of the development of perception is paralleled by two competing explanations for perception generally. These are *top-down* processing, which emphasises the influence of expectations, and *bottom-up* processing, the view that sensory data is sufficient to explain perception.

None of these theories of perception could be described as correct or incorrect; in fact, they each may account for different aspects of perception. The process of differentiation, or bottom-up processing, may explain innate systems of perception, whereas enrichment, or top-down processing, is related to those perceptual abilities which are learned. The relative contributions of each will vary according to particular circumstances.

# SUMMARY

In this chapter, we have seen that even before birth infants put innate capabilities to work and gain experience in sensorimotor development. Restricted experience during infancy appears to lead to permanent perceptual deficits and supports the critical period hypothesis. Theories of perception offer another account of the effects of experience, questioning whether what we learn to perceive is 'real' (differentiation theory) or whether it merely reflects our arbitrary way of classifying sensations (enrichment theory). This philosophical question will be considered again in Chapter 4, with reference to language and thought.

There is a tendency to regard perceptual and cognitive development as separate processes, but in reality both have origins in this early period when infants are learning to discriminate between classes of things and to co-ordinate their sensorimotor schema. We will return to cognitive development in Chapter 5.

# *chapter three*

# CHAPTER OVERVIEW

The processes of bonding and attachment begin during pregnancy and early infancy. However, they reach a critical point around the age of eight months at a time when the infant first exhibits separation and stranger anxiety. Both attachment and anxiety serve useful functions for the developing infant and, in this chapter, their value will be discussed in cognitive and survival terms. We will also look at Bowlby's theory of attachment which has been one of the most influential in developmental psychology.

# BONDING

The term *bonding* means forming a relationship. From the beginning, infants form important relationships, or bonds, with those around them. Both adults and infants probably have an innate predisposition to do this, because such bonds perform important survival functions. Infants who elicit care and attention and encourage caretakers to stay close will have a better chance of survival. The same is true of the adult responses. Caretakers feel uncomfortable when hearing a baby cry, and they find a 'baby face' appealing. This ensures they offer the necessary care and support.

# SEPARATION ANXIETY

The period of *specific* attachments is defined by the onset of separation anxiety, that is, the distress an infant shows when left alone by their main caregiver. The three typical stages are:

1  **Protest**
   The child cries but is able to be comforted. It is inwardly angry and fearful. This is a natural reaction to loss.

## 2 Despair

The child becomes calmer but apathetic, it no longer looks for its attachment figure. It may seek self-comfort through, for example, thumb-sucking or rocking.

## 3 Detachment

If the situation continues for weeks or months, the child may appear to be coping well but essentially has given up hope. When the attachment figure returns, s/he may be ignored.

**Box 3.1** The development of attachment behaviour

| AGE (APPROX.) | STAGE | DESCRIPTION |
|---|---|---|
| 0 to 2 months | Asocial stage | Infants produce similar responses to social and asocial stimuli. They react to voices and are attentive to faces. They show recognition of main caregiver(s) in terms of being more settled when held by such persons and showing a broader smile when hearing that person's voice. |
| 2 to 7 months | Indiscriminate attachments | Clear preference for any human company, infant complains when anyone puts them down. More likely to smile at familiar faces than strangers. |
| 7 to 9 months | Specific attachments | Infant protests when separated from one particular individual. Also shows 'stranger anxiety', a fear of strangers. This is the time that infants first develop a sense of object permanence. |
| 9 months plus | Multiple attachments | Very soon after main attachment formed, the infant develops a wider circle of attachments to familiar people. |

The degree of distress varies according to individual and situational differences. For example, a securely attached child whose life is generally settled will be less distressed. The presence of other familiar persons or things will also lessen anxiety, as will previous good experiences of separation. A securely attached child may experience a period of greater anxiety due to changing family circumstances, such as the arrival of a new baby or a family member going through a stressful time.

The initial response may degenerate into more pathological behaviour if the child remains separated from its attachment figure. As a child gets older, the expression of separation anxiety lessens. However, people of all ages experience such distress when separated from objects of comfort. When adults are bereaved, their responses pass through similar phases. The short- and long-term effects of separation are discussed in Chapter 8.

# RESEARCH TECHNIQUES:
## *Measuring attachment*

Separation anxiety is the visible side of attachment. Therefore, psychologists use this to define and measure attachment. The best known example of this is the Strange Situation developed by Mary Ainsworth and colleagues (1978). The procedure consists of seven three- minute episodes:

1  Parent and infant enter.
2  Stranger joins parent and infant.
3  Parent leaves.
4  Parent returns, stranger leaves.
5  Parent leaves.
6  Stranger returns.
7  Parent returns, stranger leaves.

The most important thing is what the child does when the caregiver/parent leaves and when the caregiver/parent returns. This behaviour is classified as:

■ **Type A** (anxious – avoidant): no protest when parent leaves, ignores parent's return.

■ **Type B** (securely attached): mild protest, on return seeks parent and is easily comforted.

■ **Type C** (anxious – resistant): seriously distressed, when parent returns alternately clings/rejects.

Ainsworth found that ten per cent of children tested are Type A, seventy per cent Type B and twenty per cent Type C. Type B is universally the largest group. Such children have been found to be more socially outgoing, independent, co-operative, compliant and curious, and better able to cope with stress. However, Takahashi (1990) warns about the cross-cultural use of the strange situation. He found that Japanese infants were very distressed when left alone because, in Japanese culture, infants are *never* left alone. Therefore Japanese children won't fit into the Ainsworth typology.

# COGNITIVE MATURITY

Attachment is more than bonding and includes the experience of distress caused by the absence of the attachment figure. The onset of specific attachment, after the age of six months, can be understood in terms of cognitive maturity and in particular *object permanence*. Object permanence is an ability described by Piaget as part of the fourth sub-stage of the sensorimotor period, what he calls the 'co-ordination of secondary schemes' (see page 67 for full description of Piagetian stages). A three-month-old infant who sees an object being hidden behind a pillow will cease to be interested whereas a one-year-old child realises that the now invisible object is still there, and it is this knowledge that is at least in part responsible for separation anxiety.

There is some debate as to when an infant is first aware of object permanence; Piaget claimed this ability first appears around the age of nine months.

However, others have found contrary evidence. For example, Bower (1981) showed that infants as young as four months showed surprise when an object that was hidden behind a screen was no longer there when the screen was lifted. He also observed that babies of two months old tracked an object as it moved behind a screen because their eyes showed where it should emerge. But seeing a parent disappear is different from a toy being hidden, and the anxiety this creates may well overwhelm any further thought.

There are other cognitive factors aside from the onset of object permanence which may influence the emergence of attachment and separation anxiety, most importantly consistency in cognitive schemas. At around the same age as separation anxiety develops, another fear, *stranger anxiety*, also develops. For example, a doctor in a white coat and with medical equipment may have difficulty examining an infant because of such anxiety. This can be reduced if the doctor puts on more normal attire so that the image presented fits in more easily with the schemas that the child has available. So, we might understand both stranger and separation anxiety in terms of the infant's cognitive schema. By the age of six months, these have developed to the point that they can recognise familiar animate and inanimate objects and situations, but equally they detect the unfamiliar and this causes distress. Kagan (1972) describes these as 'familiar faces in familiar places' schemas. Any violations cause incongruence and distress.

In the same way that the onset of attachment and separation anxiety can be understood in terms of cognitive maturity, the decline of such distress can also be explained in this way. Separation anxiety peaks around the age of fifteen months and then gradually declines. It may be no accident that this decrease coincides with increasing linguistic competence, when parents can inform the child beforehand about where they are going, and the child is able to express its feelings and be reassured. As children get older, they also learn that when caregivers go, they do come back. The building of schemas to cope with these situations helps to alleviate the anxiety experienced.

# THE ETHOLOGICAL VIEW

A different, but not mutually exclusive, way to explain attachment and separation anxiety is in terms of the ethological argument that any behaviour which continues to be part of a species' repertoire must serve some function. We have already noted how attachment serves obvious safety functions. Anxiety is equally an adaptive response. In general, it serves to motivate an organism to escape potential harm. In infants, it is a means of keeping parents and children close together. But why does this anxiety appear after the early months rather than being apparent from the start? It may be no accident that the nine-month-old infant is becoming mobile and may be tempted to venture from its caregiver. Such anxiety maintains closeness and therefore safety.

# PSYCHOLOGICAL PERSPECTIVES:
## *The ethological perspective*

Ethologists seek to understand and explain behaviour in terms of its adaptive or evolutionary value, that is, the extent to which the behaviour contributes to the survival of the individual and thus the species as a whole. Ethologists have introduced some important concepts, such as instinct, imprinting and critical or sensitive periods (a concept in turn taken from embryology to express the fact that, during physical development, there are specific periods when the organism is maximally sensitive to certain development). Ethologists have also stimulated psychologists to use naturalistic observation as a way of collecting data. Ethological concepts are more appropriate to explanations of animal behaviour, since human behaviour is less governed by innate factors and more influenced by learning. Nevertheless, explanations involving the concept of adaptive value provide important insights.

Evolutionary psychology is a different, though related, approach which bases all explanations on the Darwinian principles of evolution, namely that all behaviours can be understood in terms of the degree to which they enhance survival.

# OTHER FUNCTIONS OF ATTACHMENT

Brazelton et al. (1975) have described how interactions between infants and their attachment figures form the basis for learning to take place. The first interaction between parent and child is a 'dance' which has a cyclic rhythm. Several times each minute the infant seeks the mother's attention or responds to her cues, then turns away and recovers before recommencing with more attention and eye contact. Such attentional cycles, or *interactional synchrony*, allow infants control over the flow of information so that they will not be overwhelmed. They also give infants the experience of being able to control their environment rather than being a passive participant. This interaction and self-control sets up an optimal situation in which infants can learn.

Attachment behaviour also assists in other ways, such as providing infants with an emotionally secure base from which to explore the world, and acting as a model for later adult relationships and the individual's own behaviour as a parent. Children who fail to form early attachments may find security in other relationships (such as with young school friends) which provide necessary support and enable the development of empathy and eventual emotional maturity.

Attachment also assists self-development. In order for children to form a separate identity, they need confidence gained from a secure relationship with a caretaker(s). Rogers (1961) formulated this in terms of 'unconditional positive regard'. This basic parental relationship frees individuals from striving throughout life for social approval and enables them to seek self-actualisation. Where children receive conditional love, they feel they must be someone else in order to receive love. As a result, their actual self and ideal self are in conflict. We will consider self-development in greater detail in Chapter 6.

# FOCUS ON...
## *transitional objects*

Nearly half of all American middle-class children develop attachments to inanimate objects (LeFrançois, 1983). The most common non-social attachment is the security blanket which can provide comfort and reduce anxiety, especially at times of transition, such as bedtime, when the child is moving from a high to low arousal state, or when a child starts nursery school. For this reason, Winnicott (1953) described non-social attachments as *transitional objects* (TOs).

Children generally prefer soft things as TOs, though a very small number of children select hard objects. The importance of tactile comfort has been shown in Harlow's research with monkeys, described later in this chapter. The most common behaviour is to hold the object and feel it, possibly rubbing it against the face. The smell of the object may also be important. A number of children suck their thumb while holding the TO, but do not suck the TO – this is a key distinction between TOs and oral habits (dummies or pacifiers, or

thumb-sucking). Some infants spontaneously create their own TO, but a number of parents (perhaps around twenty per cent according to Litt, 1986) encourage such attachments by providing a special blanket or toy at times of need.

TOs probably serve a variety of psychological functions at different ages and for different children. Busch et al. (1973) propose that, before the age of twelve months, attachments should be classed as primary TOs, whilst later attachments are secondary TOs. At both stages, TOs offer support for anxiety, but secondary TOs may perform an additional function. Winnicott described them as part of the Freudian separation-individuation process: between the ages of two and three the child is moving away from maternal ties and developing a distinct sense of self. This is the time when TOs become most important. In Winnicott's view, TOs are not mother substitutes, but rather they are evidence of a good mother-infant relationship which enables the

FIGURE 3.1 *The use of transitional objects (TOs) is a familiar aspect of childhood. By school age, it is expected that children will have given them up. PEANUTS © 1996 United Features Syndicate, Inc. Reprinted by permission*

infant to transfer the soothing properties of the mother to some other object. On the other hand, Gulerce (1991) points out that, where an infant has an unresponsive mother, the TO may be a substitute, providing security where it is lacking elsewhere. In this case, there would be no need for mother-infant separation, since it is poorly developed in the first place.

There is evidence that TO use is associated with better long-term emotional adjustment. In a review of research, Litt (1986) reported a positive correlation between TO use and children having fewer sleep disturbances, becoming more independent, more self-confident and easier to manage. Conversely, Cohen and Clark (1984) found distinct differences between undergraduates who formerly used TOs and those who didn't. Former users were more likely to be classed as tense and outgoing, whereas non-users were significantly more relaxed and reserved. This led Cohen and Clark to conclude that TO use is necessary for those individuals who are inclined to be easily aroused. Haslam (1992) found TO attachments were more common in 'slow-to-warm-up' children (see page 100 for a discussion of temperamental types).

The common view that children who have security blankets are insecure is probably, then, at least partially true, and the use of TOs to resolve such temperamental 'problems' would be a healthy and appropriate course of action. TOs are unhealthy only when their use is associated with other emo-

tional problems, such as lack of social interaction. TOs are a symptom rather than a cause.

In contrast, Haslam believes that oral habits do not serve a healthy purpose. Oral habits are functionally different from TOs and signify a regressive form of self-soothing rather than a means of enabling the developmentally appropriate process of individuation. A dummy, for example, may be useful when a neonate has colic, but it is thought to interfere with successful breastfeeding, especially when breastfeeding has not been fully established. After the age of six months, the use of a dummy may prevent babbling because it restricts tongue movements in a way that thumb-sucking doesn't (which could be the origin of the term 'dummy'). Mike Woolridge, a director of the UNICEF UK Baby Friendly Initiative, claims that thumb-sucking and dummies are rare in traditional rural communities because babies spend more time being fed, rocked, and carried. Oral habits provide the rhythmic calming that our culture otherwise lacks.

One of the problems faced by parents of children with oral habits or TO attachments is breaking the habit. Why do adults feel uncomfortable when these habits persist past school age? Perhaps this is because they have some drive to move children from childhood to adulthood, and along the way they must discourage childish behaviours. There is also an element of sensual pleasure is the use of TOs and oral habits, and such activities are discouraged in public. It may also be that adults feel such behaviour is a sign of psychological problems. Woolridge points out that it is not surprising that children persist in their use of TOs and oral habits: 'if you find something that is terribly gratifying and comforting, it is hard to give it up.' Jalongo (1987) points out that disparaging comments may only intensify the child's need to cling to their TO and that it is mainly a question of waiting. TOs fade in importance as children develop friendships and as they overcome childhood anxieties. Jalongo lists a number of children's books which present creative solutions to the attachment object dilemma.

# Early theories of attachment: Behaviourist and Freudian views

Up until the 1950s, behaviourist and Freudian views dominated general thinking about attachment. These proposed that an infant is born with basic biological drives to satisfy hunger and thirst. Behaviourist principles suggest that infants become attached to their primary caregivers because the caregiver is associated with the satisfaction of hunger, the reinforcement of social signals and other pleasant experiences. Contented infants who smile and coo increase the caregiver's affection which completes the cycle of positive reinforcement. Freud's view of the origins of love were similar, in that he saw the satisfaction of oral pleasure leading to mother love.

These theories led to practices of infant care which were fairly rigid and emotionally distant. It was thought that healthy psychological development could be assured by well-regulated feeding schedules and attention, and that mothers should avoid 'spoiling' their babies. All this changed as a result of the work of John Bowlby.

# PSYCHOLOGICAL PERSPECTIVES: *The psychodynamic perspective*

This perspective is referred to as 'dynamic' because it attempts to explain how personality develops as well as describing what it is. Freud described personality in terms of three structures, namely the *id* (the unconscious, instinctive part which demands satisfaction), the *ego* (the conscious, intellectual part) and the *superego* (learned from others and governs moral behaviour). The way that development can be explained is in terms of an interaction between biologically determined structures, psychosexual stages and life experiences. Individual differences in adult personalities can be traced back to the specific way that early conflicts were handled during the early developmental stages (oral, anal and phallic). For example, a lack of oral gratification may lead to certain behaviours, including smoking, overeating or thumb-sucking, and also to certain personality characteristics, such as impatience, greediness or dependence.

Freud's emphasis was on innate, unconscious urges and the importance of early experience.

Neo-Freudians, such as Jung and Erikson, tended to include cultural influences and play down the role of biology.

Overall, the psychodynamic perspective has been enormously influential, both within psychology and beyond. Such popularity supports the view that Freud's analyses have some validity. However, it is essentially a reductionist account (reducing human activity to a basic set of biological structures and processes), and one which has little empirical support.

# BOWLBY'S THEORY OF ATTACHMENT

Bowlby was asked by the World Health Organisation to study the effects of maternal deprivation on children who had been orphaned during the Second World War. Bowlby published a number of books, starting with *Maternal Care and Mental Health* in 1951 and including three volumes of *Attachment and Loss* (1969, 1973, 1980). His training as a psychoanalyst explains his emphasis on maternal relations, although later on he was influenced by the ethological perspective, and sought to explain attachment as an adaptive strategy which appeared during a critical period.

An outstanding tenet of Bowlby's theory is that maternal attachment is as essential for healthy psychological development as 'vitamins and proteins are for physical health'. Behaviourists and Freudians thought that physical comfort was a caregiver's primary concern. Bowlby, however, suggested that emotional care was at least equally important. Bowlby also proposed the concept of *monotropy*, that is the need for one central caregiver, usually the mother, but alternatively the father or another person. The concept of 'mothering' does not need to imply that it is done by the child's mother or even another female. Finally, Bowlby felt that there was a critical period in the formation of attachment bonds. He believed that children who experience maternal deprivation below the age of four will suffer permanent damage.

Three landmark studies conducted in the 1950s supported his views. In 1946, Bowlby looked at the life histories of eighty-eight children who had been referred to his psychiatric clinic, half of whom had a criminal record for theft. Fourteen of the 'thieves' displayed an 'affectionless' character, that is, a lack of normal affection, shame or sense of responsibility. Almost all of these affectionless children (eighty-six per cent of them) had suffered 'early and prolonged separations from their mothers'. In practice, this meant that, at least before the age of two, these children had continually or repeatedly been in foster homes or hospitals, often not visited by their families. A pen picture of their lives presents sad reading. Of the remaining seventy-four children who were not affectionless, only seven (one per cent) had been separated. This appears to be strong evidence in support of Bowlby's hypothesis, but the data was both retrospective and, more importantly, correlational. We cannot be sure whether the maladjustment was *caused* by the separations themselves or if there was a third factor responsible for both maladjustment *and* separations, for example general family discord could be a cause of both. This was one of Rutter's criticisms (see page 43).

More support for Bowlby's views came from a piece of classic research conducted by Lorenz (1935). In this study, Lorenz became 'mother' to a brood of goslings. It was already known that many birds attach themselves to the first figure they see upon hatching and persist in this attachment, and Lorenz's work confirmed this. The phenomenon is called *imprinting*, another ethological concept taken from embryology. During pre-natal development, there are short periods when an individual is especially vulnerable. These times are called 'critical periods', and the effect is an imprint. Imprinting is an example of an instinct, an inherited behaviour pattern which predisposes an individual to certain forms of learning at critical times in development. Bowlby suggested that attachment behaviour is a kind of imprinting.

A third line of evidence came from Harlow's work with rhesus monkeys (1959). Harlow separated infant monkeys from their mothers soon after birth because he was then able to provide a better standard of physical care for the infants and reduce mortality rates. He and his co-workers noticed that the young monkeys were particularly distressed when the sanitation pads at the bottom of their cages were changed – the monkeys seemed to regard the pads as a kind of 'security blanket'. This led him to devise an experiment where a monkey was provided with two 'mothers', one a wire cylinder with a monkey-like face and a feeding bottle attached, the other with no feeding bottle but wrapped in a cloth (see Figure 3.2 overleaf). The position taken by behaviourists and Freudians would be that the monkeys should become attached to the 'mother' that offered food rather than comfort. In fact, the monkeys spent most of their time with the cloth mother, visiting the other one only for food. When they were frightened, they always went to the cloth mother. In later life, the monkeys raised without a responsive mother became socially maladjusted and had difficulty with mating and parenting.

When considering Harlow's research, it should be remembered that making generalisations from animal to human behaviour is not always appropriate. Behaviourists argue that the differences between human and non-human species are quantitative rather than qualitative, but others psychologists believe that certain unique features of the human species (such as consciousness and language) mean that non-human animal research has limited applicability. Harlow's research has also been criticised in terms of the ethics of

FIGURE 3.2 *Harlow's rhesus monkeys. The monkeys spent most time with the cloth mother, visiting the other only for food.*

allowing animals to be manipulated in this way. Such criticism can also be applied to Lorenz's work with goslings.

# Criticisms of Bowlby's views

Some of Bowlby's claims were challenged by Schaffer and Emerson (1964). They followed sixty newborn babies from a working-class area of Glasgow over a period of eighteen months. First, Schaffer and Emerson found that infants formed multiple attachments rather than just one. By the age of eighteen months, only thirteen per cent of the infants had one attachment figure, and thirty-five per cent had five or more attachments. Second, for thirty-nine per cent of the infants, the person who fed, bathed and spent most time with the infant was not the primary attachment figure. Therefore, this research supports Bowlby's view that an infant's emotional dependence on a caretaker is not related to filling physiological needs. However, Schaffer and Emerson disagreed with Bowlby's view of the importance of the caregiver's continued presence, since they found that attachment was not related to time *per se*. Ainsworth called this the *caregiving hypothesis*, suggesting that it is the quality not quantity of interaction that is important. Anxious attachment should therefore result from mothers who respond less readily to a child's needs, rather than being related to the amount of contact. Secure attachment occurs when a mother is sensitive, sees things from the infant's viewpoint, and is accepting.

Schaffer and Emerson pointed out that having multiple attachments is advantageous. There are individual differences in babies and caregivers. For example, some children and adults like cuddling whilst others don't. Equally, there are different kinds of attachment, each of which is important for healthy development. A father's style of play is often more physically stimulating and unpredictable, whereas mothers are more likely to hold their infants, soothe them, attend to their needs and read stories (Lamb, 1981). Many societies rely on multiple attachments. Ainsworth (1967) illustrated this in a study of the Ganda tribe of Uganda. She observed that most infants were cared for by several adults and formed multiple attachments. In Israel, about four per cent of the people live in kibbutzim, where everything is shared, including childminding. Mothers return to work a few weeks after giving birth, and then a nurse, or *metapelet*, looks after the child in the Children's House. All the children spend a few hours each evening with their parents, but sleep at the Children's House, spending the greater amount of time with the metapelet. Fox (1977) observed 122 children born and reared on a kibbutzim in a variation of the Ainsworth Strange Situation (see page 34) where both the natural mother and the metapelet took the role of parent. Fox found that the children protested equally when either mother or metapelet left, though some children sought their mother at reunion and were more comforted by her than the metapelet. Therefore regular, prolonged separations did not appear to damage the attachment bonds, though it is worth remembering that any study which is cross-cultural is prone to some bias because psychologists interpret behaviour in terms of their own cultural assumptions (see an example of this on page 88).

These findings suggest that Bowlby was correct in identifying the importance of attachment, but incorrect in overemphasising the single maternal role and the time factor for all children. Attachment, however, is only one part of his theory. Another part relates to the effects of deprivation. Rutter (1981) felt that the main problem with the concept of maternal deprivation was that it muddled together a range of essentially different experiences. He felt that separation is not the crucial factor in emotional disturbance. Instead, it may be that general family discord underlies the emotional disturbances observed by Bowlby. It may also be that affectionless psychopathy is due to the initial failure to form bonds (privation, see Chapter 13) rather than bond disruption (deprivation, see Chapter 8). Finally, situations where children experience deprivation, such as short hospital stays, may create emotional disturbance because of the strange and frightening environment as much as the separation and interference with attachments.

Bowlby's theory was important in changing our view of early emotional behaviour from one of *dependency*, the behaviourist and Freudian view, to one where the infant is an *active* participant in eliciting care. The criticisms served to refine this theory in several important ways: to include multiple attachments, to place less emphasis on mother-love, to consider individual differences and finally to distinguish between different kinds of deprivation. McFadyen (1994) suggests that many critics 'seem almost to have got stuck in a time warp, hanging on to [Bowlby's] early ideas, which were of course extremely controversial but also important and influential at the time.'

# SUMMARY

Infants usually form a variety of different attachments, with people and even things, which comfort them at times of stress and enable them to feel secure in exploring the world. A lack of attachment or absence of an attachment figure leads to feelings of anxiety which may be an adaptive response if the infant's distress brings help. When separation is prolonged, there may be long-term emotional consequences. Research on separation and privation is discussed further in Chapters 8 and 13 respectively.

Attachment serves to promote cognitive, emotional and self-development through interactions with significant others. Children benefit from having multiple attachments and high-quality social interactions during a sensitive period of their early development.

# *chapter four*

## THE END OF INFANCY: ACQUIRING LANGUAGE

# CHAPTER OVERVIEW

The 'official' end of infancy is marked by the onset of speech (the word infant comes from the Latin *infas* meaning 'without speech'). This chapter describes the sequence of language acquisition and looks at theories of how children learn their native language. The two main accounts are the behaviourist view that language acquisition can be explained in terms of reinforcement and imitation, and Chomsky's nativist theory which proposes that children are innately programmed to transform what they hear into a 'rule-driven' language. As well as discussing these, we will also consider functional and interactionist theories of language acquisition and, from a developmental perspective, the relationship between language and thought.

# STAGES OF LANGUAGE ACQUISITION

The sequences of language acquisition appear to be the same in all cultures. Pre-linguistic children engage in important vocal activities, such as babbling and echolalia (e.g. 'lalalala'), which develop their capacity for speech. However, before the age of six months, the nervous system and oral cavity are not sufficiently developed to form, or distinguish, different sounds. Understanding precedes production, although the fact that an infant follows an instruction may be the result of non-verbal signals as much as a comprehension of certain words. The stages of acquisition are outlined in Box 4.1.

**Box 4.1** The stages of language acquisition

| PHASE | AGE (APPROX.) | BEHAVIOUR |
|---|---|---|
| Pre-linguistic | 0 to 12 months | *Cooing* and *crying* : verbal behaviours which are non-linguistic and pre-intellectual.<br>*Turn-taking* (from two months): non-verbal conversation.<br>*Babbling* (six to nine months): producing phonemes (ma, pa). These are the same in all languages and even in deaf children. By nine months, phonemes are restricted to those of the native tongue, and deaf children have stopped babbling.<br>*Echolalia* (eleven to twelve months): the baby echoes itself, phoneme expansion (mamamama).<br>*Gestures* : a kind of pre-language which uses a grammar. |
| One-word utterances | 12 to 18 months | *First words* are often invented, a word is when a sound is consistently matched with meaning.<br>*Holophrases* : a word which conveys a complex message.<br>*Vocabulary* is typically ten words by fifteen months, fifty words by about 20 months and 200 words by the age of two. |
| First sentences | Around 2 years | **Stage 1 grammar**<br>*Two-word utterances*: from the beginning, these are not imitated, children create their own.<br>*Telegraphic speech*: only key words are used, but they are combined with rules (grammar) to convey meaning.<br>*Pivot grammar*: pivot plus open words [Braine (1963) noted that there are certain key, or 'pivot', words which appear repeatedly, in the same position and in conjunction with other 'x' or 'open' words. For example, 'see' is always first and 'it' last, and the same is true of 'throw' and 'ball'. Braine claimed that this was the earliest kind of grammatical sequencing, which becomes extended as the child matures.]<br><br>**Stage 2 grammar**<br>*Overgeneralising* or *overregularising*: applying a grammatical rule wrongly. For example, 'sheeps' rather than 'sheep'.<br>*Overextension*: using 'daddy' as a word for all men.<br>*Underextension*: limiting the use of a word to a specific context. For example, 'car' means a moving car, whereas all other references to car, such as 'parked car', must be spelled out. |

| PHASE | AGE (APPROX.) | BEHAVIOUR |
|---|---|---|
| | | *Pragmatics*: by the age of two children are proficient at using many non-verbal signals, such as raising the head to signal the start of conversation.<br>*Complex sentences*: by the age of four all children have an average MLU (mean length of utterance) of 4 which indicates the production of complex sentences. Some reach this stage as early as age two. |
| Later speech | 4 plus | *Pronunciation*: until the age of five most children usually have trouble with at least one phoneme.<br>*Complexity*: children continue to develop their language. Examples include joining sentences with a conjunction ('I am crying because he hurt me'), embedded sentences ('Here is the book I was reading yesterday'), passive constructions ('The boy was hit by the girl'), the use of tag questions ('You will go, won't you?') and distinguishing between pronouns ('Give it to her' rather than 'Give it to she'). As always, understanding precedes production.<br>*Metalanguage*: listening to and creating rhymes, poems and songs, enjoying jokes based on language. |

# First words

Pre-linguistic infants communicate in non-verbal and vocal ways, but language first appears as single words, known as *holophrases*, in which one word is used to represent a more complex meaning. For example, 'milk' may mean 'I want more milk' or 'I spilled my milk'. Adults interpret and amplify the meaning. Nelson (1973) studied the early speech of a group of eighteen infants and found that the first words tended to be objects which were prone to change (movement) such as 'ball' or 'car'. She also found that, from the beginning, children used all types of words and ones which were quite specific, such as 'pigeon' rather than 'bird' or 'cornflakes' rather than 'cereal'.

# Two-word utterances: grammatical speech

The next stage in language acquisition is combining words into two-word utterances. One index of children's speech development is their mean length of utterance (MLU). For example, a child aged two might have an average MLU of 1.5 morphemes ('to' and 'toe' are one morpheme whereas 'today' and 'toes' are two morphemes).

Brown (1973) and his colleagues recorded the speech of two children, Adam and Eve, by visiting them for two hours a week over many months. The children were twenty-seven months and eighteen months old respectively at the start of the study; Adam's average MLU was 1.84 morphemes, and Eve's was 1.4. Nine months later, this had increased to 3.55 and 3.27 morphemes respectively. These differences indicate that, although children begin to speak at different ages, their rate of acquisition remains fairly stable.

Brown and his colleagues noted some key features of Adam and Eve's development. First, they recorded frequent examples of the children imitating what their mothers said. Such imitations always preserved the order exactly, but not the content of what they heard. For example, the mother might say 'He's going out' or 'No, you can't write on Mr Cromer's shoe', whereas the child would repeat 'He go out' or 'Write Cromer shoe'. Brown considered this preservation of order to be a critical demonstration that children are beginning to produce grammatical expressions. In this context, 'grammar' refers to the way that the arrangement of words expresses meaning. For instance, 'man bites dog' means something different to 'dog bites man'. From the start, children place gestures and words in an order consistent with adult usage. Children say 'two shoes' not 'shoes two' and they say 'hit balloon' rather than 'balloon hit'. It could be that they are imitating the order they have heard, but they also produce novel phrases using order appropriately. Thus, a child might say 'Mummy sock' to mean 'Mummy's sock', or 'sock Mummy' to mean 'give the sock to Mummy'. When children imitate adult speech, the fact that they reduce what they hear to two or three words at a time is not just due to limitations of memory or the amount they can process at any one time. If this was the case, they would just repeat the first two or three words. Rather, they carefully select the key words and sustain the meaning of a sentence.

A second feature of Adam and Eve's linguistic interactions with their mothers was the reverse of this 'imitation with reduction', that is, 'imitation with expansion'. Brown and his colleagues observed that when the children uttered a telegraphic message (containing key words only), the mothers responded by expanding the sentence with the order preserved. For example, 'Eve lunch' became 'Eve is having her lunch'. From the mother's point of view, the expansion is a 'meaning check'. For the child, it is a lesson in how to create detailed meaning.

A third universal aspect of children's language development is the use of *overgeneralisations*, such as 'sheeps' and 'goed'. These cannot be imitations of what the child has heard because no adult uses them. Children must be inventing the language for themselves on the basis of grammatical rules. Berko (1958) checked this by showing children a picture of a 'wug'. She then showed a picture of two of them and asked them to complete the sentence: 'There are two......'. Children invariably said 'wugs', demonstrating their knowledge of the appropriate grammatical rule. Berko did the same for other grammatical rules. For example, 'This is a man who 'glings' every day. Today he 'glings'.

Yesterday he ......'. Adults will offer a variety of answers, such as 'gling', 'glang', 'glung' or 'glought', but children promptly say 'glinged'.

# THEORIES OF LANGUAGE

A theory of language attempts to account for the facts, and explains rather than describes how language is learned. The key features of acquistion are that children imitate what they hear, they produce rule-driven and novel utterances almost from the beginning, they acquire language with amazing ease and speed, and their speech is driven by a desire to comminicate meaning to other people.

## Learning theory

Skinner's (1957) view was that language is not different from any other behaviour, and therefore the same laws of learning apply. Skinner's account is based on principles of association, reinforcement and shaping. The random sounds, or *mands*, that a child produces are selectively reinforced by the child getting what it wants, such as a biscuit or parental attention. Through the process of *shaping*, these sounds become closer and closer to the real thing. A child also learns to produce actual words through *imitation* and is helped to do this by adults' use of 'motherese' (or Baby Talk Register (BTR), a less sexist term). This is a special form of language that adults use when talking to children. It is repetitive and uses a simplified grammar. For example, 'Look at the doggie', 'See the doggie', 'Pat the doggie'.

Skinner's theory explains some aspects of language acquisition, such as learning speech sounds, simple meanings, vocabulary and accent. However, it cannot account for overgeneralisations. Nor does it explain the speed at which children acquire language, and the fact the sequence of language acquisition is the same in all cultures.

# PSYCHOLOGICAL PERSPECTIVES:
## *The behaviourist perspective*

Behaviourists focus on observable behaviour rather than internal processes. They explain behaviour in terms of how it is learned (experience) rather than in terms of innate factors. In particular, learning occurs through conditioning (classical learning theory) and reinforcement and shaping (operant conditioning). For the behaviourist, the mind is a 'black box'. In order to understand behaviour, all we need to know is what goes in and what comes out. Skinner is considered a radical behaviourist because, in his view, *all* behaviour is caused and maintained in this way.

Learning theory is a powerful framework for understanding behaviour, and almost all explanations of behaviour incorporate behaviourist concepts. On its own, however, it rarely accounts for the complexity of human behaviour, nor for consciousness and subjective experience. It is a mechanistic, deterministic and reductionist account, and few psychologists today would regard themselves as 'strict' behaviourists.

## Social learning theory

Social learning theory (SLT) extends learning theory to include indirect forms of learning which occur through *imitation* or *modelling*. In so-called vicarious learning, reinforcement is observed but not personally experienced. SLT is therefore behaviourist *and* cognitive and draws on the ability to symbolise, imagine and think. It also incorporates the psychoanalytic concept of identification. The term 'social' indicates that learning occurs not just through interactions with the inanimate environment, but also within a social context. It is sometimes called *observational* learning, *indirect* learning, or *neo-behaviourism*.

SLT is particularly important in explaining how children learn new behaviour. They imitate others, especially parents, and model their behaviour on what they see around them, such as through the media. SLT has all the advantages of classic learning theories and avoids many of the disadvantages, since it allows for cognitive factors and indirect forms of learning.

## Nativist theory

According to Chomsky (1959, 1965), the universal sequence of language acquisition can be best understood in terms of children possessing an innate program to develop linguistic structures. Children acquire language by constructing the necessary rules (called *syntax* or *grammar*) when they are provided with appropriate input, that is, their native language. Chomsky's key point is that this ability to generate rules is an innate feature of the human brain which is similar to our capacity to walk or form particular cognitive structures. Chomsky described this capacity as a *language acquisition device* (LAD or, to maintain a sense of gender balance, a *language acquisition system*, LAS). Children learn the actual vocabulary of their native language, but the means of organising this data is innate and universal.

Chomsky's theory explains overgeneralisations, novel utterances and the fact that children manage to develop language while working on a usually incomplete sample of speech. It also explains why there is a universal sequence of language acquisition and why there are universal aspects of language, such as nouns.

If language acquisition is innate, then there may be a critical period for its acquisition, as is the case for visual perception (see page 24). Lenneberg

(1967) was the first to propose such a critical period for language and the evidence described in *Language Acquisition in Deaf Children* (see below) supports this view. The ability to learn words appears to be present in humans throughout life and is also an ability found in some animals, such as chimpanzees and parrots. However, the capacity to develop grammatical language appears to be available only during a sensitive period (before puberty) and only in human development. This suggests that grammatical language is biologically determined and that the specific areas of the brain responsible for it degenerate if not used.

# FOCUS ON...
# *language acquisition*
# *in deaf children*

Deaf children offer us a unique insight into language acquisition through a kind of 'natural experiment'. In normal children, exposure to language is inevitable. In deaf children, it is often limited, and this enables us to observe the effects of innate processes and learning.

When the Sandinista government reformed education in Nicaragua in 1979, they created the first schools for the deaf, who until then had been isolated from each other. During their play times, the children invented their own sign system, which very quickly spread and became known as the Lenguaje de Signos Nicaragüense (LSN). It had no grammar, but was an efficient communication system. The most interesting thing about it was that when deaf children around the age of four were exposed to LSN, they developed something much more fluid and stylised. In fact, their version was sufficiently different that it was given a different name, Idioma de Signos Nicaragüense (ISN). The most notable difference was that ISN was grammatical.

The older children were presumably beyond the age of acquiring grammar, but the younger children were taking a communication system (LSN) and turning it into a language (ISN). Presumably, they were applying their innate linguistic acquisition device to a linguistic input, something which had been unavailable to the older children at the appropriate age (Pinker, 1994).

Singleton and Newport (1993) have recently been studying a nine-year-old profoundly deaf boy. His parents are also deaf and only learned American sign language (ASL) after the age of fifteen. Their grasp of ASL is without grammar. However, the boy, who was exposed to this defective version of ASL from infancy, is a competent grammatical user. Again, the conclusion must be that the boy's parents were beyond a critical age for the acquisition of grammatical language, though they could learn a vocabulary and use it to communicate.

Exposure to language at an appropriate age

may be necessary, but it is not sufficient. Sachs et al. (1981) studied a young boy whose parents were both deaf and dumb. Although the boy heard language from TV and briefly at nursery school, by the time he was four his speech was below age level and structurally idiosyncratic. Since his speech therapy led to quick improvements, this suggests that language will develop only when it is placed in a social context. A similar conclusion might be drawn from the Nicaraguan deaf children described earlier. The schools tried to teach the children lip reading and speech, but were unsuccessful. However, where social forces dictated the necessity for language (in the playground), the children developed their own sign language. Thus the social function of language must also be considered a key factor in acquisition.

All of these findings are supported by other types of research. Several psychologists have tried to teach animals to use language (for example, Savage-Rumbaugh, 1991). Although some chimpanzees can learn ASL or other symbol systems, they never truly acquire the grammatical abilities of anything more than a two-year-old. Presumably, their brains do not have the requisite ability (Wallman, 1992).

A different line of research has been to look at children who learn a second language. If learning occurs before the age of seven, their performance is the same as native speakers in terms of their grammatical ability. However, this is not true of older children or adults (Newport, 1990).

Perhaps the best-known studies have been of children who have suffered extreme early deprivation. Do they learn language when exposed to it? Curtiss (1977) observed a girl called Genie over many years. Genie was thirteen when first discovered and initially showed great linguistic promise, but in the end it was clear that her word combinations could never be called grammatical. This particular case is much quoted but not very helpful because of its unique features. Possibly, Genie was brain damaged from birth and this could explain her abnormal development. In fact, the reason her father had locked her away in the first place was because he thought she was retarded. In any case, her mother reported that she *had* been exposed to language in her early years. Further, the emotional and social deprivation she suffered could equally explain her lack of recovery. In other cases of extreme early deprivation, children have recovered the ability to use language, but they were either younger when 'discovered' or they had been isolated with a brother or sister, as in the case of the twins studied by Koluchova (1972). These case histories are described in more detail in Chapter 13 (page 168).

## Functional theories

Alone, neither Skinner's nor Chomsky's account fully explains language acquisition. Halliday (1975) has criticised Chomsky's approach for the fact that it refers almost exclusively to structure and ignores function. Halliday points out that early language has functional importance: smiling, crying gestures and eye contact all communicate things of immediate importance. Bruner (1983) felt that Chomsky's LAD was not sufficient to explain acquisition, and that children require social interactions of the kind described by Halliday to provide the necessary linguistic input. Bruner termed this the innate acquisition system (LASS – language acquisition support system) and he has applied his ideas to the study of autistic children. In Bruner's view, it is lack of social interaction that explains the reason why they do not develop normal language.

Vygotsky (see page 73) also underlined the importance of pre-intellectual language as serving a largely social purpose, and language generally as being an embodiment of culture. However, if language was merely a reflection of culture, then stone-age cultures should have stone-age languages, but this is not the case. It would also follow that blind children, whose social interactions are limited because they cannot engage in mutual eye gaze or other non-verbal proxemics, should not develop normal language. Yet they do.

## Interactionist theories

Piaget sees language as being but one outcome of a general intellectual ability. Instead of proposing an innate specialised processor, he proposed a sophisticated brain which matures slowly and predisposes children to develop the same ideas at roughly the same age. These general cognitive changes are reflected in the sequence of language development. For example, the fact that children of a certain age start producing two-word utterances may be because of a general cognitive rather than linguistic maturity. Language, like cognitive development, is the result of interactions with the environment. The language produced by young children is influenced by their environment. They talk about those things immediately around them, such as the toy they are using or about aspects of their experience. Children also enrich the input they receive from the environment and they actively shape their perceptions using existing cognitive schemas. This view of language acquisition is referred to as *enrichment* or *input* theory (see page 29). Thus, children acquire language through their assimilation of new words/concepts (a 'top down' process) and their accommodation of existing words/concepts (a 'bottom up' process).

## Conclusion

Obviously it is possible to combine the various views. For example, Bruner's LASS is both social, learned and biological. According to Pinker (1994) the key to language is its innateness: 'Language is universal because children actually reinvent it ... not because they are taught it, not because they're generally smart, not because it's useful to them, but because they just can't help it'.

# COGNITIVE AND
# LINGUISTIC DEVELOPMENT

Another issue is whether cognitive changes precede linguistic advances, as proposed by Piaget, or whether children who have mastered certain linguistic forms of expression are then stimulated to make cognitive advances, as suggested by Vygotsky (Piaget's and Vygotsky's views are described in Chapter 5). Vygotsky sees language and thought as having different origins. Thinking originates in the need to restructure a situation (pre-linguistic thought), whereas language starts with the need to communicate (pre-intellectual language). Around the age of two, Vygotsky sees language taking on a thinking function as well as a social one, and then it shapes thought. Language embodies cultural concepts, and learning these concepts may affect our perception of reality. In the words of Whorf (1956), 'we dissect nature along the lines laid down by our native languages ... the world is presented as a kaleidoscopic flux of impressions to be organised by our minds'. We raised the same issue in Chapter 2 when we considered perception and the extent to which what we perceive is directly related to sensations or whether it is altered by our conceptual expectations (see pages 29–30).

It is true that vocabulary helps young children make discriminations within the mass of sensory data around them. It is also true that learning a new subject or skill generally involves learning a new vocabulary, so that, at the very least, language aids in concept formation. Experiments testing memory have shown that the labels given to objects or colours will influence the way they are later recalled, supporting the view that language is affecting cognitive processes (Carmichael et al., 1932). The classic example used to demonstrate the effect of language on thought is the existence in certain languages of special groups of words. It is thought that this enables native speakers to distinguish features not available to speakers of other languages. However, Pinker (1994) is critical of this line of argument. First of all, with respect to the 'Great Eskimo Vocabulary Hoax', he points out that the Eskimos actually only have around twelve words for snow rather than the fifty or so that has been claimed, and that there are about the same number of 'snow' words in English: snow, sleet, slush, blizzard, avalanche, hail, hardpack, powder, flurry, dusting. Even if Eskimos did have more words, it wouldn't be surprising, because the more contact one has with a particular kind of thing, the more one needs to make and represent finer distinctions. For example, people working in publishing have many words for printing fonts, and horse breeders have various names for the sizes, shapes and ages of horses. It is therefore the cognitive *need* to make distinctions which influences the vocabulary that a person develops, rather than the other way round. Vygotsky (1987) suggests that the acquisition of a new word is the *beginning* of the development of a concept rather than the finish.

Some concepts may exist independently of the language we use, and are based on innate discriminations (as suggested by the differentiation theory of perception, see page 30). Rosch (1978) tested members of the Dani, a culture from New Guinea. They have only two colour words corresponding to black and white. Rosch found that the Dani were quicker at learning a new colour category based on 'fire-engine' red than a category based on an 'off-red'. The human eye records colour using cones which respond best to certain colours (such as fire-engine red). Therefore the Dani's performance in learning colour labels suggests that some concepts are physically rather than linguistically influenced.

Bruner (1966) believed that the onset of language enables qualitatively different thinking, and therefore thinking *depends* on language. Bernstein (1961) argued that only a certain kind of language ('elaborated code') allows users to articulate abstract concepts, and that children who use a 'restricted code' are unable to engage in these kinds of intellectual activity. Of the many criticisms of Bernstein's work, the main ones are his failure to recognise the subtleties of some forms of non-standard English and his confusion between social and linguistic deprivation (Labov, 1970).

We can use common experience to demonstrate that thought can exist without language, as in knowing what you feel but not having the words to say it. Thinking certainly begins at an earlier developmental stage than language. In Piaget's view, the onset of language does not alter the pace of cognitive development. Evidence supporting this comes from Sinclair-de-Zwart (1969). She divided a group of children into those who could or could not conserve (see page 69 for an explanation of conservation). She found that the children who could not conserve also showed differences in their linguistic development. Mainly they used absolute rather than comparative terms, such as 'big' rather than 'larger'. They also used a single term for different dimensions, such as 'small' to mean 'short', 'thin' or 'few'. These findings suggest that cognitive and linguistic development are tied together. In a further experiment, Sinclair-de-Zwart tried to teach the non-conservers the verbal skills they were lacking. However, ninety per cent of these children were still unable to conserve. This supports Piaget's view that cognitive maturity is a prerequisite for linguistic development because provision of an appropriate vocabulary did not result in cognitive advances.

The conclusion must be that language and thought are interdependent much of the time: cognitive operations underlie linguistic development and language can affect the way we categorise things or how we think. However, the two processes can, and do, exist independently.

# SUMMARY

The key feature of human language is grammar. There is strong evidence for a critical period in development during which children, given linguistic input, will generate a set of linguistic rules (or a grammar). Children cannot be simply imitating what they hear because they produce novel phrases which are grammatical. However, imitation and reinforcement are part of the account of language acquisition. Also part of the account are the functions that language serves, both social and cognitive. Early infant language is social and thought is non-verbal. Ultimately, thought is much influenced by our linguistic concepts, though it continues to exist independently of language.

# *chapter five*

## CHAPTER OVERVIEW

In this chapter, we will evaluate claims that cognitive abilities and intelligence can be speeded up or increased through, for example, compensatory education or parental stimulation. We will also look at ways of measuring IQ in children, and finally at the theories of cognitive development proposed by Piaget, Vygotsky and Bruner.

## NATURE VERSUS NURTURE

The question of whether cognitive abilities are largely a result of inherited factors or whether experience can have a significant effect on cognitive development has at least three practical implications. Firstly, many parents want to know whether they can speed up their child's cognitive development and increase the child's intelligence through extra stimulation. Secondly, people concerned about the inequalities which exist between certain classes of persons believe that compensatory education can alter the course of a disadvantaged child's cognitive development. Finally, educators generally wish to know the best way to approach teaching.

Piaget's view was that children advance their knowledge because of biologically-regulated cognitive changes. For Piaget, outside influences have a minimal effect, and children should therefore be offered stimuli which are moderately novel only when they are ready for them. Self-discovery and self-motivation are critical in developing intrinsic satisfaction. As Piaget remarked, 'Each time one prematurely teaches a child something he could have discovered himself, that child is kept from inventing it and consequently from understanding it completely.' (Piaget, 1970). Bruner and Vygotsky took a different view and felt that cognitive development depends on the guidance of those with greater knowledge. This intervention enables children to fully exploit their current capabilities; without it, the process of development will be at least slower.

Both Piaget and Bruner's approaches are sometimes referred to as *discovery learning*, emphasising the child's active role in their learning as opposed to the behaviourist view of passive reinforcement. Skinner (1948), for example, described an ideal world where the environment is designed in such a way to shape human behaviour rather than behaviour shaping the learning process.

# SPEEDING UP COGNITIVE DEVELOPMENT: THE EVIDENCE

Some features of cognitive development are obviously tied to maturation. For example, language or certain physical activities depend on the development of requisite muscular apparatus. Mental abilities may also be affected by maturity, but equally they could result from the progressive development of a hierarchy of higher order skills. For example, reading depends on linguistic proficiency, which in turn depends on the ability to discriminate sounds and shapes. Gibson et al. (1962) showed a set of letter-like figures (see Figure 5.1) to children aged four to eight years old, and asked them to pick out the stimuli which were identical to the standard figure. The under-fives had diffi- culty with this task, but older children could identify the distinctive features. Such an age difference suggests that maturational factors were responsible, as the children would have had differing kinds of experience.

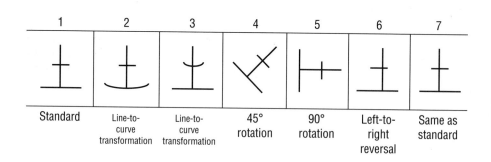

FIGURE 5.1 *Letter stimuli used by Gibson et al. (1962)*

Another study looked at the ability to categorise sounds. Bradley and Bryant (1983) found a high correlation between those under- fives who could do this well and their later ability to read. To test whether teaching could affect this, they worked with a group of children whose original ability to discrimi- nate was very poor and spent two years teaching them sound categorisation skills. Bradley and Bryant found that this intervention did lead to significant improvement in reading. One teaching approach to pre-reading skills is to use alliteration and rhyming, such as appear in many traditional nursery rhymes (for example, Ba Ba Black Sheep). This research suggests that such guidance can have a significant influence.

More support for the value of training comes from Bryant and Trabasso (1971) who worked on *transitive inference tasks* (knowing that if A→B and B→C, it follows that A→C). Piaget had predicted that such tasks were beyond the grasp of a seven-year-old, but Bryant and Trebasso felt that such failure was due to the demands placed on memory. They thought that if children were taught the initial comparisons (A→B, B→C, C→D, and so on) very thoroughly this would help. In their experiment, they used five coloured rods of different lengths and demonstrated that children as young as four could manage the task. Therefore, it would seem that the inability to do the transitive inference tasks was due to limited memory and not because the seven-year-olds couldn't cope with the logic. Increased memory capacity develops as a consequence of maturation, thus this research supports the maturational hypothesis as well.

Freund (1990) also investigated the value of intervention with pre-school children. She asked children to help a puppet furnish a doll's house. This was to establish a baseline of what the children were currently capable of in the way of identifying furniture and placing it appropriately. Then she divided the children into two groups. One group played on their own, the other played with their mothers. Finally, the children were assessed on a furniture-sorting task. Those who had worked with their mothers showed dramatic improvement whereas the other group had changed very little. This supports Vygotsky's view that guidance increases learning.

Taken altogether, this research suggests that cognitive abilities can be speeded up, though the long-term effects may still be negligible. We also cannot know how much the children's understanding, as opposed to their performance, has improved.

# FOCUS ON...
## *compensatory programmes*

In the 1960s, educationalists and politicians came to the view that disadvantaged children should be helped by receiving the pre-school educational experiences and health care that they otherwise lacked. In this way, it was hoped that they would start school on equal terms with other children and avoid a self-perpetuating cycle of failure. Probably the best-known example of this is Operation Head Start, a scheme set up in 1965. The programme resulted in initial IQ gains, but these turned out to be small and short-lived, and the costs were high; the first summer's bill came to over a billion dollars for half a million children (Zigler and Muenchow, 1992).

Follow-up studies (for example, Lazar and Darlington, 1982) have found that participants were less likely to become pregnant, need welfare assistance or become delinquent when compared with non-participants. They were also more likely to complete high school, to be employed after high school and/or to continue in further education. This suggests that the scheme did have some positive effects. IQs may not have altered, but critical attitudes towards achievement had changed. Weighing costs versus benefits is difficult, but one estimate suggests that for every $1,000 spent, $4,000 was saved in terms of welfare, health and policing (Davenport, 1991). The Head Start programme should also be evaluated in terms of its effect on subsequent generations. The fact that participants' attitudes towards achievement were changed may well be passed on to *their* children.

Some psychologists believe that even the Head Start project came too late in the child's development, which might explain the lack of success in terms of IQ. It might also be better to have greater parental involvement. The Milwaukee Project, conducted by Heber et al. (1972), worked with newborn infants and their low social class black mothers who had IQs below 75. Half the group were 'controls' and received no extra treatment. The mothers in the experimental group were given help with job-related skills, parenting and house-keeping, and their children were involved in a regular day-care programme from the age of three months. This included pre-school skills and parental involvement. By the time the children entered school, the experimental group had a mean IQ of 124 whereas the control group's mean IQ was 94. This enormous gap decreased later, although at age fourteen the experimental group were still 10 IQ points above the controls.

# INCREASING
# INTELLIGENCE: THE EVIDENCE

Intelligence is a measure of cognitive abilities, and the study of the development of intelligence focuses on how people come to possess more or less of this ability. The evidence suggests that intelligence clearly owes something to inherited factors, but a large amount of variation can be attributed to the environment. This can be expressed in terms of Gottesman's (1963) concept of an innately-determined *reaction range*. A person's genotype sets a possible range for their intelligence, whereas a person's actual IQ (intelligence quotient) will be determined by the degree to which their environment is intellectually enriching. This same principle can be applied to other aspects of human development, such as height and sociability.

What experiential factors lead to increased intelligence? Nutrition is an important factor from the moment of conception. When a pregnant woman is malnourished, her foetus will be underdeveloped, most critically in terms of brain development. This pattern continues throughout childhood. As we saw in Chapter 1, breastfeeding is linked with higher intelligence, possibly because of the presence of certain fats in breast milk which facilitate brain development (see page 17). Other factors are important, too. For example, Benton and Cook (1991) reported that vitamin supplements given to six-year-old children can lead to increases in IQ. Participants were given either vitamin or placebo tablets using a *double blind* procedure. When tested after six weeks, the children taking the vitamins showed improvements on measures of IQ, reaction time and the performance of a difficult cognitive task. Other research supports the importance of improved diets. Lynn (1986) reports that the average gains in IQ per decade in Britain, the US and Japan are 1.7, 3.0 and 7.7 IQ points respectively. This is unlikely to be due to genetic change, but more probably because of improved education and improved diet.

A second key influence on intellectual development is the amount of cognitive stimulation a child receives. Zajonc and Markus (1975) suggest that this can be used to explain birth order effects. They used data from a Dutch study of 40,000 males born in 1944, and found that eldest and only children had significantly higher IQs, and that IQ tended to decline with family size. Zajonc and Markus explained this in terms of a *confluence model*: the intellectual climate of the home is enhanced by older members, and younger members detract from it. Older children receive a greater amount of parental time, and parents have higher expectations for them, whereas subsequent children have to share attention and family resources. Other research has suggested that the reason why children from middle-class homes do better at school is that they receive greater stimulation at home (Smith and Cowie, 1991). Stimulation has also been used to explain why some children become creative 'geniuses' or child prodigies (see page 13–14).

A third line of evidence takes a more global look at the effects of various 'risk' factors. Children may fail to develop their full potential because of a poor environment, much in the way that a plant might fail to thrive in poor soil. Sameroff and his colleagues (1987, 1993) conducted the Rochester Longitudinal study, following a group of over 150 children from birth and testing them at the age of four and again at thirteen. They identified ten fami-ly risk factors, such as mental health, education, occupation, extent of family support, stressful life events and family size, and found a clear negative corre-lation of about 0.60 between the number of risk factors and IQ . At age four, those children who had most risk factors (high-risk) were twenty-four times as likely to have IQs below 85 than low-risk children. Sameroff calculated that, on average, each risk factor reduced the child's IQ score by 4 points. These factors are all associated with low socio-economic class. However, it is not certain which is the cause and which is the effect. For example, the rea-son that social class is correlated with intelligence could be because with low socio-economic status families have poorer nutrition (class as a cause), or it could be that adults of lower intelligence tend to become members of the lower social classes, and then their children's lower IQ could be ascribed to inherited low intelligence (class as an effect).

Of course, evidence also supports the alternative view that intelligence is largely a fixed quantity at birth and that environmental influences only result in small variations. If this is true, then the only way to change intelligence would be through eugenics (selective breeding). Classically, support for this position comes from studies of twins and adopted children. For example, Shields' (1962) study of twins found almost identical correlations (+ 0.76/0.77) for identical (monozygotic, MZ) twins, whether they were raised in the same or different environments. Non-identical (dizygotic, DZ) twins were less similar (+ 0.51). Shields' study has been criticised for involv-ing a small sample who often shared similar environments, such as going to the same school, despite being labelled 'separated'. The Minnesota Study of Twins (Bouchard et al., 1990) has kept track of more than 100 sets of MZ and DZ twins and triplets who were reared apart since 1979. The evidence continues to supports the view that IQ is at least partly inherited, finding that about seventy per cent is due to genetic variation. The Swedish Adoption/Twin Study of Ageing (SATSA, Pedersen et al., 1992) recorded data on over 300 MZ and DZ twins reared apart or together from an early age. When they were tested at an average age of sixty-five they found that MZ twins reared apart or together had IQ correlations of about 0.79, whereas DZ twins reared apart were 0.32 and together were 0.22. This suggests that about eighty per cent of IQ is inherited. Finally, the Texas adoption study (Horn, 1983) followed 300 children whose biological mothers had given up their children within one week of birth. At the age of eight the children's intelligence was correlated 0.25 with their biological mothers and 0.15 with their adoptive mothers, evidence for a stronger genetic than environmental link. Overall, this evidence suggests a large genetic component and a small environmental influence.

There are conditions in which intelligence is clearly linked to inherited fac-tors. Mental retardation may arise because of certain genetic disorders, such as Down's or fragile-X syndrome (see page 143). In both of these cases, the expression of the disorder is by no means uniform. Environmental factors, such as the amount of stimulation a child receives, have a significant influence over the severity of retardation. In another genetic condition, phenylketonuria, a faulty gene means that proteins are not correctly metabolised, and their poisonous residue leads to permanent brain damage. If this condition is detected at birth and the infant given a diet low in protein, it suffers no ill consequences. In this case at least, the environment is crucial in determining the child's IQ. In fact, all the evidence examined demonstrates that inherited factors underlie intelligence, but they do not fix it.

# RESEARCH TECHNIQUES:
## *Comparing nature and nurture*

Developmental psychology is particularly concerned with trying to distinguish the separate effects of nature and nurture. The best-known form of natural experiment is the use of twins because they provide genetic and/or environmental controls. Monozygotic twins (MZ) have identical genes, since they develop from a single egg. Dizygotic twins (DZ) are only as similar as siblings because they grow from two separate eggs. If twins are reared apart, we can observe the effects of a different environment on the 'same' person. Or we can compare MZ and DZ twins to see if greater genetic similarity is associated with more similar abilities, presuming that both kinds of twins share very similar environments.

However, these suppositions are not entirely correct. From birth, MZ twins are not actually identical because of different pre-natal experiences, such as nutrition. Twins reared together may not have had the same experiences, whereas those reared apart may have had more similar experiences than was thought, either because they were reared by relatives or because people who look the same produce the same responses in others,

the genotype creating the phenotype as described in Chapter 1 (see page 5).

A second approach is to study adopted children, another form of natural experiment. Psychologists compare adopted children with their natural parents (shared genes) and with their adoptive parents (shared environment).

Cross-cultural research can also provide evidence about nature versus nurture. Where cross-cultural behaviours are the same, despite different life experiences, we can propose that the behaviours are innately rather than culturally determined. However, there are many problems with such research. For example, a non-native observer may not understand the language or practices of different peoples, the observations are only a sample of that culture's behaviour and may not be typical, and one can't be certain that an observed child-rearing practice is actually the cause of a cultural trait.

The main problem facing investigations of nature and nurture is that it is hard to separate the two causes. Most studies rely on correlations rather than deliberate manipulations. For example, intelligent parents (good genetic strain) are most likely to provide a more intellectually stimulating home and diet (good environment), so that any correlation between parents' and their children's intelligence is in fact due to environment, but may appear to be genetic. This is true even when a child is adopted, because attempts are made to match adoptive and natural parents.

# RESEARCH TECHNIQUES:
## *Assessing intelligence in early childhood*

All of the theories and studies of intelligence rely on a means of being able to assess or test them. A person's IQ is calculated by giving them a series of tasks and scoring what they accomplish. This is then adjusted for age, since a younger child will be able to do less, even though they have the same potential intelligence as an older child. The items in intelligence tests may be divided into different sub-scales, such as performance, verbal, non-verbal, or creative. Some tests examine different processes, such as a child's attention span, their ability to learn from examples or performance on Piagetian tasks. Some intelligence tests are specifically 'non-verbal' or 'culture-free' so that less literate persons or those from different backgrounds have an equal chance to those who can read or who are similar to the test designer in terms of culture or class.

For children under the age of three, there are scales which provide a 'developmental quotient' (DQ). This assesses the rate at which the infant has achieved important milestones. The best and most widely used are the Bayley Scales of Infant Development, for use with infants aged two to thirty months (Anastasi, 1990). It includes a motor scale (looking at, for example, head balance, sitting or grasping a cube), a mental scale (for instance, reaching for a desirable object or searching for a hidden toy) and an infant behavioural record (which documents such things as the child's temperamental characteristics, attention span, goal directedness and social behaviour).

DQ may not bear much relationship to later IQ because progress under the age of three is much more controlled by maturational factors, whereas later in life experience becomes more important. However, such tests are useful in the early identification of problems such as mental retardation or deafness.

Children over three are tested using non-verbal or individual tests, because their use of language is limited. The Wechsler Performance Scales involve tasks such as saying what part of a picture is missing, reproducing a design using blocks of red, white and red/white blocks, arranging pictures to tell a story, and mazes. Testing children of this age requires special skills because of their short attention spans and their susceptibility to 'suggestion' from the tester, a kind of experimenter bias.

# PIAGET'S THEORY OF COGNITIVE DEVELOPMENT

Piaget's (1926, 1950, 1970) view has been called *genetic epistemology*, that is the study of knowledge (epistemology) from a biological perspective. It has been variously described as cognitive, structural, interactionist, dynamic and functional. His theory extends to moral development and play (see Chapters 7 and 9) and has had enormous influence on psychological theory, research, educational practice and attitudes towards children generally. Piaget described development in terms of a fixed sequence of biologically determined stages. Piaget based his theory on the observations he made while working in Binet's laboratory on the first intelligence test to be developed. Piaget noted that children of the same age tended to make similar mistakes. These observations were confirmed in the observations he made of his own children's cognitive development and, later, in experiments with young children using what he called the 'clinical method'.

# RESEARCH TECHNIQUES: *Interviewing children*

One way to assess behaviour is to observe it. Another way is to ask people what they think themselves. This is called the self-report method and can be oral (an interview) or written (a questionnaire), and may be highly 'structured' or 'unstructured'. Such self-report methods are collectively called surveys. They usually rely on linguistic competence and therefore are not particularly suitable for children unless the interviewer provides some assistance, which may result in tester bias.

Piaget used a technique he called the 'clinical method', a form of unstructured interview where the interviewer determines some of the questions to ask, but many of them are determined by the child's answers. The technique therefore allows for the possibility that the child will give unexpected answers and that further questioning will lead to new discoveries about thinking. This maximises the amount of information that is gained, and the more informal atmosphere is good for child participants. However, it is highly susceptible to tester bias and relies on the interviewer's skill.

Piaget's account is more than just an 'ages and stages' theory. He also described how the human intellect works in terms of an adaptive structure. The complementary processes of *assimilation* and *accommodation* enable a child, or an adult, to incorporate new experiences into existing knowledge (schema) or to modify existing knowledge in the light of new experience, that is, to learn. The driving force behind this is the human desire for equilibrium. In general, information is assimilated using existing schema. When these do not fit, a state of disequilibrium prevails, and the schema must be modified or accommodated, thus returning the organism to a state of equilibrium. This drive ensures that cognitive development will take place. In Piaget's view, intelligence is the degree to which a person can adapt to a changing environment and maintain equilibrium.

This process can be used to explain common observations and experiences. Suppose that a three-year-old is given a new toy, a small box with several buttons which can be pushed. What happens next? The child might, for example, push the buttons to see what happens or stand on the box. In other words, the child is trying to fit (assimilate) the object into an existing schema. If any of these actions results in a new discovery (for example, the child may find out that pushing the button results in the box opening), this leads to cognitive disequilibrium requiring the accommodation of existing schema. Similarly, calling an animal with four legs a 'cow' is an example of assimilation; but if the child then discovers that the animal does not make a mooing sound, this requires accommodation, and a new category of animals must be formed.

We constantly adapt existing knowledge or schema to fit new situations to advance our understanding and mastery of the world. The cognitive structures which enable us to do this are innate, appearing in sequence as a child matures. Infants are born with certain innate schemata which are equivalent to reflex responses, for example grasping or sucking schema. With experience, these schema change and are thus *variant*. Other structures are *invariant*, such as assimilation and accommodation, because they remain the same throughout life. Operations are also variant structures which develop with age. They are the thoughts that a person has which are subject to rules of logic and may involve physical or symbolic manipulations. As children mature they are progressively capable of more abstract and less egocentric operations.

# Evidence for Piaget's theory

Many of Piaget's observations fit our everyday observations of children. Take object permanence, for example. Infants of less than six months will lose interest in an object hidden under a pillow because, once an object is no longer visible, it ceases to exist as far as they are concerned. Slightly older children will search for the object, and the game of 'peek-a-boo' exploits this

**Box 5.1**   Piagetian stages of cognitive development

| STAGES | AGE IN YEARS (APPROX.) | MODE OF THINKING | SUB-STAGES/CHARACTERISTIC BEHAVIOURS |
|---|---|---|---|
| SENSORIMOTOR | 0 to 2 | Beginnings of language and symbolic thought, but child mainly focused on sensory and motor experiences. | • Reflex activities (birth to one month), e.g. sucking.<br>• Primary circular reactions (one to four months) 'Circular' means repetitive, e.g. smiling, kicking.<br>• Secondary circular reactions (four to eight months), repetitive actions with external objects, e.g. shaking a bottle.<br>• Co-ordination of secondary schemes (eight to twelve months): schemas used to solve problems. Object permanence develops around nine months, but is only firmly established in the final sub-stage.<br>• Tertiary circular reactions (twelve to eighteen months), experimenting with actions.<br>• Symbolic problem-solving (eighteen months +), end of sensorimotor stage because infant no longer relies on physical representation of things. |
| PRE-OPERATIONAL | | The ability to form and use symbols, as seen in the use of language and numbers. Thought processes are developing but are still unsystematic (syncretic). Language is an outcome of thought. | |
| Pre-conceptual | 2 to 4 | Concepts not fully formed. | • Animism.<br>• Egocentric thought.<br>• Centration.<br>• Inability to perform concrete operations such as conservation, reversibility. |
| Intuitive | 4 to 7 | Reasoning doesn't use adult logic. | • Moral realism (see Chapter 7). |
| CONCRETE OPERATIONS | 7 to 11 | More adult-like thought, but still not abstract nor always using adult logic. | • Can now cope with conservation, centration, seriation, class inclusion, understanding numbers, reversibility.<br>• Problem-solving still tends to be random.<br>• Moral relativity and empathy (see Chapter 7). |
| FORMAL OPERATIONS | 11 on | Formal logic and abstract thought. | • Systematic and organised deduction/induction.<br>• Strong idealism.<br>• Own values, beliefs and philosophies. |

developmental stage. Another example of the onset of object permanence can be seen in attachment behaviour (see page 34). Only when children realise that their caregiver or parents are permanent can they begin to note their absence. Object permanence relies on the ability to form mental representations and make inferences.

As children mature, they exhibit certain ways of thinking which are characteristic of their age. For example, two-year-olds might bump into a chair and apologise to it. This is called *animism*, the willingness to attribute life-like qualities to inanimate objects. Children in this pre-operational stage also find it difficult to see things except from their viewpoint, an *egocentric* outlook. A four-year-old girl would be able to say that she had a brother, but might find it difficult to see that her brother has a sister. Piaget's three mountains experiment (see Figure 5.2) demonstrated such egocentric thinking. Children aged between four and twelve were shown a doll placed in various positions around a model of three mountains. In each position, the children were asked to identify the doll's view of the scene from a selection of pictures. An egocentric child cannot do this, being only able to imagine the scene as they see it. By the age of nine, the children were sure of the doll's perspective.

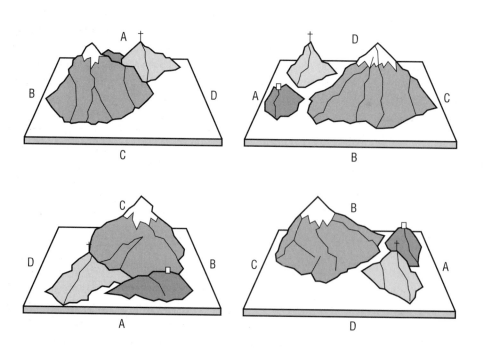

FIGURE 5.2  *A model of the mountain range used by Piaget and Inhelder*

Probably Piaget's most widely known experimental work is the research relating to *conservation*. This term describes the ability to perceive that volume, length, number and mass (weight) remain constant, even when they appear to change. For example, when water is poured from a tall, thin beaker into a short, fat one, it looks as if there is less, but of course the volume remains constant. By the age of nine, all children realise this, whereas very few five-year-olds do. Piaget demonstrated similar conservation skills using rows of beads (number conservation) and balls of clay (mass).

In terms of Piaget's theory, this evidence demonstrates the unsystematic nature of the pre-operational children's thought. In a sense, their thought does demonstrate some logic. The fact that a beaker has a higher water level can mean more water. However, it is a flawed logic and would not hold up under questioning. In the case of animism, for instance, a child could not cope with the question 'how can a chair be alive when it does not breathe?'. Their thought is logical to the extent that it has some internal consistency, but this is not the same as the logic used in the adult world.

Around the age of seven, children's quality of thought changes. This has major consequences for what children are now capable of; for example, they are now able to learn mathematical operations, to develop a sense of empathy for others and engage in activities with rules, such as rounders or chess.

However, children's thought during the concrete operations stage continues to lack systematicity, in particular inductive and deductive reasoning. Transitive inference tasks (as described earlier in this chapter) should be understandable only if given in a concrete form, for example using dolls or sticks. The game of *Mastermind* involves deductive reasoning; a person must work out the colour and position of four pegs given limited feedback; they present a guess and are told how many are right but in the wrong position, and how many are right and in the right position. By developing various hypotheses, the player can deduce the correct answer. Children of any age can play the game, but until they have reached the level of formal operations, they will not make systematic guesses. Piaget suggested that this stage is reached around the age of 11, though Parker, who manufacture the game of *Mastermind*, suggest that six-year-olds might be capable of such thought.

It is not just reasoning which shows stages of development. Artistic development also follows a regular sequence. A child's early scribbles are the first steps in the development of writing skills. Children quite often draw hundreds of circular-type figures, which may be related to the development of muscular co-ordination and pre-writing skills. In time, children can produce recognisable objects, though invariably pre-school children draw what they know rather than what they see (called *intellectual realism*). For example, if you ask children to draw a picture of a house, it is rarely a picture of an actual house, but a representation of their concept 'house'. One study demonstrated this by asking children between the ages of five and nine to draw exactly

**69**

what they saw. They were shown some simple shapes and then a cup positioned so that the handle was out of sight. Children younger than seven invariably include the handle, whereas older children didn't, though when asked to draw an imagined cup, they did include a handle (Freeman and Janikoun, 1972).

# Criticisms of Piaget's theory and research

It is claimed that Piaget underestimated the age at which children exhibit each ability, and also overestimated the abilities of adolescents and adults. One reason for this may be the research methods he and his co-workers used. Firstly, much of Piaget's account is based on his detailed observations of his own three children. Such 'case studies' are unreliable and not objective. Nevertheless, Piaget's records are an extremely rich source of data and many of his observations cannot be disputed. Secondly, Piaget collected data using the clinical method which is open to experimenter bias. This might explain why he got the answers he expected. Finally, the most well-known criticism is that some of his tasks simply did not make sense. This problem is compounded by the fact that very young children may not understand what is expected of them, and look for other cues to guide their behaviour. For example, in the conservation experiments, Piaget asked children the same question before the transformation and again afterwards. Children who could conserve should give the same answer both times. However, a younger child may think that a second question implies a different answer. Experiments by Rose and Blank (1974) and Samuel and Bryant (1984) found that, by asking the question only after the transformation had occurred, many younger children were, in fact, able to conserve. However, there were still age differences, although the boundary had shifted downwards. McGarrigle and Donaldson (1974) used a 'naughty teddy' to 'mess up' the display of counters 'accidentally', and found that nearly double the number of four- to six-year-olds were able to conserve, presumably because the task made more sense to them. Donaldson (1978) also believed that the reason children have difficulty with the class-inclusion question, 'Are there more black cows or more sleeping cows?' is because it doesn't make sense. She changed the question to 'Are there more black cows or more cows?' and found the percentage of those who answered correctly rose from twenty-five per cent to forty-eight per cent.

Piaget's age errors may also be because children today are more able. Intelligence has certainly increased (see earlier in this chapter) and so has physical maturity. Therefore we might expect that children are able to do certain tasks at a younger age than they could forty years ago.

However, simply to criticise age limits is to miss the central point of Piaget's theory, that qualitative changes occur during cognitive development, and these are tied to maturation. A more critical and practically oriented dispute is about the extent to which children can be trained beyond their current level of functioning, the issue discussed at the beginning of this chapter. The evidence does not suggest that Piaget was wrong, but that he places insufficient emphasis on the value of practice.

# Neo-Piagetians

Neo-Piagetians suggest that certain adjustments can be made to Piaget's theory to accommodate these criticisms. First, a more fluid approach should be taken to ages and stages. Fischer's (1980) skill theory proposes that development proceeds through a series of skill structures called levels. Specific skills at one level are built directly from specific skills at the preceeding level. There is gradual movement from one level to the next as the skills are gradually transformed. Fischer therefore believes that there are discrete stages in cognitive development which are tied to maturation, but, at the same time, this process is continuous. In fact, Piaget did not claim that there were abrupt changes between stages. He claimed that there would be a period when a child could do some of things of the next stage but not all, calling this horizontal décalage. However, he felt that it was not possible to fully proceed to the next stage until all the earlier elements had been learned.

Second, Neo-Piagetians explain individual differences as a function of learning experience, and maintain that development should be seen as an interaction between both biological and environmental factors. This accounts for uneven rates of development – the effects of practice – and acts as a bridge between biological and learning theory accounts of cognitive development. Even learning theory relies on some biological basis for development, as the ability to learn itself is innate in the same sense that Piaget's structures for acquiring knowledge are innate.

Third, cognitive development is seen as the acquisition of skills or strategies for problem-solving, organising information (memory), selecting relevant information (perception and attention) and so on. This differs from Piaget's approach because it suggests that children's thinking differs across different domains of thinking. It may be possible to explain, for example, changes in logical reasoning in terms of increased memory. As children get older, their memory capacity increases. Since many logical tasks involve memory, this would lead to and explain improvements in logical reasoning (see Bryant and Trabasso, page 59). This means development could be 'measured' in terms of the number of items a child can recall.

# VYGOTSKY'S THEORY
# OF COGNITIVE DEVELOPMENT

Lev Vygotsky's work had little impact on Western psychology until it was translated into English in 1962. His ideas were very influential in post-revolutionary Russia, but his books were banned during the Stalinist regime because they ran counter to the preferred theories of Pavlov. In this way, his ideas were similar to Piaget's. Both of them presented theories which contrasted with behaviourism, describing cognitive development as the result of the child's active construction of their knowledge rather than passive conditioning. However, Vygotsky's views differ from Piaget's in their emphasis on social or cultural influences, especially language, as the driving force behind cognitive development. Vygotsky's work has a strong political theme and supports the Marxist position that the only way to bring about psychological change is by altering social conditions.

For Vygotsky, the structure of the intellect consists of elementary mental functions, that is, innate capacities such as attention and sensation. Cultural influences transform elementary functions into higher mental functions, such as problem-solving and thinking. Without culture, an individual would not progress further than the elementary functions. Culture is largely transmitted via language and the help of persons with greater knowledge ('experts'). At any time, the distance between a child's current and potential abilities is described as the zone of proximal development (ZPD). This zone is critical in leading cognitive development. Instruction 'wakens a whole series of functions that are in a stage of maturation lying in the zone of proximal development' (Vygotsky, 1987). Additionally, the process of learning creates a motive to learn more; children must learn to be motivated rather than vice versa.

Vygotsky's central interest was in the relationship between language and thought, and he attempted to explain how these interact developmentally. In his view, language and thought at first develop independently, which he called pre-intellectual language and pre-linguistic thought. Around the age of two or three, this changes so that language and thought interact. Children move from a stage where language serves a largely social purpose (social linguistic stage) to an egocentric stage, where they use language to control their own behaviour and thought. This kind of 'self-talk' in young children is often spoken out loud. After the age of seven, this self-talk becomes silent (inner speech) and differs in form from social speech. Throughout life, language serves these dual purposes, for thought and for social communication. Since social processes shape language, they also shape thought. This emphasises the cultural nature of Vygotsky's approach.

# Evidence for Vygotsky's theory

Vygotsky himself did little empirical research. He summarised the work of a colleague, Shif (Vygotsky, 1987), who asked seven- and nine-year-old pupils to complete sentences which ended in 'because' or 'although' and found that they were better able to finish the sentences which dealt with scientific rather than everyday concepts. Vygotsky argued that this demonstrates a greater understanding of scientific concepts, presumably because these are learned through instruction, whereas everyday concepts are assimilated through self-directed activity. It therefore follows that instruction increases understanding. The study by Freund (1990), described at the beginning of this chapter, also found that expert intervention improved children's task performance.

Vygotsky's view was that the concept of the ZPD should enable a better understanding of the learning process and recommend better approaches to education. Expert intervention should be most effective when the expert is aware of the limits of the ZPD. Thus, the more sensitive an adult is to a child's competence and the more the adult exposes the child to processes necessary for successful problem-solving, the more the child should improve. Smith and Cowie (1991) offer a description of nursery school activity to illustrate this: a teacher gives her pupils cardboard toilet rolls to experiment with, and their first response is to use them as trumpets. After a suitable interval, she gives them other objects which can also be used to make noise, such as watering cans and bowls of water. This intervention is intended to contribute to the children's inventiveness rather than destroy it. Later still, the teacher records some of their sounds and asks the children to identify what each sound is, and to decide which is funniest or shrillest. This shows how sensitive intervention can expand the children's process of discovery and learning, in this case, to categorise, sort and listen, and that such learning motivates them to continue.

Newman and Holzman (1993) give support to Vygotsky's views by describing various pedagogies which have reorganised the learning environment along the lines suggested by his concept of the ZPD. One Danish project had a collective goal, to create a class ZPD so that both the teacher and the children acted as 'experts' and shared a group motivation. In Chapter 1 (pages 13–14) we saw evidence of the relationship between motivation and special talents. Children working together may promote learning not just because others may have greater knowledge but also because conflicting views necessitate negotiation which forces the individuals to reconstruct their ideas (see page 122).

Vygotsky's analysis of the developmental relationship between language and thought is supported by the evidence explored at the end of Chapter 4. It seems clear that the origin of language lies in its social function and that children think long before they are able to use language. The later relationship between language and thought is one of independence and mutual influence.

# BRUNER'S THEORY OF COGNITIVE DEVELOPMENT

Jerome Bruner started his career in psychology as a theorist interested in thinking generally rather than the developmental perspective. This is reflected in his early description (Bruner, 1966) of cognitive development as a progressive acquisition of the three modes of adult thinking (see Box 5.2). Bruner describes the structure of intellect in terms of categories (concepts) which are hierarchically organised. This notion of hierarchies (or coding systems) enables us to explain how people remember and assimilate knowledge (i.e. learn), and is widely used in memory and other areas of cognitive research.

**Box 5.2** Bruner's modes of thought and stages of cognitive development

| MODE | AGE IN YEARS (APPROXIMATE) | DESCRIPTION AND FUNCTION |
| --- | --- | --- |
| Enactive | 0 to 1 | Thinking is based entirely on physical actions. We learn by doing rather than through internal representation. This mode continues later in many physical activities. |
| Iconic | 1 to 7 | The use of mental images (icons) which may be based on sight, hearing, smell or touch. |
| Symbolic | 7 onwards | Representation of the world through language, and other symbolic systems, such as number and music. |

As far as development is concerned, Bruner (1973) proposed a theory of skill acquisition, arguing that cognitive development can best be described in terms of the growth of skills. Infants learn physical skills, such as grasping, during the enactive stage. These become automatic and act as modularised units which can be combined in different ways to build up a repertoire of new skilled behaviours and to allow attention to be freed for other things. As children grow older, they also develop representational skills.

Like Vygotsky, Bruner considered that language has a critical influence on cognitive development. Language allows us to categorise things and thus facilitates the formation of our coding systems. In this way, it doesn't just reflect thought, but actively shapes it. Language is the driving force behind the change from iconic to symbolic thinking. Evidence for this comes from Frank (1966), who demonstrated that if you encourage a pre-symbolic child to use language, they can overcome their reliance on the iconic mode. Frank conducted the volume conservation task with four- to six-year-olds. First she checked that her pre-conservation participants could not conserve. Then she placed a screen in front of the beakers so that the children could not see the water levels. This freed them from iconic dominance (seeing the water levels change) and encouraged them to use language to describe the activity to themselves. Now the children were able to conserve, and on a later trial without the screen, they remained able to conserve. This change from iconic to symbolic thought was attributed to the use of language. On the other hand, Furth (1966) studied deaf children and concluded that language may increase the *efficiency* of concept development, but it is not a prerequisite for the basic capacity to abstract and generalise (the same conclusion that was drawn at the end of Chapter 4).

The practical importance of Bruner's theory lies in his development of Vygotsky's concept of expert intervention. Bruner used the metaphor of *scaffolding* to explain how an adult advances children's thinking by providing a framework on which children can climb. The tutor has the task of engaging and maintaining children's interest, simplifying the task so as to reduce the number of steps required to reach the target, highlighting those that are relevant, and providing demonstrations for children to imitate. Such a technique demands special skills of the tutor, chiefly to ensure that the demands they make are within children's ZPD, but also that they guide children rather than telling them what to do. For this reason, Bruner's approach has also been called discovery learning; children must organise new information for themselves by integrating it into existing hierarchies or adapting hierarchies to fit new situations.

# SUMMARY

The evidence described in this chapter shows that intelligence and cognitive development are in part determined by inheritance, but equally a significant amount of variation can be attributed to environmental factors such as nutrition, stimulation and practice. This means that children who fail to reach their potential could be given suitable enrichment, but it doesn't follow that such enrichment, if given earlier in children's life, will increase a child's eventual cognitive abilities.

Piaget's theory of cognitive development has continued to be enormously popular because it is a comprehensive account and a useful tool for thought and research. Some critics may have interpreted his ideas too rigidly. Perhaps the main flaw in Piaget's theory lies in the minimal role given to social influences, particularly language. The current popularity of Vygotsky's work is probably due to its emphasis on social influences and relevance to education. He argued that it is educationally more valuable to know what children can do with some assistance rather than what they can do unaided. Ultimately, therefore, the theoretical approach, which is concerned with expert intervention, should be the more valuable one. Bruner's approach to education is very similar to Vygotsky's. His theory of skill acquisition is largely a cognitive account and lacks social elements, but it has the advantage of trying to combine Piaget's view of maturation with behaviourist views of learning.

PART
2

# Influences on Development

## NON-STAGE THEORIES

A different way of looking at development is in terms of experiential rather than maturational factors. This might be described as a non-stage approach, since it does not identify changes which occur at a particular age, but instead focuses on factors which lead to certain outcomes. For example, we can understand aggressive behaviour in terms of social learning theory: children model their behaviour on their parents or what they see on TV. Alternatively, we can understand aggression in terms of biological influences, such as hormones. In both cases, development is described in terms of influences rather than as a progressive sequence.

This part of the book will look at the influence that parents, other family members, peers and the media have on the development of gender, self, moral attitudes and behaviour, aggression, emotion and play. We will also examine alternative explanations, such as the influence of hormones and maturation.

# chapter six

## SOCIALISATION

# CHAPTER OVERVIEW

This chapter describes the development of gender and self, which are both examples of how biologically governed processes are profoundly affected by the child's social world. The general topic of socialisation is briefly discussed. Also included in this chapter are a look at the possible causes of homosexuality and a consideration of culture bias, considered in the context of self-development.

# ENCULTURATION

*Socialisation* or *enculturation* is the process of learning the norms and values of one's society, including things like language, gender role behaviour, moral principles and ways of aggressive expression. In lower animal species, behaviour is almost entirely governed by innate predispositions; the higher up the evolutionary scale, the more behaviour is culturally rather than genetically determined. Cultural transmission is considerably more powerful and flexible than the biological process of evolution, because it is faster. For example, it took 200 million years for the first marine mammals to evolve into amphibians, whereas it took only fifty years for man to move from flying in the air to space travel. Cultural inheritance is analogous with genetic change and subject to pressures similar to the process of evolution: those behaviours which are successful will be imitated and passed on the the next generation.

# PSYCHOLOGICAL PERSPECTIVES:
## *The sociocultural perspective*

Some of the approaches so far described in this book lack one important element, namely a consideration of the social context in which behaviour occurs. The sociocultural perspective, or more traditionally 'social psychology', is distinct from sociology. The latter is less concerned with the individual as a separate entity and more concerned with the structure and functioning of social groups. In contrast, social psychology is interested in explanations of individual behaviour in terms of group processes: social and cultural influences.

Cross-cultural studies of child-rearing help us to identify what behaviours may be universal, and therefore innate, and what are due to experience. They serve to remind us that our own view of development is an *ethnocentric* one. Any account of development is necessarily culturally based, which is not unreasonable, since the process of raising children is essentially one of enculturation. However, it is important to remember that such understandings of human behaviour are not universal. What is true for middle-class white Europeans is not necessarily true in other parts of the world.

# GENDER DEVELOPMENT

Gender development is a good example of the combined effects of innate factors and socialisation. Sex is a physical matter of being male or female. During normal pre-natal development, the genetic code (XX for a girl and XY for a boy) leads to the production of sex-appropriate hormones, which in turn influence the development of external genitalia. Nature's impulse is to create a female, and the absence of male hormones results in the external genitalia remaining female. Testicular Feminising Syndrome (TFS), for example, occurs when an XY individual has an insensitivity to the male hormone testosterone. As a result, such individuals remain female externally but internally are male and are therefore sex-typed at birth as a female. Often their true sex is only discovered when they fail to start menstruating. They remain content with their assigned sex despite biologically being male (Goldwyn, 1979).

Sex hormones also affect the developing brain. Some researchers believe this may ultimately predispose individuals to masculine or feminine behaviour, as opposed to just affecting their sex organs. Experiments with guinea pigs showed that injections of testosterone (male hormones) into pregnant individuals produced genetically female offspring who not only developed a penis but also behaved sexually rather like males (Vines, 1992). Similar effects have been observed in humans. One opportunity for this arose when pregnant women, who had previously suffered miscarriages, were given testosterone to prevent reoccurrence. This treatment resulted, in some cases, in a normal XX infant who developed external male genitalia, called Androgenital Syndrome. Money and Ehrhardt (1972) studied a group of twenty-five such girls, all of whom received corrective surgery. They appeared content with their sex, but were described as more tomboyish than normal, preferring vigorous outdoor activity and having less interest in dolls or games involving mothering roles. However, such descriptions are relatively subjective, and ultimately this evidence does not convincingly demonstrate that pre-natal exposure to male hormones has a significant effect on gender behaviour. Money and Ehrhardt also studied individuals with TFS and found that, despite exposure to male hormones and indeed their genetic maleness, such individuals developed normal female gender identity and sexual orientation towards males. This illustrates that such biological accounts of sexual development may be appropriate to non-human behaviour, but upbringing is more important where human behaviour is concerned, a bio-social approach.

# PSYCHOLOGICAL PERSPECTIVES:
## *The biological perspective*

The term 'biological' refers to all the physiological systems we find in the body: muscles, blood, hormones, nerves and the brain. It also includes genetic factors. Biological accounts clearly explain behaviour at a particular level. However, they are *reductionist* explanations, and are not always appropriate or adequate.

Even if we knew all the biological foundations of memory, learning, emotion and so on, we might still lack an explanation of human behaviour, because it omits cognitive, emotional and environmental influences, and subjective experience.

## Gender role development

A person's gender identity is generally established at birth, as in: 'It's a boy!'. Many first-time parents expect that what follows, in terms of gender-related behaviour, can be consciously directed by them, only to be dismayed by how sex-stereotyped their child's behaviour becomes. The common observation of gender-related preferences, even in young children, is supported by research. Smith and Daglish (1977) found that boys aged between one and two usually prefer cars and lorries, whereas girls of the same age prefer to play with soft toys and dolls. It is likely that, unconsciously, parents and other people communicate a wealth of information regarding gender-appropriate behaviour to infants in an effort to socialise them. A number of studies have shown that this happens. For example, Smith and Lloyd (1978) asked mothers to play with a six-month-old baby as part of a supposed investigation into play. There were feminine-type toys (a doll and squeaky Bambi), masculine-type toys (a squeaky hammer and a rabbit wearing trousers) and neutral toys (a squeaky pig, ball and rattle). When the baby was dressed and named as a boy, the mothers encouraged more motor activity and offered the masculine toys. On the other hand, studies which have sought to demonstrate actual differences between male and female babies have been relatively unsuccessful (Williams, 1987). This would suggest infants have no innate gender behaviours, but quickly learn these through selective reinforcement and gender models.

This was the conclusion reached by Mead (1935) in her classic studies of three primitive societies in New Guinea. She found completely different gender roles in each society. In the Arapesh tribe, both men and women exhibited maternal, nurturant behaviour and neither sex was particularly aggressive. The Mundugumour were the opposite, and both sexes were highly aggressive, ruthless and conformist. In the third tribe, the Tchambuli, men and women performed gender-related roles, but these were the reverse of typical Western male/female stereotypes. Mead's conclusion was that sex differences were cultural creations. However, she also felt that there were some universal gender behaviours and these must be innately determined. For example, she felt that in comparative terms, men were always the more aggressive. It is true that the male hormone testosterone is associated with aggressive behaviour, which would be needed for the task of hunter-gathering, whereas the female hormone oestrogen appears to be related to nesting or nurturant behaviour. Psychologists have also found evidence that women are more oriented towards interpersonal goals, whereas men function on a level of principles, that women are more cautious, conformist and emotionally sensitive; and that girls are superior in terms of verbal ability whereas boys are better at visuo-spatial tasks and are generally more intelligent. However, when Maccoby and Jacklin (1974) undertook a massive review of more than 1500 studies of gender differences, they concluded that the differences observed were minimal and that most popular gender-role stereotypes are 'cultural myths' that have no basis in fact. Such myths are perpetuated by expectations arising from gender stereotypes.

There are some real sex differences, referred to as sexual dimorphism (morph meaning 'form', therefore two forms). These include such familiar things as size (throughout childhood, boys are generally bigger, but not especially stronger) and changes at puberty (girls develop breasts and boys develop facial hair). There are other differences which might explain some seemingly psychological differences. For example, boys have a higher metabolic rate from birth, which means they often appear more boisterous than girls. Girls develop motor skills earlier than boys, which may explain the fact that girls tend to be toilet-trained earlier and have fewer problems with bedwetting than boys. Finally, boys are genetically more 'vulnerable' than girls because of the lack of genetic information on the Y chromosome, which allows recessive genes on the X chromosome to be expressed. This is why boys are more likely to have haemophilia, reading disabilities, speech defects, emotional disorders and some forms of mental retardation. For the most part, however, gender differences are social constructions, subtly perpetuated by cultural stereotypes. From a very early age, children have a desire to learn such behaviours as a means of establishing their own identities.

## Learning sex-appropriate behaviours

The study by Smith and Lloyd indicates that an important route for learning sex-appropriate behaviours is through selective reinforcement. Such rewards and punishments are generally verbal, as in 'you look very pretty' or 'little girls shouldn't do that'. These come from parents, other adults, siblings and peers. Lamb and Roopnarine (1979) observed three- to five-year-olds at play at nursery school, and noted that children were quick to criticise sex-inappropriate play. The children responded most readily to same-sex reinforcement, which shows that they already knew what was sex-appropriate and their peers were just reinforcing that knowledge. The fact that, from an early age, children appear to prefer playmates of their own sex, will emphasise this peer reinforcement of sex-appropriate behaviours. When Jacklin and Maccoby (1978) introduced unfamiliar two and a half-year-olds to each other and dressed them in neutral clothing, they found that interactions were most lively and positive with same-sex pairs. This may well reflect an early incompatibility between girls and boys, partly based on biological differences, such as boisterousness, and partly due to learned preferences for toys and activities.

The second way that children acquire sex-appropriate behaviour is through modelling or imitation, which are indirect forms of learning. Young children observe and practise much adult behaviour through role play, observing what others do and trying it out. The third route is the self-generation of cognitive schema (cognitive developmental theory), which serve to organise existing information and generate appropriate behaviours. Therefore, the children aren't simply passive recipients of gender knowledge but actively seek such information.

Between the ages of three and seven, as these schema are developing, children show the most rigid polarisation of masculine and feminine roles. It is probably important for them at this age to adhere carefully to their fledgling schema. Before the age of three, children are aware of their gender but

FIGURE 6.1 *From an early age children engage in sex-appropriate behaviour and this is reinforced by peers and adults*

tolerant of doing things which are not gender-appropriate. For example, a boy will imitate his mother and role play activities such as ironing. Later, both sexes will often justify their activity in terms of it being something that boys do or don't do. At all ages, it is more likely that a girl will have an interest in masculine things, probably because such behaviour is more highly valued in our society. This means that girls are freer to engage in all types of behaviour whereas boys are more limited to masculine-type activities.

## Healthy gender stereotypes

Mead (1972) observed that there are three possible courses of action for any society with regard to the gender development of their children. First, a culture may emphasise a difference in roles between the sexes. Second, it may promote a unisex model of behaviour. The result of both of these is that any non-conforming person becomes labelled a 'deviant', a situation which leads to unhappiness and disequilibrium in the society. The third 'solution' is to de-emphasise gender. Bem (1974) introduced the concept of *androgyny* as a means of better describing gender roles. She pointed out that most people actually possess both masculine and feminine characteristics. Furthermore, healthy development is associated with people who can be adaptable in terms of their sex roles. This is because an androgynous person, when faced with a decision as to how to behave in any particular situation, can choose from a wider variety of responses; to have to behave 'like a man' leads to a limited behavioural repertoire. Androgyny is a more flexible cognitive style which is becoming increasingly common in our society as men and women take on cross-sex roles and present such models to their children.

Androgyny does not mean one has to deny one's masculinity or femininity, but instead children should learn to distinguish between what biologically makes them a boy or girl and the associated gender stereotypes which suggest masculinity or femininity. Bem illustrates this with an example from her son Jeremy's experience. When he was four, he wanted to wear barrettes (hairslides) to nursery school. Another boy told him that he was a girl because 'only girls wear barrettes'. Jeremy explained that 'wearing barrettes doesn't matter, being a boy is having a penis and testicles.' (Bem, 1983). In the struggle for liberation from feminine stereotypes, many women forget this. A healthy and gender-neutral approach is to give children of both sexes the same toys and opportunities, and allow them to select which are personally most appropriate, whilst underlining the fact that the essence of being male or female is a different matter.

# FOCUS ON...
# *homosexuality*

Freud's classic account of homosexuality was that, during the phallic stage of development, around the age of three, a boy fails to overcome his strong attachment for his mother and therefore cannot resolve his conflicts with his father. The result of this faulty resolution of the Oedipus complex is that the boy cannot identify with his father, and this prevents the boy reaching a mature stage of sexual development and developing a desire for the opposite sex.

Such a view has never had substantial empirical support, but it is in line with some intuitive feelings about homosexuality. This view is that homosexuality is due to abnormal parental relationships, is pathological and needs to be 'cured'.

A second possibility is that homosexuality is caused by biological rather than social factors, which means that it is unavoidable and therefore 'normal' and acceptable. There is a growing body of evidence which supports this alternative position. LeVay (1991) conducted post-mortem examinations of brain tissue to see whether there were differences between homosexual and heterosexual men and women. His interest lay in the third interstitial nucleus of the anterior hypothalamus

(INAH-3) because the hypothalamus has been found in other animals to be different in males and females. He found that the INAH-3 tended to be bigger in men than in women or male homosexuals. He concluded that this demonstrates a biological basis for sexual preference. Other anatomical differences have been found. For example, the suprachiasmatic nucleus and the anterior commissures are larger, on average, in homosexual men than in heterosexual men (Vines, 1992). The cause of such anatomical differences is suggested to be lack of pre-natal exposure to male hormones in the brain.

The classic test of whether a behaviour is innate is to look at concordance rates in twins. Kallmann (1952) found a maximum of 100 per cent concordance for homosexuality for MZ twins but less than fifteen per cent for DZ twins. Other researchers have claimed to find evidence of a 'gay gene'. For example, Dean Hamer et al. (1993) studied the X-chromosome in forty pairs of homosexual brothers and found that in thirty-three pairs, there were five identical gene markers.

However, there are methodological problems with much of this research. For example, in LeVay's studies, sexual preference was presumed rather than established. Also, in all of the anatomical evidence, heterosexual and homosexual brains were only 'on average' different. The INAH-3 in some presumed homosexuals was actually larger than heterosexual ones. Studies of twins raised together fail to separate biological from environmental influences, so the concordance rates may be in part due sharing similar life experiences.

The third kind of explanation offered for the cause of homosexuality is that it is a learned preference (social learning theory). If a young person has an early sexual encounter with a member of the same sex which is pleasurable, this may induce a homosexual preference through positive reinforcement. This might be particularly likely in situations where contact with the opposite sex is limited, such as in single-sex schools. The main objection to this account is that most homosexuals report that homosexual feelings usually occurred at least three years before they engaged in any homosexual activity (Bell et al., 1981).

One of the problems in establishing a cause for homosexuality is that it is not a discrete condition. There are people who are exclusively homosexual or heterosexual, but there are many people who are somewhere in between; the Kinsey scale ranks individuals on a seven-point scale, ranging from strictly homosexual to strictly heterosexual. Therefore there must be many causes for many outcomes. Even where a condition has a genetic cause, such as Down's Syndrome (see page 143), there is enormous individual variation in part due to differential susceptibility of the embryo and in part due to post-natal environmental influences. Therefore, finding a biological cause does not necessarily mean that this is the ultimate explanation for an individual's homosexuality.

# THE SELF-CONCEPT:
# SELF-DEVELOPMENT

A child's gender concept is a part of their wider self-concept. Like gender, self-development depends on social interactions. Argyle (1978) has suggested four important social factors which influence the development of the self-concept. First, the reactions of others provides us with a reflection of ourselves. Cooley (1902) called this the *looking-glass self*. Such reactions do not just provide a picture of yourself, but also convey expectations and esteem. If your parents tell you that you are clever, you come to believe that yourself. It makes you work harder and do well, so their expectations are self-fulfilling.

Second, others provide a means of comparison. Many self-concepts are comparative, such as 'tall' or 'clever', and therefore require the standards to be set by others. One of the reasons people may seek the company of others is to make such comparisons.

Third, social contact also influences self-development through the process of imitation. Children identify with and model themselves on significant others. They 'try out' various identities or take another's persona, such as identifying with a pop idol. People with lower self-esteem are most ready to imitate others. This aspect of self-development can explain why children appear to be so impressionable. It is also why children and adolescents become besotted with their idols. Role play is not only important for generating appropriate behaviour, but is also a means of moving from the egocentric world of the young child to the broader perspective of understanding other people's points of view. In turn, this increases self-awareness. Selman (1980) has suggested that the growth of role-taking skills underlies a mature understanding of the self and other people. To 'know' another person, one must be able to take on another person's perspective and understand their thoughts and feelings, a development of cognitive competence.

Fourth, an outcome of imitating others is learning social roles which dictate much interpersonal behaviour and generate self-expectations. For example, the roles of daughter, son, schoolchild or friend all involve behavioural expectations. Goffman (1959) suggested that life is a series of theatrical performances, and each role is acted out in accordance with expectations. These roles are incorporated into our self-concept. When Kuhn (1960) asked children to answer the question 'Who am I?', he found that a quarter of their answers were role-related.

# PSYCHOLOGICAL PERSPECTIVES:
## *The humanist perspective*

Humanists describe behaviour in terms of self-concepts. They emphasise subjective experience, individual uniqueness and the importance of personal control as opposed to being controlled by external forces. Carl Rogers, the father of counselling, felt that unconditional positive regard from significant others was critical in healthy personality development. It leads to high self-esteem and frees people from striving for social approval so that they can seek self-actualisation.

The humanist perspective has encouraged psychologists to accept the view that there is more to behaviour than objectively discoverable facts, which may be statistically significant but humanly insignificant. However, as a theoretical approach, it is unscientific, being less concerned with scientific methods and more concerned with enabling individuals to achieve their potential, especially in a therapeutic setting.

## Self-recognition

Self-recognition is the beginning of social awareness. Before you can 'know' others, you must know yourself, and before that, you must recognise what is and isn't you. The infant's first experiences of self-recognition involve matching the action of their own hand with what they can see or feel. This may even happen in the womb (see page 29). Infants also hear their own noises. However, it is probably not until the end of the first year that the self schema is established. Lewis and Brooks-Gunn (1979) found that children as young as nine months show some ability to distinguish pictures of themselves, indicated by the fact that they smile longer at pictures of themselves rather than other same-age babies. They also found that children of this age will smile at themselves in a mirror, and reach out and touch themselves. True self-recognition comes later, as they demonstrated using an ingenious technique first used by Gallup (1977) to see whether chimpanzees ever developed self-awareness (they did, but gorillas didn't). Lewis and Brooks-Gunn put some rouge on the child's nose, reasoning that children who responded by touching their own nose rather than the mirror image must have self-recognition. They found that few children under one year of age did this, whereas by the age of twenty months, seventy per cent of the children did. It is noteworthy that people raised in isolation often don't have self-recognition, underlining the importance of experience and social interaction in self-development.

By the age of three or four children can distinguish a thinking, psychological self from their physical self (mind and body). Eder (1990) has studied children of this age and found that they have an understanding of how they behave in various situations. For example, such children might say, 'I like to play by myself at nursery school'. However, most of their self-concept is concerned with their physical attributes, interpersonal relationships and actions of which they are proud. Children of this age tend to describe themselves in concrete terms such as, 'I am a boy' and 'I have a sister', rather than, 'I like people'. They are learning to distinguish their 'self-as-knower' and 'self-as-known-by-others', the division between a private and public self. During this same period, it should be remembered, their cognitive development is described as 'egocentric' (see Chapter 5).

In middle childhood, there is a shift towards a more abstract self, in line with cognitive changes generally. The process of distinguishing 'me' from others continues until adolescence, when a child truly takes on its own identity.

# FOCUS ON...
# *a cross-cultural view*
# *of the self-concept*

Nobles (1976) has argued that Western psychologists need to be aware of the cultural assumptions they make when describing human behaviour, particularly in their theories about intelligence and self-concepts. The African worldview is guided by two principles: 'survival of the tribe' and 'oneness with nature'. This creates culturally esteemed values of co-operation, interdependence and collective responsibility. In contrast, Nobles describes the European worldview as 'survival of the fittest' and 'control over nature' bringing an emphasis on individuality, uniqueness, competition, independence and separateness. The African philosophical tradition leads to the development of an extended self, a sense of a collective self, 'we' rather than 'I':

> 'African people ... realise that one's self is not contained only in one's physical being and finite time.... [it] transcends through the historical consciousness of one's people, the finiteness of both physical body, finite space and absolute time.'

Therefore we can see that our culture's ideal for establishing a sense of individual identity as a prerequisite for mental health is something that we have all learned through socialisation; it is not an innate feature of human behaviour.

# Other self-concepts

The self-concept is the image you have of yourself. This includes appearance, race, gender, nationality and abilities. There are a constellation of other self-concepts which all have important consequences for behaviour and achievement: the ideal self and self-actualisation motivate you, self-efficacy is your understanding of your own abilities which generates expectations of future success, and self-esteem is the value you place on all your self-concepts.

Coopersmith (1968) studied the effects of self-esteem in pre-adolescent boys. One method of assessing their level of aspiration was the 'beanbag experiment' (see Figure 6.2). A boy has to throw a beanbag at a selection of targets, some of which are closer than others; the more distant the target, the higher the score. The boys were asked to name their target before throwing, and to say the ideal score they would like to get, and the score they expected to get. Those boys high in self-esteem had higher goals and were more successful in achieving these goals. Those low in self-esteem had lower ambition and also did less well. Therefore, both low and high self-esteem affect performance and confirm the original expectation. A person's self-esteem may reflect their true ability or it may develop from what others tell you about yourself. Once it is established, it can be self-perpetuating.

In an experiment to illustrate the value of self-efficacy, Weinberg and his co-workers (1979) artificially manipulated participants' sense of expectation by asking them to test their leg strength using a machine which gave a false feedback. Performance was then assessed on a muscular endurance task (sitting down and extending their leg in a horizontal position as long as

FIGURE 6.2 Coopersmith (1968) studied the self-esteem of boys using the beanbag experiment

possible). The participants who had been given a sense of lower self-efficacy did less well than the high self-efficacy subjects, and their performance deteriorated even more after experiencing failure. The Russian programme for training athletes puts this into practice by showing young students edited films of their performance to make it look better, thus raising their self-efficacy.

The main factor here is that expectations of personal success are of greater importance than ability itself. The secondary factor is that, once the cycle of success or failure is begun, it is self-perpetuating. Seligman's (1975) work on learned helplessness and depression is worth consideration here. His view is that 'depressives' are people who tend to blame failure on internal, global factors rather than external ones, for example blaming lack of skill rather than lack of luck. Early experiences of failure may therefore lead to an unrecoverable cycle of continued failure and helpless despair rather than leading to the more positive approach that the situation can and will be changed. It would seem that success does little to alter low self-efficacy once it has been established. Ideally, parents should teach their children how to make external attributions and to have a high sense of self-efficacy, thus avoiding a cycle of failure which is hard to alter.

# SUMMARY

In this chapter, we have looked at gender and self-development as examples of how socio-cultural factors combine with biological processes. In terms of gender development, there are some inherited sex differences, but most are the result of early and subtle reinforcements. Each culture establishes gender-appropriate behaviours which are perpetuated unconsciously so that they may appear to be innate. Ultimately, such behaviours are important for the roles that adults take within their society, such as hunter-gathering and childcaring. However, psychological health is best served by allowing some flexibility.

The development of self is also related to social experiences, through the reactions of others, social comparison, imitation and modelling, and learning social roles. Children raised in isolation fail to achieve self-recognition, one of the most basic self-concepts. Self-esteem and self-efficacy are critical ways of explaining behaviour; these are learned early and have lasting consequences for achievement, acceptance of failure and even depression.

# chapter seven

# PARENTAL INFLUENCES

## CHAPTER OVERVIEW

The most important influence in any child's life must be their parents. Our aim in this chapter is to look at kinds of child-rearing or parenting styles and the effects these have on the development of prosocial and moral behaviour, prejudice, aggressiveness, cognitive skills and personality.

## PARENTING STYLE

Erikson (1963) suggested that the two main dimensions of the parent-child relationship are parental warmth and parental control. Warmth is important for emotional development and the growth of self-esteem. Control is a vital ingredient of moral development: through discipline the child learns self-control. Such parental control, or power, needs to be exerted with reason and firmness in order for the child to develop autonomous discipline without a sense of hostility. These conclusions come from various studies of parents and their children. For example, Baumrind (1971) worked with many pre-school children and their parents. The children were rated in terms of sociability, self-reliance, achievement, moodiness and self-control. Baumrind also interviewed their parents and observed parents and children interacting at home. She concluded that parenting styles fall into one of three categories, shown in Box 7.1.

Hoffman (1970) also distinguished parenting according to styles of discipline: love withdrawal (creating anxiety over loss of love), power assertion (techniques that may generate fear, anger or resentment) and induction (explaining why a behaviour is wrong, its effects and how it might be undone). He found that the induction method was associated with positive behavioural outcomes, such as fostering empathy and moral behaviour. Furthermore, children prefer induction as a method of discipline, and consider it most effective; physical punishment is a second best.

**Box 7.1** Baumrind's parenting styles

| PARENTING STYLE | BEHAVIOUR | ASSOCIATED BEHAVIOURAL PROFILE IN CHILD |
|---|---|---|
| Authoritarian | Adult imposes rules, rarely explains reasons and often relies on punitive measures to ensure obedience. May use disciplinary strategy of power assertion or love withdrawal. | *Conflicted-irritable*: fearful, moody, passively hostile, vulnerable to stress, aimless, unfriendly, achievement-oriented, prejudiced. |
| Authoritative | A flexible approach combining some freedom within set guidelines, parents use reason as well as power to get obedience (inductive discipline). Parents are responsive to child's point of view. | *Energetic-friendly*: self-reliant, self-controlled, cheerful, co-operative with adults, curious, purposive, achievement-oriented. |
| Permissive | Child is relatively free to express own feelings and determine own choices, parents rarely exert any control, but take warm interest in children. | *Impulsive-aggressive*: rebellious, domineering, low in self-reliance and self-control, aimless, low in achievement. |
| Baumrind's scheme assumes that parents are reasonably involved, but this is not always true. Therefore a fourth category is needed: | | |
| Uninvolved parenting | Some parents reject their children, possibly because of their own stresses and problems. They are uncontrolling, overpermissive and aloof. | Hostile and rebellious adolescents, involved with antisocial behaviour and drugs. |

# REWARD AND PUNISHMENT

The differences between the child-rearing styles are described by Baumrind largely in terms of the kind and extent of discipline that a parent uses. For example, the authoritative or inductive approaches emphasise the internalisation of behavioural control rather than relying on the more traditional methods of reward, punishment and/or explicit instruction as a means of teaching moral behaviour. Clearly, children learn *some* sense of what is right and wrong through conditioning and direct teaching, but there is much evidence to show that these methods are not very effective ways of learning and may even be counterproductive.

Where punishment is delayed, the connection between the wrong-doing and negative reinforcement is lost and no learning may take place. Bower and

Hilgard (1981) consider that punishment must be prompt, intensive and clear if it is to be effective. If punishment is used too frequently, children may habituate and no longer respond to it. Punishment may produce hostility and a desire to rebel, or children may enjoy the attention associated with punishment so that it is positively reinforcing instead of acting as a deterrent. For this reason, 'time out' is a method of punishment which has been advocated by psychologists for difficult children. In order to break the cycle of positive reinforcement, unacceptable behaviour is treated with time in temporary isolation until the child calms down. Many parents intuitively employ such measures by sending a child to their room or sitting a child in the corner, facing the wall. To be effective, this method should be balanced by attention for good behaviour.

In a different way, rewards may also be counterproductive. External rewards can destroy intrinsic motivation. Lepper et al. (1973) showed this experimentally by asking a group of children to draw a picture. Some of the children were told beforehand that they would receive a certificate for good drawing, whereas the others did not know about the certificates. Some weeks later, the children were again asked to draw a picture. Lepper et al. found that the no certificate group were more willing to do a drawing. This finding supports the view that it is more valuable for children to be allowed to develop their own internal sense of control. (At the end of the experiment, all the children did receive the certificate.)

# TEACHING MORAL BEHAVIOUR

The idea that morals can be taught simply through reinforcement may be erroneous, but so too is the idea that explicit instruction will work. Children may learn moral *principles* in this way, but not moral *behaviour*. In fact, Hartshorne and May (1928), in their classic study of moral development, concluded that methods of direct moral instruction, such as Sunday Schools, made children less rather than more honest. Hartshorne and May questioned over 10,000 children aged eight to sixteen to evaluate moral and religious education. They gave the children tests of moral behaviour, such as the Planted Dime Test, which involved giving each child a box with several puzzles, one containing a dime which the tester never referred to. When the box was returned after the test, they checked to see whether the dime was still there. They also asked children questions about their moral principles, such as 'Do you usually pick up litter?' or 'Did you ever pretend to understand a thing when you did not really understand it?' They found very little correlation between moral principles and moral behaviour and suggested that deceit is a social problem which can best be tackled by controlling a child's experiences in such a way as to make lying unnecessary. At the same time, children should be taught a series of behaviour habits which are honest.

Moral or prosocial behaviour may be learned indirectly through parental style, specifically parental warmth which facilitates the development of empathy. Rosenhan (1970) looked at why some people behave more altruistically than others. He interviewed some of those who had been involved in the US civil rights movements in the 1960s. Rosenhan distinguished between the fully committed, who had given up their homes and careers for the movement, and the partially committed. The fully committed had warmer relations with their parents, and their parents were liberals who expressed outrage about moral issues and did something about it. The partially committed described their parents in negative or ambivalent terms. Some of them had run away from home or were openly hostile. Their parents were also liberals, but they did not practise what they preached in terms of moral behaviour. Rosenhan concluded that a combination of prosocial parental models, closer attachments and a better developed sense of empathy led to greater prosocial behaviour.

# PSYCHOLOGICAL THEORIES:
## *Prosocial or moral development*

## Learning and social learning perspectives

This approach suggests that right and wrong are learned through reward, punishment and imitation. It is a simplistic account which omits the fact that most people develop at least some of their moral sense through reasoned thought rather than as a conditioned response. For instance, decisions to become a vegetarian or to truant from school are unlikely to be conditioned responses. However, this approach can account for the fact that moral principles are different from moral behaviour.

## Psychodynamic perspective

Freud's (1935) description of moral develop-

ment is based on the concepts of identification and imitation. Freud suggested that moral behaviour is controlled by the super-ego, which develops during the phallic stage, around the age of three. At this time, children feel desire for their opposite-sex parent (the Oedipus complex in boys, the Electra complex in girls). They see their same-sex parent as a rival, and this leads to feelings of unconscious hostility, guilt, and a fear of punishment should their true desires be discovered. Resolution occurs through identification with the same-sex parent, that is, the process of 'taking' on the attitudes and ideas of another person. Identification also leads to the development of a 'conscience' and an 'ego-ideal'. The conscience punishes us when we do something wrong and is a source of guilty feelings (an internal representation of the 'punishing' parent). The ego-ideal rewards us when we behave in accordance with parental moral values (acting as the 'rewarding' parent). The ego-ideal is a source of feelings of pride and self-satisfaction. Identification is also important for gender identity and attitudes towards authority. Unsatisfactory resolution can result in problems such as amorality, homosexuality and rebelliousness.

Freud's theory predicted various interesting outcomes. For example, a more threatening parent should produce a greater fear of punishment in a child, leading to a stronger sense of identification. This would explain why there are often strong bonds between domineering parents and their children. In general, Freud's account is rather exaggerated and fanciful, though it nonetheless contains some important elements. It suggests how moral development relies on both social factors (parental influences) and biological factors (innate desires).

# Cognitive-developmental perspective

Stage theories, such as those of Piaget (1932) or Kohlberg (1969), tie moral development to cognitive maturity; each child goes through a predictable series of moral stages on the way to adulthood. Piaget's theory describes the pre-school child as *'pre-moral'* and unable to understand rules. During the next four years, children go through a stage of *moral realism*, in which rules are regarded as unchangeable, a person's actions are evaluated in terms of consequences, and morals are *heteronomous* (rules supplied by others). The final stage is *moral relativism* where actions are judged in terms of a person's intentions, rules are *autonomous* (created by oneself), and punishments should fit the crime.

Kohlberg proposed a more detailed series of ages and stages in the development of moral reasoning, as shown in Box 7.2. His conclusions were drawn from a long-term study of fifty-eight males (Colby et al., 1983) which has been criticised for its gender bias and cultural assumptions. The values Kohlberg describes are those of Western society and are not, as he claimed, innate. Kohlberg's account is specifically about moral principles, which means that it may tell us little about moral behaviour.

**Box 7.2**   Kohlberg's stages of moral development

| LEVEL | AGE | STAGE | |
|---|---|---|---|
| Pre-conventional | 6 to 13 | 1 | Heteronomous, obeys rules to avoid punishment, deference to authority. |
| | | 2 | Egocentric, seeks rewards, does good to serve one's own interests. |
| Conventional | 13 to 16 | 3 | 'Good boy/girl', conforms to avoid disapproval, able to care for others. |
| | | 4 | Law and order, conforms to avoid blame, unquestioning acceptance of authority. |
| Post-conventional or principled | 16 to 20 | 5 | Concerned with justice, questions law and authority, interested in individual rights. |
| | | 6 | Universal ethical principles, acting on basis of own principles, a stage probably not be reached by everyone. |

Cognitive accounts of moral behaviour assume that people behave consistently and that moral principles are universal. Both of the assumptions are questionable. Piaget probably underestimated children's moral sophistication in some situations and overestimated adult moral behaviour. People of all ages find it difficult to determine morally correct behaviour in terms of consequences and intentions. (Consider Kohlberg's moral dilemma where a man wants to obtain a very expensive medicine for his wife who is dying from cancer. He was able to borrow half the necessary money from friends, but the chemist refused to sell the medicine for less or let him repay the amount later. The husband broke into the shop and stole the medicine. Was such behaviour right or wrong?)

## Biological perspective

We must also consider the fact that some children may be born with psychopathic or sociopathic personalities (also called 'antisocial personality disorder'), which may explain why some people commit the sort of crimes which exhibit a lack of empathy. A genetic view is supported by research, which has found that sociopaths tend to be under-aroused in terms of activity in the autonomic nervous system and therefore less susceptible to conditioning (Rosenhan and Seligman, 1989). Even if this is the case, it is clear that certain home backgrounds interact negatively with this condition, because most sociopaths come from low socio-economic classes. However, this also means that some aspects of moral behaviour are not the parents' or offenders' 'fault'.

## Humanist perspective

The route to moral conduct is through warm family relationships which are conducive to emotional development and which lead a child to identify with appropriate prosocial models. People who have troubled relationships with their parents are in some ways prevented from fully developing their personalities. Instead, they are forever trying to find social approval and establish their own identity.

# PARENTS AND PREJUDICE

Children learn many of their attitudes and prejudices through their parents. Aboud (1988) points out that there are important age differences in the way children display prejudices. Below the age of seven, children are cognitively immature and therefore cannot avoid making judgements based on learned prejudices which tend to simplify the world.

As children mature, they learn to make important differentiations in their stereotypes. However, various experiences may decrease the likelihood of this happening. It may be that a child is exposed to supportive stereotypes in the media (see page 134) or it may be that certain parenting styles predispose a child to retain a prejudiced cognitive style. This was the conclusion reached by Adorno et al. (1950). They interviewed about 2,000 white, middle-class Americans and concluded that those people who tended to be prejudiced also had a favourable impression of themselves, a rigid cognitive style and a greater interest in status and success rather than solidarity. They tended to favour a law-and-order position with regard to morals and were not interested in psychological interpretations. Adorno et al. followed their initial survey by asking eighty of the most prejudiced participants about the child-rearing styles used by their parents. Their descriptions matched what has been described as the authoritarian style (see page 92), which makes intuitive sense. However such retrospective and subjective data should be regarded with some caution, because they are likely to be biased.

A further reason why some children are more prejudiced than others may be due to frustration. When a person is frustrated, for example through lack of opportunity, this leads to aggression which is projected on to other less powerful people or objects; we blame these scapegoats rather than blaming ourselves (Weatherly, 1961; Geen and Berkowitz, 1967). Aboud suggests that tolerant sensitivity to children's frustrations with authority will make prejudice less likely.

# PARENTS AND AGGRESSIVENESS

Punishment is often thought to be associated with high levels of aggression in children. However, this may not be the only kind of parental interaction which increases aggressiveness. Patterson and his associates (1991) conducted a large-scale study of over 200 families. They compared those families who had at least one highly aggressive boy with other families of the same size and socio-economic status who had no problem children. Assessments were made through questionnaires and interviews with children, parents, peers and teachers, as well as home observations. They identified coercive home environments: families where little affection is shown; where family members are constantly struggling with each other and using aggressive tactics to cope; and where parents rarely use social reinforcement or approval as a means of behaviour control, and instead use physical punishment, nagging, shouting and teasing. The children in such families are typically manipulative and difficult to discipline. Patterson et al. suggested that this kind of home environment may create aggressiveness in a number of ways:

1 Harsh discipline and lack of supervision results in disrupted bonding between parent and child, and lack of identification.
2 Parental behaviours provoke aggressiveness in their children through, for example, nagging. Poor housing, marital strife and so on may cause stress, frustration and aggressiveness.
3 The children are experiencing aggressive means of solving disputes at home and are not being given clear examples of alternative methods. Therefore, they learn through imitation. This may be emphasised by the media (see page 131 for a discussion of violence on TV).
4 Such children become resistant to punishment, and progressively harder to restrain.

5   This aggressive behaviour leads them to be rejected by their peers, to join deviant peer groups and to fail at school.

Patterson suggests that families need to be offered training in conflict resolution, plus alternative means of expressing their anger and ways to form closer emotional bonds. In addition, antisocial children need social skills training to prevent rejection, and remedial help to counteract their failure at school.

# PSYCHOLOGICAL THEORIES:
## *The development of aggression*

## Biological perspective

In a recent murder trial in America, the defendant was described as a 'natural born killer' who could not be blamed for his behaviour. Support for this view comes from studies of identical twins and adopted children. In Denmark, every pair of twins born since 1870 has been registered with the authorities. Psychologists have cross-checked this data with criminal records, in general concluding that a Danish man who has a twin with a criminal record is fifty per cent more likely to have been in prison himself as compared with the average Danish male (Connor, 1995). Mednick and Hutchings (1978) found that adopted children with biological fathers who were criminals were more likely to become criminals themselves.

Aggression has also been linked to high levels of certain chemicals or hormones. Brown et al. (1979) found levels of serotonin were lower in marines who had a record of violence. High levels of serotonin are associated with sleep, which suggests that low levels might be related to high arousal. It is possible that some people are born with lower serotonin production rates which would lead to greater arousal and aggression. High levels of

testosterone (a male hormone) are also associated with increased aggression, which could explain why men are generally more aggressive than women. In women, there is evidence that pre-menstrual syndrome and increased levels of progesterone are correlated with increases in irritability, hostility, child abuse and crime (Floody, 1968). Nevertheless, such evidence cannot account for cultural differences in aggressiveness and cultural differences in the way that aggression is expressed.

## Ethological perspective

Ethologists argue that aggression is a highly adaptive response. An individual who is aggressive can control resources such as food, territory and mating. These advantages increase the individual's chances of surviving to reproduce. Even though aggression in animals is an innate tendency, it is triggered by environmental signals. For example, the male stickleback behaves aggressively when it sees anything red (Tinbergen, 1952). In animals, aggression is rarely harmful. Any species where aggression leads to death or serious injury will eventually become extinct unless it evolves a form of natural regulation, such as ritualised fighting. Lorenz (1966) believed that the same rules apply to humans as to all animals because humans are governed by the same laws of natural selection. It is possible that aggressive humans are particularly insensitive to non-verbal appeasement signals so that aggression escalates to an unhealthy extent.

However, human behaviour is less governed by innate factors because of higher conscious control, which means that learning must be part of any account. Any parallels between man and animals may be oversimplified.

## Psychodynamic perspective

Like the Ethologists, Freud (1920) believed that aggression comes from unconscious, instinctive drives. Freud emphasised the need to release this natural energy which would otherwise remain pent-up and cause psychological disorders, such as depression, suicide or masochism. The act of release is called *catharsis*, and may be achieved either through violent behaviour or by being channelled into more socially acceptable forms, such as sport. However, sports activity is often associated with increased rather than decreased aggression.

## Social learning perspective

If an aggressive act is seen to be positively reinforced, it is more likely to be repeated. This may be experienced directly from, for example, parents, or indirectly, as in watching a role model on TV. This account explains how diverse cultures come to be more or less aggressive and how they each display aggressiveness differently. Mead (1935) described how various child-rearing practices encouraged such behaviour. The main criticism of the social learning approach, in general, is that it is oversimplified. For example people are not consistently rewarded for aggression; in fact, they are often punished.

# PARENTS AND COGNITIVE DEVELOPMENT

Parents can influence their children's cognitive development in a number of ways. This influence may be in terms of the amount of stimulation and attention a child receives, or the diet they are given (see Chapters 1 and 5). Another obvious way that parents exert cognitive influence is in the provision of suitable toys and materials to encourage play, an activity which is vital for practising cognitive and physical skills (see Chapter 9). Equally, books will be important for pre-readers in developing skills such as being able to distinguish between different sounds. Research described in Chapter 5 (see page 59) demonstrated how nursery rhymes contribute to this development. In addition, simply looking at picture books or seeing adults reading to themselves gives children the desire to read. Once children are learning to read, research shows that parents can help by presenting reading as a useful and pleasant activity (Topping and Wolfendale, 1985). They should teach word-building skills and avoid constant corrections or attempts at blindly guessing the word.

# PARENTS AND PERSONALITY

Children may learn some aspects of their personality through selective reinforcement and imitation. The problem with this behaviourist view is that it doesn't explain why siblings may develop considerably different personalities despite experiencing relatively similar child-rearing styles. Thomas and his associates (1970) have proposed that the reason for intra-family differences lies in innate temperamental patterns, that is, the child's individual style of emotional response. Their research, the New York Longitudinal Study, followed over 100 children in some cases for a period of more than twenty years. They found strong support for five major dimensions of temperament which are apparent from the first months of life and which may persist over time. These are activity levels, emotionality (how easily or intensely the infant is upset), soothability (how easily the infant can be calmed down), fearfulness and sociability (receptiveness to social stimulation). These traits tend to cluster together, forming broader temperamental profiles. The 'easy' child is even-tempered, positive, adaptable and predictable, whereas the 'difficult' child is active, irritable, irregular, finds newness distressing and responds by withdrawing or crying. The 'slow-to-warm-up' child is inactive, moody, slow to adapt but puts up passive resistance rather than crying like the difficult child. Most children fit into the 'easy' category.

Personality isn't simply an outcome of innate temperamental differences. According to Thomas, the fit between temperament and environment is critical in determining eventual personality. When a person's environment is suited to their particular temperament, this is considered a good fit, and the result is a well-adjusted individual. If the fit is not good, then early, 'difficult' traits may be amplified into troublesome, maladaptive behaviours. This helps us to understand why a particular style of parenting might cause one child to be anxious and submissive, whereas another child might become defiant and antagonistic. Thomas and Chess (1986) give the following example of a boy named Carl who had an extremely difficult temperament from infancy. The fact that he didn't develop a behaviour disorder was mainly due to optimal handling by his parents and the stability of his environment. Carl's father was easy-going, took delight in his son's 'lusty' characteristics, recognised his son's negative reactions to new experiences and had the patience to wait for his eventual maturing to occur. His father felt that his son's difficultness was not due to himself or his wife. New demands on Carl always caused his 'difficult' traits to re-emerge. When he went off to college, he was faced simultaneously with a host of new situations and demands and he became depressed and constantly irritable. He was advised by Dr. Thomas to drop some extra-curricular activities and to limit his social contacts. Once he felt more positive, he was then able to take on these additional demands. The message for parents is that they should respond to their children's innate temperament and adapt their parenting style to make a better 'fit'.

# LEARNING TO BECOME A PARENT

To some extent, our parenting skills are the result of our own upbringing. In Harlow's classic research (see page 41), he found that monkeys raised by a wire 'mother' became very poor mothers themselves. The reason for this may be because the deprived infant has no appropriate model for maternal behaviour.

*Are you a parent?*

Being a parent is the most important job in the world

*...and it isn't always easy!*

**Parent-Link**

---

### What is **Parent-Link**?

**Parent-Link** *is a programme of 12 sessions run in small groups and led by a specially trained parent. Parents often carry on to meet together after completing the 12 sessions to exchange 'good listening', practise new skills and continue with their learning.*

### Who is **Parent-Link** for?

Parent-Link is for ALL parents and any adult living or working with children and young people. In some areas Parent-Link is run specially for parents of Teenagers.

### How does **Parent-Link** work?

Parents meet with other parents and ...

Learn practical ways to help our children be more confident, independent, caring, considerate and co-operative ...

Practise listening, assertiveness and communication skills, and look at the everyday ups and downs of family life.

Think about our own upbringing and how this can affect the way we bring up our children.

Parent-Link helps us to increase our self-confidence as parents and feel better about ourselves.

Bringing up children is the most important job we ever do and most of us manage as well as we can. Coping without much training, support or appreciation ...

Parent-Link can help change that!

Some comments made by parents who have done Parent-Link ...

66 *The communication skills I learnt have helped in all areas of my life, with my children and also with my partner, friends and work colleagues.* 99

66 *I know I'm not alone with my difficulties and I can see how we are all doing the best we can. I have become more accepting of myself, my children and others.* 99

66 *Shouting at my children when they were fighting didn't help. I learnt that listening to one another calmly helped us to find out about the problem.* 99

FIGURE 7.1 There are a number of organisations such as Parent-Link who offer support and advice for parents about, for example, how to deal with conflict situations, improve communication techniques and increase confidence about parenting.

Social workers or family therapy clinics may offer special assistance for families who are having difficulties, and courses may be available in schools where pupils are likely to become parents of 'problem' families. In addition 'normal' parents may want help. A recent survey by the voluntary organisation Exploring Parenthood (1994) obtained responses from 14,000 parents who shopped at Sainsbury's and sixty-four per cent of them said they would welcome some form of education or training. One mother commented that she wanted to do things differently from the way she had been brought up, but found that difficult. Such courses aim to promote many aspects of behaviour, such as developing ways of dealing with conflict situations, improving communication techniques and increasing self-confidence as a parent, as well as the specific skills related to child-rearing. The Children's Society has suggested that parenting should be on the National Curriculum.

# SUMMARY

Parenting is an awesome responsibility and a position of enormous power. In this chapter, we have seen that parents who try to rule with a rod of iron create certain kinds of children, likely to be morally principled but less likely to behave prosocially, and more prone to prejudice and aggressiveness. This is not to say that parents should not discipline their children, but they should use an authoritative style involving firmness, warmth and reasoned explanations. Parents also have responsibility for encouraging and stimulating their children, and acting as appropriate models. It is assumed that parenting is something that we can all do, but it may be beneficial to offer people more direct help in this difficult task.

# chapter eight

## SEPARATION AND DEPRIVATION

# CHAPTER OVERVIEW

In Chapter 3, the consequences of maternal deprivation were described as having a lasting and serious influence on emotional development. Deprivation results when the child is separated from its parents or main caregiver(s). In this chapter, the effects of different kinds of separation are explored. The areas we will look at are: childcare, hospitalisation, fostering, divorce, parental death, adoption and neo-natal special care.

# ATTACHMENT AND LOSS

Bowlby's theory proposed that attachment behaviour serves to maintain maximal closeness between mother and infant. If a child is distressed, it will seek out its mother or caregiver and receive comfort. When such a figure is not present, the child remains distressed and, in time, such anxiety will develop into deeper emotional problems which ultimately affect physical and cognitive progress. Bowlby referred to mother-infant separation as 'maternal deprivation'. Rutter (1981) argued that the main difficulty with the concept of deprivation is that it covers 'a most heterogeneous range of experiences and outcomes due to quite disparate mechanisms'. For example, it fails to distinguish between the loss of a maternal attachment (deprivation) and the lack of one altogether (privation). It also ignores the possibility that the very factors which led to a separation were the ones that led to emotional maladjustment, rather than separation per se causing emotional problems. This is the case when parents divorce and there is discord prior to the divorce, which is responsible for the separation and maladjustment. There may also be situations where separation is preferable in terms of healthy emotional development, as when a child is fostered because of abuse in the home.

Such arguments suggest that we should distinguish between the variety of causes, many of which co-occur, and their outcomes. In this chapter, our focus will be on situations of separation (where the loss is not permanent) and deprivation (where it is), rather than cases of privation, which are discussed in Chapter 13.

# FOCUS ON...
# *childcare provision*
# *for parents who work*

## Day nurseries

John Bowlby and other psychologists in the 1950s and 1960s felt that the mother was the child's best source of consistent physical care, emotional security and cognitive challenge. Children placed in day care would lose this care and suffer short- and long-term consequences. At the same time, there was some feeling that working-class children might benefit from day care to enrich their lives, such as compensatory pre-school programmes like the Head Start project which involved day care (see page 60). Kagan and his co-workers (1980) argued that this suggests a dual standard, where privileged children have access to their own mothers but the poor have substitutes. Kagan et al. were also aware that there were a large number of mothers who were working or wanted to work, and this led them to set up a longitudinal study to assess the actual effects of day care. Kagan et al.'s nursery, the Treemont Street Infant Centre, was located in a working-class area of Boston. Each member of staff at the school had special responsibility for a small group of children, thus ensuring close emotional contact. The children themselves came from middle- and working-class families and various ethnic backgrounds, including white and Chinese.

The sample consisted of thirty-three infants aged between three and a half and five and a half months, none of whom had any particular personal or home problems, and a matched control group who were looked after at home. When the study ended two years later, the children were assessed on temperamental traits, social interaction, general attachment behaviour (in the Strange Situation, see page 34) and cognitive development. Though there was large variability between the children, Kagan *et al.* found no consistent difference between the groups, suggesting that nursery care had no detrimental effects.

Fox (1977) came to a similar conclusion in his study of kibbutzim in Israel (see page 43). The children remained most attached to their mothers, despite the fact that they spent more time with their nurses. This may be because there is quite a high turnover rate of metapelets on kibbutzim; if the metapelet was a more permanent figure, attachment might be stronger.

There is conflicting evidence about the effects of day care on cognitive development. For example, Burchinal et al. (1989) tested the IQ of children entering school and found that those who had been in day care usually did better than those who had been at home with their mothers. However, this might reflect the fact that working mothers are less likely to be middle class. Tizard (1979) found that conversations between mother and child, rather than teacher and child, were more complex, involved more exchanges and mothers elicited more from the children. Such differences might have a negative affect on the nursery child's cognitive development.

Childcare may also affect sociability. Various studies have found that children who go more often to a day nursery become more active, outgoing and playful and less aggressive (Shea, 1981). Moreover, the ones who go on to attend school together like school better than those who have little or no nursery experience (Ladd, 1990). However, this is not true for all children; when children are shy and unsociable, the nursery experience can be threatening, which may have a negative effect on their school career (Pennebaker et al., 1981).

Research suggests that the effects of day care are not universally negative and may often be positive. Hoffman's (1989) review of research findings indicated that working mothers are still able to give their children quality time and, in fact, may compensate for their absences by being especially responsive. Employment does not lead to loss of attachment *per se*, but it may appear to do so because employment is correlated with other factors, such as low socio-economic grouping and a disordered home life. It may be these that are responsible for poor bonding (Howes, 1990).

Finally, we should consider the benefits to the mother of having a working life rather than remaining at home. According to Williams (1987), work increases a woman's sense of achievement, personal worth and self-esteem. Contributing to the family income gives women a greater sense of equality, a wider circle of friends and more

varied experiences. Research has also found that women who don't work and have several young children to care for are more likely to become seriously depressed (Brown and Harris, 1978). The children of working mothers tend to be more confident in social settings, hold higher aspirations and are more independent and less stereotyped than those who have remained in their mother's care (Shaffer, 1993). The fact that working women have such attributes may be because they are working, or it could be that these personality characteristics are a causal factor in why some women choose to work. Whatever the cause and effect relationship, working mothers should feel that there are compensations for their children.

# Childminding

One alternative to day nurseries for many mothers in this country is to place their children in the care of a registered childminder. Mayall and Petrie (1983) looked at British childminding, observing and interviewing sixty-six pairs of mothers and minders in London. The children were under two years of age. Mayall and Petrie found that the quality of care was very variable, many minders were highly competent, but certain children spent the day in an under-stimulated environment, lacking love and attention. Some of the children displayed signs of emotional disturbance, though this may be because they had problems at home. In general, Mayall and Petrie concluded that childminding need not be disruptive but it may be. The things which moderate the effects of childcare arrangements are the quality of the care, the stability of the arrangement and the strength of the original attachment bond.

Bryant and his colleagues (1980) conducted a similar study in Oxfordshire, as part of the Oxford Pre-school Project. They observed ninety-eight children, their mothers and child-minders and found that at least a third of the children were 'failing to thrive' and some were actually disturbed. Many minders felt that they did not have to form emotional bonds with the children nor did they have to stimulate them. In fact, minders rewarded quiet behaviour, reinforcing a kind of emotional withdrawal. Bryant et al. claim that two 'government-sponsored myths' about child-minding have no basis in fact. These are that childminding is a good form of care because it approximates more closely to being at home with mother, and that the only qualification a minder needs is being a mother herself. Childminding is politically popular because it is a cheap form of care; it can be excellent but sometimes can be very poor.

## In-home care

The third form of care which is available to working parents is to arrange for childcare in their own home. Some in-home care is under-taken by relatives of the child, whereas other families employ trained nannies or *au pairs* to work in their homes. In the US in 1983, thirty per cent of more than five million working mothers used in-home care for under fives (Readdick, 1987). Such arrangements tend to be private and not monitored by social services, which means that they are not easily accessible to psychologists. Contrary to popular opinion, it is not the very wealthy who employ such help, but two-career families from the business or professional community.

## 'Self-care' or 'latchkey' children

Working parents continue to need childcare after a child has reached school age. Their children need to be supervised for after-school hours and in the evenings, if parents do shift work. Ideally, such children need more than just 'supervision'. In the US, it was estimated that, in 1984, about two million children between five and thirteen were looking after themselves with little or no adult supervision (Padilla and Landreth, 1989). This lack of care may lead to bond disruption, feelings of neglect and loss of self-esteem, all of which might be associated with antisocial behaviour in adolescence. Alternatively, it is possible that such experiences have positive benefits, such as developing independence and responsibility, and many children enjoy looking after themselves. Padilla and Landreth report that there are no universal effects, and it is important to consider the kind of self-care setting, the degree of parental involvement at other times, and the style of parenting. For example, rural children may feel less fearful, and parents who are authoritative (see page 92) will be able to foster sufficient self-control in their children so that being left alone will not led to problems and loss of confidence. A study by Vandell and Ramanan (1991) of nearly 400 children aged between eight and eleven found that after-school care *per se* is less important than the quality of children's experiences with their families. Again, quality care appears to compensate for loss of time together.

# THE EFFECTS OF SEPARATION

How does separation lead to emotional and cognitive deficits? The absence of familiar figures leads to feelings of anxiety (separation anxiety, see page 32). Conversely, the presence of known people or objects enables children and adults to cope better. Evidence for this comes from Kamarck et al. (1990).

They asked participants to perform a series of difficult tasks either alone or with a friend, and recorded the participants' cardiovascular reactions. These were lower when a friend was present, demonstrating that social support does reduce stress responses. It has also been shown that there may be a link between stress and health because of a reduced immune response. The immune system protects us from disease chiefly through the action of anti-bodies. The presence of adrenalin, which is produced as part of a fear response, seems to inhibit the production of these components. Kiecolt-Glaser et al. (1984) found evidence that immune responses were lower during examination periods in a group of medical students. It was particularly low for students who reported feeling most lonely, again emphasising the importance of social support in psychological and physical well-being.

Anxiety creates arousal, which affects performance in a curvilinear fashion. Too little or too much leads to depressed performance, whereas a moderate amount has a positive effect. This relationship is termed the Yerkes-Dodson law (see Figure 8.1). It is dependent on task complexity and on individual differences: a more complex task requires greater arousal and some people cope better with arousal than others. A person who is just waking up (low arousal) is slow to respond. Equally, a person in a state of panic (high arousal) can become inactive, as occurs in stage fright. Arousal and anxiety interfere with both cognitive and physical performance. Hembree (1988) cites over 500 studies concerned with test anxiety. He concludes that such anxiety causes poor test performance and that persons with low self-esteem will be most affected. Anxiety also affects learning (McKeachie, 1984): highly anxious students profit less from instruction, especially when it is unstructured.

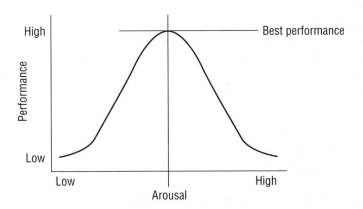

FIGURE 8.1 *The Yerkes-Dodson law*

This evidence suggests that children left on their own may experience anxiety, depressed health and reduced ability to think and learn. Where anxiety is lessened, from, for example, making friends or bringing attachment objects from home, the effects should also be minimised.

# DIFFERENT KINDS OF SEPARATION

It is clear that not all separations lead to long- or even short-term distress, and that different children exposed to similar separations respond differently. Why? First, it may be that those children who are more securely attached will experience fewer ill-effects. This has been found in studies of childminding, described earlier in this chapter, where the children who failed to thrive were the ones having difficult relationships at home.

Second, some children maintain attachment links in the form of transitional objects, friends or substitute attachments. This can be seen in cases of divorce; where children maintain contact with their non-custodial parent, they appear to suffer fewer problems. This was also what Robertson and Robertson (1968) concluded from their film study of four different children during a period of separation in their lives. All the children were between one and two years of age. One boy was filmed being admitted to hospital, and another boy had to stay in a residential nursery for a short time. The Robertsons considered that both of these boys experienced loss of their mother-figure *and* had no adequate substitute, though they were adequately cared for. They called this *bond disruption*. They also filmed two girls who were separated from their mothers, but spent the time in a family setting (the Robertsons' home). They had visited the home beforehand, and were encouraged to talk about their mothers during their stay. The boys showed clear signs of acute distress, whereas the girls were only mildly stressed and generally adapted well. The Robertsons concluded that separation need not cause distress as long as bonds are not disrupted. For them, bond disruption is deprivation, but separation is not.

It should be noted that this research has a number of methodological flaws. The sample was very small, the observations were rather subjective, and the children studied were at a critical age (we cannot be sure that the same effects would be observed in older children). In addition, the situations studied were not equivalent, because the children in hospital were in a more threatening situation, regardless of the maternal care they received.

# LONG-TERM EFFECTS

Ainsworth (1972), in a review of research, concluded that children who experience separation from their parents for at least a month during their early years do have a slightly increased risk of later psychological disturbance. However, she also commented that it is difficult to see how such short separations alone might have such consequences. It is more likely that a cluster of factors are involved, so that separation is important only when other factors are also disturbed. Ainsworth notes that this is of course often the case and that separation concurs with other problems such as discord in the home, poor housing, inadequate parenting, ill-health and so on. Perhaps the most useful way to understand the situations where children are separated from their main caregivers is to think in terms of risk factors: where children have inadequate personal resources or where they may have to cope with too many potentially detrimental factors, they will be affected by emotional deprivation. Some children are more vulnerable than others because of their age, temperamental differences and/or other life experiences. In general, children are very resilient and many are not permanently damaged by experiences of separation.

# OTHER CHILDHOOD EXPERIENCES OF SEPARATION

## Hospitalisation

Spitz and Wolf (1946) carried out a number of studies of children admitted to hospital, and found that apparently 'normal' children reacted to this separation by becoming quiet, apathetic and sad (a condition they referred to as *anaclitic depression*). Spitz and Wolf found that the children recovered quickly when restored to their mother if the separation lasted less than three months. However, longer separations were rarely associated with complete recovery. Support for these findings came from a study by Douglas (1975), who used data from the National Survey of Health and Development, a longitudinal study of 5,000 boys and girls born in Great Britain during one week in 1946 (excluding illegitimate births and twins). The children were contacted every two years over the next twenty-six years. The survey kept a record of pre-school hospitalisation and assessed behaviour in adolescence. There was a strong association between a child having experienced a hospital admission of more than a week, or repeated admissions in a child under four, and an increased risk of behaviour disturbance and poor reading in adolescence.

However, the reason for this may not be because separation *caused* adolescent problems. Clarke and Clarke (1976) looked at the same data and found that the reason for this apparent association was because many of the children were in hospital because of problems associated with disadvantaged homes. Therefore, it might be more accurate to say that social rather than maternal deprivation was the main cause of later delinquency.

Another source of confusion in such studies is between the effects of separation alone and the effects of deprivation of maternal care. Bowlby's (1946) original work *Forty-four Juvenile Thieves* involved children who had experienced repeated, short separations, often in hospital, without any substitute care or contact with their own families (see page 40). Bowlby et al. (1956) also studied children who had been cared for in a TB sanatorium and found little in the way of cognitive, emotional or behavioural ill-effects. This may be because of better substitute care, the conclusion offered by the Robertsons' study described earlier in this chapter.

With hindsight, it appears obvious that children in hospital are placed under a considerable amount of stress and having to face this alone must invariably be traumatic. One solution to the problem of hospital separation has been to encourage parents to stay in hospital with their children, thus providing continuing emotional support. Psychologists have suggested other means of reducing anxiety, such as play therapy to enable the children to act out their fears. Schwarz et al. (1983) compared the effects of different kinds of play on children who were hospitalised for dental treatment. One group had 'hospital toys', such as stethoscopes and bandages, while another group had 'non-hospital toys' such as Lego and puzzles. A third group received no special treatment. The first group showed less distress and greater co-operation during treatment than either of the other groups, though the provision of any toys seemed beneficial. Other studies have shown that allowing children to act out their fears with puppets or making the treatment more like 'fun' reduces distress and improves recovery rates. Providing a healthy psychological environment, then, will have positive consequences for the child's recovery. The fact that hospitalisation may be associated with later problems may be because of a particularly traumatic experience and/or poor home environment rather than separation.

# RESEARCH TECHNIQUES
## *Studying children over time*

Developmental psychology is particularly concerned with discovering how children change over time. Longitudinal studies involve following one group of individuals over a long period of time, taking periodic samples of the target behaviour. An alternative, the cross-sectional or cohort study, is to observe a target behaviour of two groups of children at the same point in time, one group younger than the other. The samples are matched in terms of important variables.

Longitudinal studies have the advantage of offering greater control so we can be sure that the difference in behaviour is due to experience. However, such studies are very time-consuming and participants invariably 'drop out', leaving a biased sample in later years. In any case, the sample used may only be representative of its generation (the cross-generational problem). For example, children of the 1960s are different to those of the

1980s because of economic changes.

Cross-sectional studies are a much cheaper and more flexible alternative, though it is obviously impossible to ever match the samples perfectly. In fact, differences between participants may be due to social changes from one generation to another rather than age (the cohort effect).

The case study is another means of looking at behaviour over time. Where a particular influence is rare, such as early childhood deprivation, it may be the only way to study the effects on behaviour. The study may be of an individual or a small group, institution or event. The participant(s) may be followed over time or retrospective data collected about their experiences. Such studies have limited applicability, though they provide rich data and unusual insights.

## Fostering

Children may spend some time away from home, fostered by the social services department, because it is in their 'own best interests'. The difference between adoption and fostering lies in the transfer of parental rights. Where a child is adopted, parental rights are given to the adoptive family, and children have no contact with their natural family (in future the law is likely to change to allow the natural parents continued contact). Where a child is voluntarily placed in care, the rights remain with the parents, although if this is the result of a court order, the rights are with the social services department. Fostering involves no permanent commitment and usually finishes when the child leaves home aged eighteen. A fostered child may be allowed supervised visits from their natural parents.

The decision to place a court order on a child is based on the idea that the child will suffer greater emotional deprivation by remaining at home than the child will by being separated. What are the consequences for those involved? A child taken into care may suffer from feelings of guilt, rejection and/or maternal deprivation. A warm foster placement may offer better maternal care. In a review of studies of substitute parenting, Shaw (1986) suggested that a foster mother usually brings valuable mothering skills to a child who may well be in need of such expert care. Such mothering may act as a useful example to the biological mother; alternatively, the natural mother may feel a greater sense of inadequacy in the shadow of a more experienced mother.

Of course, in some situations, foster parents turn out to be unsatisfactory or even abusive themselves, and another matter for psychologists is to understand what sort of people offer themselves as foster parents. They tend to be older women whose own children have left home. They are sometimes regarded as people who have some problem of their own to resolve, though there is no evidence to support this (Berryman et al., 1994). It is useful for foster parents to be offered professional support. For example, they need advice about how to cope with emotionally disturbed children and help with their own fears about the eventual loss of their foster children.

An alternative approach to fostering is to leave the child in their own home, but provide day nursery care where the parents can also attend to learn new skills. This is becoming a more popular choice rather than the disruptions caused by fostering, especially when it is not likely to be permanent.

# Divorce

There is a commonly held belief that a good divorce is better than an unhappy home because the stress caused by family rows may be worse than problems created by divorce. A recent study by Cockett and Tripp (1994) tested this view. They assessed 152 children in late childhood and their parents. Some participants came from 'reordered families' (their parents were separated or divorced and some had remarried and taken on a step family). The 'control' children had lived with both their natural parents since birth and were matched to the experimental children on key variables, such as age, sex, socio-economic status and mother's educational background. This group was subdivided into those whose parents had regular conflict, and those whose parents had no serious conflict.

Cockett and Tripp found that the children from reordered families were more likely to have health problems, need extra help at school, experience friendship difficulties and to suffer from low self-esteem. Those who had experienced multiple changes were worse off than those with a one-parent or stepfamily. Most importantly, those children living in intact families where there was marital discord did less well than the control children, but were better off than those from reordered families. Therefore, it seems that marital breakdown causes more problems for children than discord alone, and that the more disruption a child suffers, the worse the adjustment.

Other research has found lower levels of academic achievement, a higher incidence of conduct disorder, problems of psychological adjustment generally, and a somewhat earlier social maturity in children from divorced families. The differences between these children and those from 'normal' homes are significant but small, the size of the effect being of the same order as the difference between children from 'normal' middle-class and working-class homes (Richards, 1995). The difficulty with this evidence is that it is correlational. Divorce may not be the sole cause of disturbance, because separated families tend to have a cluster of other problems as well. Cockett and Tripp found that reordered families were also more likely to be receiving social security benefits, had moved house more often and were less likely to own their own car (indicative of low income).

Amato (1993) has identified five main reasons why divorce may lead to maladjustment. These are: the absence of the non-custodial parent (Bowlby's view), the poor psychological adjustment of the custodial parent (poor parenting), economic hardship, stressful life changes (the Exeter study) and inter-parental conflict (Rutter's view). Amato concludes that no model accounts satisfactorily for all the research findings and that the reason why research has uncovered only small differences between children from divorced and non-divorced families is because of the variability found amongst children. Some children adjust well, and even show improvements

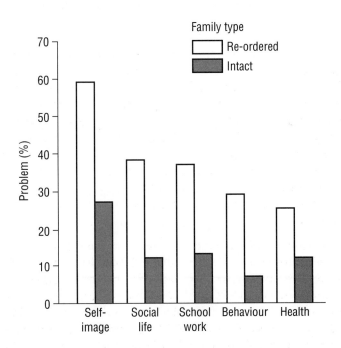

FIGURE 8.2 *Cockett and Tripp (1994) found that children from reordered families experienced more problems than children from intact families*

in behaviour, whereas others experience problems. Amato suggests that the two concepts of *resources* and *stressors* can be used to understand why some children cope while others don't. Children have various emotional, financial and personal resources to help them cope with the variety of stressors present in their lives. A child who has a warm relationship with both parents, despite a separation, will be able to cope with financial hardship and parental conflict, whereas separation and hardship might lead to depressed performance in other circumstances. It is the total configuration which counts.

Such an understanding of how divorce affects children's well-being highlights better ways of coping. For example, in Cockett and Tripp's study, twenty-one per cent of the children had received no explanation of why their parents had separated, probably because parents found it difficult to talk with each other. Such communication problems led to difficulties arranging visitation; in fact, only thirty per cent maintained regular contact with their non-resident parent. Children also lost contact with grandparents, with whom they may have had close relationships. Ideally, both parents should explain their decision to the child and make it clear that the divorce is not the child's fault (it is common for a child to feel that they in some way caused the separation or could have prevented it). Continuing strife between separated parents places a difficult burden on an emotionally vulnerable child who may be forced to take sides. Loss of contact might led to understandable feelings of abandonment. Realistically, parents who do separate have many problems of their own to resolve and are unable to give their children the amount of consideration they deserve. Such problems peripheral to the separation itself may be more central to the ill-effects of divorce.

# Parental death

Parental death is a special kind of separation because, unlike divorce, it is unlikely that there was a history of discord, though in some cases the period prior to death may have been difficult. Parental death may be associated with feelings of helplessness and an increased risk of depression rather than delinquency (as is the case for separation and divorce). For example, Bifulco et al. (1992) studied a group of 249 women who had lost their mothers before they were seventeen either through separation (for more than a year) or death. The group as a whole had twice the normal rate of depression and anxiety disorders in adulthood. However, there was a particularly high rate of depression among those whose mothers had died before the age of six. This was not true where separation occurred before the age of six. This suggests two things. First, that there is a critical early period before the age of six. Second, that there is a difference between permanent deprivation (even where there is substitute maternal care from a father, grandparent or step parent) and separation.

There are some similarities between the experience of death and other forms of separation. Robertson and Robertson (1968) noted that separation leads to grieving because, for children aged two, their mother might as well be dead. The initial stages of separation anxiety show the same kinds of behaviour as mourning generally (see page 32).

As with divorce, a number of other factors modify the effect of parental death, such as the degree of substitute care which is subsequently provided and the effect the death has on the rest of the family (particularly the remaining parent). Recovery may depend to some extent on how well children are helped to cope with their mourning. As with divorce, children may feel at fault in some way. Adults often feel the same, and see the death of a loved one as some form of punishment. Many parents and relatives prefer not to discuss the matter with their children, in part because they have yet to come to terms with their own grief, but also because they don't know how to explain it. Some children feel that they must not show distress because this will upset everyone even more. This has the effect of denying children the opportunity to express their grief. A distressed child will be in particular need of emotional support, which may well be lacking, leading to even greater denial of emotions.

## Adoption

In the past, when unmarried mothers were regularly forced to give babies up for adoption, it was common for them to nurse their infants for a significant period of time before passing them on. In such cases, infants will certainly have begun the process of bond formation with these caregivers and will have been profoundly affected by the wrench. Most adoptions today take place within the first week of birth, and where adoptions take place after the age of six months, the child is considered a special care case (see Chapter 13). Even when adoptions take place early on, we should remember that the process of bonding may start even before birth (the infant in the womb hears its mother's voice and becomes used to the rhythms of her body). This suggests that all adopted children probably experience some sense of loss (deprivation), but rarely lack emotional care – in fact the care lavished on them by desperate parents-in-waiting is an advantage that other infants may lack. As long as infants are separated from their natural mothers at an early stage it appears that adoptive mothers and infants are just as securely attached as non-adoptive families (Singer et al., 1985).

Adoptees may suffer long-term emotional problems not because of a disturbed attachment but because it is difficult to come to terms with the knowledge of being rejected by one's mother. For this reason, many adopted children seek to find their birth parents and become acquainted with their family histories. Such conflicts, called 'genealogical anxiety', usually appear during adolescence as part of the maturing child's search for self-identity.

In recent years, there have been a number of disturbing court cases in America where natural parents have sought to regain the custody of a child they gave up for adoption. In such proceedings, psychologists are called upon as expert witnesses to advise upon what is in the child's best interests (Johnson and Torres, 1994). Currently, the courts tend to favour natural ties, despite the fact that the child has often formed strong bonds of attachment with the adoptive parents, having spent a number of years in their care. It is hard to understand such decisions in terms of what is known about attachment but legal decisions have to be based on a variety of belief systems, of which attachment theory is only one.

# Neo-natal special care

Neonates receive special care (special care baby units, SCBUs) for various reasons. These include: prematurity, very low birth-weight (VLBW), illness, congenital malformation or disability. For such babies, there may be a number of obstacles to parent-infant bonding, such as difficulty holding the baby because of medical equipment and the baby's size. The parents may also have anxieties about the baby's survival and development and therefore are reluctant to enter into a relationship with the baby. Some parents may experience feelings of horror where an infant is disfigured, or grief for the baby they were expecting, as well as feelings of failure. Ultimately, lack of early physical contact may not matter (see page 15), but once separation between an infant and its parents has become established, it may be hard to overcome. The parents may experience lack of confidence about dealing with their baby, and feel that their baby is a stranger which makes it difficult to anticipate its needs and establish reciprocal interactions. Too little contact with the infant may well have short-term consequences for the mother-child relationship, though Douglas (1975) points out that too much contact with sick infants may lead to overprotectiveness from the parent and nervousness in the infant.

Immediate consequences are of relatively little concern if special care babies do not suffer permanent emotional or cognitive consequences. The effects of VLBW on cognitive development appears to be largely reversible, as long as post-natal care is good. In terms of the effects of disrupted bonding on subsequent development, there also appears to be an association between quality of subsequent care and recovery. Minde et al. (1989) followed sixty-four VLBW infants and found, at the age of four, that forty-three per cent were rated as having behavioural disturbances such as overactivity, poor concentration and restlessness. However, the presence of behavioural disturbance was not correlated with neo-natal illness score, attachment rating at one year or socio-economic status. They concluded that long-term behaviour was most dependent on the subsequent nurturing that the child received.

The research reported here applies to premature or low birth-weight babies. Those infants with clear sensory or physical disabilities also benefit from quality of parenting or family relationships, but obviously their deficits persist.

# SUMMARY

In the past, it was thought that early experiences fixed a child's personality. The wealth of research undertaken in the last fifty years has shown that this is not necessarily the case. We have seen that permanent deficits do not necessarily result from experiences of, for example, multiple carers, discord in the home, early emotional deprivation and lack of cognitive stimulation. The distress and ill-effects related to separation can be reduced by offering the child such things as quality time, substitute maternal care, continuing contact with early attachment figures and cognitive enrichment. Privation is distinguished from deprivation; this concept and its long-term effects are explored in Chapter 13.

*chapter nine*

# OTHER FAMILY MEMBERS AND FRIENDS

# CHAPTER OVERVIEW

In this chapter, we will look at other key members of the child's social world: siblings, grandparents, peers and friends, and the influence these people exert over the child's emotional and cognitive development. The consequences of having no siblings will also be discussed. One of the things that siblings, peers and friends offer is increased opportunities for play, and at the end of this chapter, we will look at the value and functions of play.

# SIBLINGS

Eighty per cent of children have a sibling. Siblings can act as models and teachers, offer the opportunity to practise social skills, and serve as confidants and caregivers. All of these enhance both the younger and older child's social, cognitive and emotional development.

For a first-born child, the arrival of a brother or sister is usually greeted with great interest and protectiveness, as well as some distress and ambivalence. Dunn and Kendrick (1982) conducted the most extensive research into sibling relationships, following forty first-born children whose parents were expecting a second child. They observed that the mothers typically devoted less time and were less warm and playful with older children when the new baby arrived. This can lead to feelings of resentment which may be expressed towards the baby or redirected towards the mother or father. The older child may also regress, behaving like a baby in order to get the same kind of attention.

There are ways to minimise early feelings of sibling rivalry. Fathers can spend more time with the older child, and mothers can include the older child in making decisions about the baby's care. It is important for mothers to devote quality time to their older child, but it is probably not helpful to be over-attentive, as Dunn and Kendrick found when they looked at relationships between older siblings and their infant brother or sister at various ages. The older girls who got most attention around the time of the birth played least with, and were most negative towards, their baby brother or sister fourteen months later. This may be because over-indulgence supports the child's belief that the baby is annoying and that they are right to feel resentful. Positive relationships were fostered by encouraging a friendly interest in the new baby and discouraging any negative responses.

Dunn (1984) concluded from the available evidence that there are no consistent effects which can be related to gender or age gap. Some studies have found that conflict is greater between children closer in age, but such siblings are also closer emotionally. In general, the kind of relationship that a parent has with the child acts as a model for the sibling-sibling relationship. Despite the fact that children often regard sibling relationships as conflict-ridden, they rate siblings as more important than friends (Furman and Buhrmester, 1985).

The positive side of the sibling relationship is associated with the older child's role as an attachment figure, role model, playmate and socialising influence. The attachment role may develop into a mutual one, with siblings enhancing each other's emotional development and offering emotional support throughout life. Older siblings may play an important caregiving role. This is especially true in other cultures and in large families, where children are raised by an older sister rather than their mother. However, not all siblings are willing to take on this role. Stewart (1983) placed fifty-four pairs of infants and older siblings (aged thirty to fifty-eight months) in the Strange Situation (see page 34) and found that, when the mother left, just over half of the older children responded to their brother or sister's distress by hugging them or saying something reassuring. Their actions were effective in reducing anxiety. The other half of the sample ignored or moved away from the infant. Other research has found that older siblings who themselves are securely attached to their mothers are most inclined to comfort younger brothers or sisters (Teti and Ablard, 1989).

Older brothers or sisters are also strong role models, important for gender and social development. They act as teachers, instructing their younger siblings in useful cognitive and physical skills, such as children's games, early reading skills and appropriate playground behaviour. Siblings learn about social relations from each other, how to share and negotiate, how to feel empathy for another, and about helping behaviour. This may assist them to get along better with their peers. The presence of siblings, whether older or younger, increases the amount of children's toys and books which are available. Older children involve younger siblings in their more advanced fantasy play, which may promote emotional and cognitive development.

Most siblings feel very protective towards each other. This can be explained in terms of the socio-biological concept of 'kin selection'. In all species, parents have an innate drive to protect their offspring as a means of ensuring the survival of their genetic line. Siblings have a similar genetic interest to parents, since they share at least fifty per cent of their genes. Consequently, there is good reason to think that they will have an innate drive to behave more prosocially towards their immediate kin. However, siblings also compete for limited parental resources. This means that the relationship is inevitably an ambivalent one. Dunn (1984) suggests that this ambivalence gives siblings their sense of 'emotional urgency', which explains why the relationship is such a strong one.

## Ordinal position effects

Later-born children have been found to be more popular amongst their peers than first-borns, possibly because they have to learn to co-operate with older and more powerful siblings, and this helps with peer interactions (Shaffer, 1993). Other research has found the opposite, that first-borns tend to be more popular because they are more likely to be sociable and friendly, more accepting and less demanding (Miller and Maruyama, 1976). First-borns are also more likely to develop leadership skills and to be more dominant because they are given roles of responsibility with respect to younger children (Dunn, 1984). They also experience a greater sense of their own competence in comparison with younger siblings, which increases their sense of self-efficacy; caring for younger siblings promotes emotional and prosocial development. Later-born children tend to have lower IQs because of having to share resources such as parental attention (see the confluence model, page 61). The social and cognitive climate of the home is very different for the first-born; they have at least nine months of individual attention, and parents often have higher expectations for their oldest child.

Newson and Newson (1970) found that parents were more rigid with their first-born child, becoming more flexible with subsequent children. For example, they were more willing to indulge later bedtimes, encourage the use of transitional objects, allow food fads and leave toilet training until the child was older. It makes sense that, emotionally, first-borns have been found to be more prone to feelings of guilt, more dependent on others, less aggressive and more conformist (Mussen et al., 1984). Mussen et al. cite a historical curiosity: the majority of scientists who publicly opposed the theory of evolution between 1750 and 1870 were first-borns, whereas ninety per cent of the non-conformist advocates, including Charles Darwin and Alfred Wallace, were later-borns.

The ordinal position effect is increased along with the size of the family. The larger the family, the more the children have to learn how to negotiate and share. There is a tendency to think of large, *happy* families. However, Dunn (1984) suggests that life in such families is not 'a bed of roses', though it does teach one that there are other people in the world with equal rights. This experience of co-operation is less true for smaller families and, since small families are the current norm, this may go some way towards explaining today's 'me' society.

# FOCUS ON...
## *only children (SINGLETONS)*

One of the reasons parents give for having more than one child is the benefits of having siblings. As we have seen, siblings offer reciprocal emotional support and encourage both cognitive and emotional development. A pre-school singleton may lack playmates and thus miss out on important learning opportunities.

However, there are advantages in being an only child. Like first-borns, they receive individualised attention and a sense of importance. This helps them establish good relationships with other children when given the opportunity, and they don't have to lose out on experiences which facilitate their social development. Any lack of social interaction with siblings may be compensated for by greater stimulation from, and socialising, with their parents and other adults. Singletons may not learn social negotiation at home but, conversely, they don't have to share their possessions, which may make self-definition easier

and enhance their self-confidence.

The Chinese have a special interest in this question because of their one-child family planning programme. One study of nearly 1000 Chinese schoolchildren found that singletons were more egocentric, whereas sibling children possessed the positive qualities of persistence, co-operation and peer prestige (Jiao et al., 1986). A study of pre-university students in India found that, on all measures, only children stood out as being the most maladjusted, whereas fourth- and fifth-born were the best adjusted (Doss, 1980). Alternatively, Polit and Falbo (1988) conducted a review of the literature and concluded that, whilst only children scored considerably better than all other groups on achievement motivation and personal adjustment, in general there was little difference between singletons and their sibling counterparts.

# GRANDPARENTS

The other major family relationship is between grandparents and their grandchildren. Tinsley and Parke (1984) suggest that an important indirect influence of grandparents is the way they raised their children, now parents, which will affect their grandchildren's experience of parental discipline and care. Grandparents may also offer financial or emotional support to the parents. Direct influences might include a grandmother looking after grandchildren on a regular basis, and caring for them during school holidays when parents are at work or on holiday. In some cases, grandparents take on the parenting role completely, for example in the case of a teenage pregnancy.

Grandparents are often able to take a less disciplinary role, and can offer a special emotional relationship. Some children find this particularly helpful in times of parental conflict. This emotional relationship also offers children a wider variety of attachment figures, which is advantageous, as there are individual differences in children and their caregivers so that some children may be closer to their grandparents than their parents.

In the past, more grandparents lived close to their grandchildren, but even distant relationships can be conducted by letter, telephone and visits. If parents separate or become divorced, this sometimes causes a break in children's relationships with one set of grandparents, although there are now laws which help grandparents petition for visitation rights.

FIGURE 9.1 *Grandparents can give children a special emotional relationship and act as important attachment figures*

# FRIENDS

Friends and peers are a key part of growing up. Relating to others is a means of learning about yourself, through social comparison and the reflection of yourself in others (see page 88). Friends also provide emotional support and an opportunity for emotional development, in particular learning empathy. Peer interactions give practice in things such as how to resolve squabbles and conduct relationships, which lays the foundation for later adult relationships. Peer groups also exert normative pressures, guiding the group in appropriate and inappropriate behaviour; children are particularly sensitive to such forces. In this way, peers act as an important source of cultural influence. Finally, friends are important in cognitive development, since disagreements allow a child to be aware of alternative views. Friends are more valuable this than acquaintances because they communicate more information, both positive and negative (Nelson and Aboud, 1985).

There are individual differences in the 'need to affiliate' (naffiliation), although it is a basic human need to seek social contact, perhaps most importantly for later reproductive purposes! Schachter (1959) found that participants who were isolated from all human contact experienced hallucinations and became highly disturbed within a period of two days, similar to the effects of sensory deprivation. His participants thought and dreamt about people. Most children readily seek out the company of others, though there are some children who are isolated. This may be due to poor social skills, but it may also be just because some people are less interested in human relationships.

## Stages of friendship

We talk loosely of 'friendship', but this covers a number of relationships. A friend is more than an acquaintance or a peer. Friendship is an emotional relationship which includes elements of mutual trust, assistance, respect, understanding and intimacy. Young children are too egocentric to truly engage in such relationships. The development of empathy and formation of peer groups comes later, and relies on greater cognitive maturity. However, the development of friendship and peer relations is not solely dependent on cognitive maturity – prior experience of social interactions and negotiation are important in teaching children necessary social skills. As we have seen earlier in this chapter, these may come from early sibling interactions.

## Popularity

Psychologists classify children as popular, rejected, neglected or average. Dodge et al. (1983) looked at how differing social skills were related to such status. They observed five-year-olds in the playground, and looked at how individual children coped with trying to join in with two other peers who were already at play. Popular children tended to watch and wait, gradually joining a group by making group-oriented statements. Neglected children also watched, but shied away from attempts to engage their peers. By contrast, rejected children tended to be highly active and aggressive. They disrupted play and were unco-operative, self-serving and critical. Of course, such a deficit in necessary social skills could be an effect of lack of social contact rather than a cause. When rejected children are placed with unfamiliar peers, they sometimes end up with the same status they normally have, but this is not always true (Shaffer, 1993). It may be that peer group rejection leads to an expectation of social failure and a lack of opportunity to practise important skills. Rejected children can be given social skills training in interpersonal skills. For example, Oden and Asher (1977) coached eight- and

| DESCRIPTION OF PEER INTERACTIONS | |
| --- | --- |
| | Infants show an interest in peers from an early age; at the age of one they will look more at another unfamiliar baby than an unfamiliar adult. |
| 2 to 4 | By the age of two children are ready for nursery school and activities involving their peers, though much of it is parallel not co-operative play. They have very little understanding of another's feelings. 'Friends' are not necessarily the same sex, though they are aware of gender-appropriate behaviour. |
| 4 to 7 | Children have their first mutual friendships. Play with friends is different from with acquaintances. Friends show each other affection and approval, but the relationship still lacks empathy. Friendship largely involves common activity, proximity, sharing things. A friend is someone who does things for you. |
| 8 to 11 | Friends have psychological similarity, shared interests, traits and motives. There is now an element of trust and responding to others' needs. Friendships are more genuine, though they tend to be 'fair-weather', lasting only as long as is pleasing to both friends. Emergence of the peer group and loosely formed gangs. These gradually become more elaborate, involving membership requirements. |
| 10 to 12 | Friendship involves reciprocal emotional commitment. Deeper, more enduring friendships, where thoughts, feelings and secrets are shared. This is related to the development of empathy. Friends give comfort and support, act as confidants and therapists. |
| 12 + | Relationships incorporate the conventions of the society. |

nine-year-old social isolates on how to participate in play activities, how to take turns and share, how to communicate effectively and how to give attention and help to peers. The children became more outgoing and positive, and even a year later had improved social status. Another strategy is to encourage mixed-age social interaction. This allows an immature child to learn how to direct the activities of younger children and take responsibility, which improves their social skills (Duck, 1992).

In general, the factors which govern who children choose as their friends are the same as those which affect relationships at any age. Physical features, such as attractiveness, the possession of some enviable characteristic, or the fact that a child has matured early, are important. At twelve months, infants already prefer attractive to unattractive strangers (Langlois et al., 1990). Such preferences may create a self-fulfilling prophecy: attractive children know they are better liked and therefore they learn to behave pleasantly, which increases their likeability. There is even evidence that children with attractive first names, such as David or Karen, tend to be more popular than those with unusual names, such as Bertha or Elmer (Harari and McDavid, 1973).

Status or perceived competence are desirable characteristics for most children. For example, children who are good at school or at sports tend to be popular, though the opposite applies in delinquent groups, where the leader may be the one who possesses the most antisocial traits. The fact that someone is similar to you, or familiar, or even just lives nearby will also influence choice of friends.

Early rejection appears to be related to problems later in life. In a longitudinal study of over 800 children in Monroe County, New York, conducted by Cowen et al. (1973), it was found that those children who received negative peer ratings at the age of eight, were three times more likely to have sought psychiatric help within the next eleven years. Duck (1991) reports that, if children were unpopular at school, they are more likely to become alcoholic, depressed, schizophrenic, delinquent or psychotic. One reason for such associations is that poor social skills are involved in all of these outcomes. It is also possible that rejected children tend to band together to form delinquent cliques and are then more likely to become involved in antisocial conduct, or that such children develop poor self-esteem, leading to psychiatric problems.

# PLAY

Much of the activity that friends, peers and siblings engage in might be called 'play'. We tend to regard play as something which is fun and extracurricular, yet throughout life it has a serious role in our development and well-being. Garvey (1977) describes the following characteristics of play: it is pleasurable and enjoyable, it has no extrinsic goals, it is spontaneous and voluntary, and it involves some active engagement. It is not just children who play. Adults continue to play, both in organised games or less informal non-work activities. The desire to play appears to be innate and, interestingly, it is only found in higher mammals and so must be related in some way to intelligent activity.

The kinds of play which children engage in change with age. Piaget's (1951) stage theory of play is derived from his general views of cognitive development. Perhaps even more well known are the stages first presented by Parten (1932), which are more concerned with the social aspects of play (see Box 9.2 overleaf).

## The value of play

In some ways, 'play' is an unhelpful term because much of what the preschool child does is called 'play', yet a lot of it is not especially playful. When children are playing with a jigsaw puzzle, they are clearly practising certain skills. In a similar way, we should distinguish 'play' from 'exploration play'.

**Box 9.2** Stages of play

| AGE (APPROX.) | PARTEN'S STAGES | PIAGET'S STAGES | DESCRIPTION |
|---|---|---|---|
| 0 to 2 | Solitary activity | Mastery play | Practice and control of movements and language, exploration, repetition gives pleasure. |
| 2 to 4 | Parallel activity | Symbolic play | Children enjoy playing together, watching, imitating but not truly interacting. By the age of three children are starting to use toys rather than themselves as an active agent. They also engage in fantasy and make-believe. |
| 4 to 7 | Social activity | | Associative or co-operative, peak of social pretend play, sex segregation becomes apparent. |
| 7 + | | Play with rules | Children can engage in games with rules, either formal rules such as football, or they spontaneously invent their own. |

Hutt (1966) showed children aged between three and five a 'supertoy' which consisted of cogs and buzzers, levers and bells. Initially, they explored the toy, being very serious and focused in their activity. The second stage was what Hutt considered true play, where the child moved from the question 'What does this object do?' to 'What can I do with it?'. She suggested that it is play which furthers a child's knowledge.

The value of this play is supported by various studies. For example, Hutt and Bhavnani (1972) found that children who were judged as being low in exploratory play when they were pre-schoolers tended to be low in curiosity and to experience problems in their social adjustment five years later. In contrast, active explorers were more likely to score high on tests of creativity and show evidence of being independent and curious.

Games of make-believe and fantasy are also thought to have important consequences for children's development. Such activities allow them to try out different social roles, to act out their emotional concerns or to explore their relationships with other objects or people. Connolly and Doyle (1984) observed nearly 100 pre-schoolers and found that the amount and complexity of fantasy play was positively correlated with social competence. Smilansky (1968) has suggested some children suffer a 'play deficit' as a result of a lack of complex fantasy and sociodramatic play. She proposed that this leads to developmental lags and difficulty in school integration. Her views are based on observations of a wide variety of working-class children and children from certain cultures (such as North African or Middle Eastern). However, the studies have been criticised for poor methodology and for her European middle-class bias about what constitutes good play. Nonetheless, Smilansky's ideas were very influential, especially because they first appeared in the 1960s when the prevailing mood was for compensatory education for pre-school children, which could include play (see Operation Head Start, page 60).

## Encouraging play

If some children are suffering play deficits, then what might be done about it? One suggestion has been to develop methods of 'play tutoring'. This involves the provision of suitable apparatus and suggestions about the kind of adult interactions which facilitate play. Equipment might include relatively 'unstructured' materials, such as sand, clay or building bricks, which encourage problem-solving, creativity and emotional catharsis. Play houses, dressing-up clothes and household items enable children to engage in role and fantasy play. Curry and Arnaud (1984) recommended that adults should say aloud what the child is doing, ask questions to help elaborate play and suggest further ideas to the child.

This is actually no more than many parents do. Slade (1987) found that the pretend activities of two- to three-year-olds are longer in duration and more complex when the mother joins in. Cohen (1993) suggests that children do gain a great deal from playing with parents (and vice versa), and that parents can encourage imaginative play by accepting and respecting their child. So it isn't just peers who are important for play. Play with parents gives a child confidence to explore the world and try out different roles. Play with familiar children in familiar situations is especially significant and children are more likely to play in such situations (Smith and Connolly, 1980). It appears that play is facilitated more by the emotional climate than the provision of stimulating equipment; it should be remembered that children have long been able to make toys and games out of coat hangers and the like. Adults and children today may be influenced by attractive advertising for a wealth of toys, whereas other factors may be more critical.

# PSYCHOLOGICAL THEORIES:
# *Play*

## Biological perspective

Spencer (1873) suggested that children play because they have surplus energy. Certainly, some aspects of play might be regarded as rough-and-tumble: play fighting, tickling, chasing each other and generally running about. The fact that such play is usually accompanied by laughter and smiling shows that it is non-serious and distinct from disputes.

## Social perspective

Play is clearly an important element in social life. It is what we often do when we are with others. Play also provides an opportunity to rehearse social routines (as when children engage in make-believe) or to learn important social skills, such as sharing. Role play is often part of school drama lessons as a means of increasing empathy, social awareness and acting out emotions.

## Psychodynamic perspective

It is the emotional aspect of play which largely concerns psychoanalytic theorists. Psychoanalysts see play as a cathartic experience which relives and relieves pent-up emotions. Some kinds of play, such as with dolls, provides an opportunity for projection, regression or displacement. For example, playing with mud instead of faeces is a means of sublimation. Different kinds of play are associated with different psychosexual phases. For example, in the oral phase (see page 40), play is centred around the mouth. Erikson (1972), a neo-Freudian, saw play as a safe escape from the boundaries of reality, as in saying 'I was only playing' and fantasy play. It also allows the child to establish autonomy.

Play therapy is a means of helping children with emotional problems express those things which are troubling them and then work through them.

## Cognitive perspective

Play offers a means of practising physical and cognitive skills. For Vygotsky, play was a means of operating beyond one's current level of capability, the 'zone of potential development'. When a child is confronted with a new problem, it is incorporated into play as a means of working through the problem. Play with others also allows a child to become more aware of the discrepancies between their own perspective and that of their playmates. Language play allows the prelinguistic child to practise sounds through echolalia, and older children enjoy nursery rhymes as continuing practice in sound discrimination and understanding words.

# SUMMARY

In this chapter, we have seen that siblings and friends provide important emotional support and help cognitive and social development. They do this by acting as attachment figures and role models, providing the opportunity to practise social skills, and discuss newly acquired knowledge. Being a singleton may be both a disadvantage and an advantage: there is a decrease in peer contact, but an increase in parental attention. Grandparents exert both direct and indirect influences, acting as important attachment figures. Siblings, peers and friends all act as playmates. Play is seen as a critical ingredient of development, aiding physical, social, emotional and cognitive development.

# chapter ten

## MEDIA INFLUENCES

## CHAPTER OVERVIEW

The term 'media' covers more than television and video. However, as they are relatively recent developments and figure largely in children's lives, psychological research focuses on their positive and negative influence. These media may have a negative influence on children, in terms of teaching them unwelcome stereotypes and displacing more desirable activities, such as reading or socialising. Alternatively, the media may be seen as stimulating and enriching. This chapter also looks at the special case of television violence and aggression.

## WHAT ARE 'THE MEDIA'?

Media are channels through which information is transmitted. The term 'media' covers written material (books and magazines) and the spoken word (radio and pop songs), as well as visual multimedia (television, computer games, videos and films). These have always been recognised as powerful means of altering opinions and attitudes and thus have been the object of considerable censorship. Traditionally, such censorship was concerned with preventing the spread of certain ideas. Today, however, psychologists are also concerned with the way in which we model ourselves on media characters and how such influences alter our behaviour towards others. If this is the case, then we should censor undesirable media stereotypes and behaviours.

## HOW THE MEDIA EXERT THEIR INFLUENCE

Everyone is influenced by what they see and hear in the media, but young children are especially impressionable because their opinions, stereotypes and emotions are just developing. Pre-school children often have very little

**130**

experience of the real world, and what they learn about other people and situations is largely through television and books. Some children may continue to have little contact with the world because of an isolated rural existence or limited life experiences. The media, especially television and video, may even have a greater influence than the real world because of the appealing and persuasive way that they present their material. The media are a particularly powerful means of cultural communication. This is especially true of advertising, a fact exploited by the makers of *Sesame Street*, who realised that this was the ideal way to teach children: short bursts of colourful and exuberant information which leaves the audience wanting more. Other programmes use similar techniques to attract large audiences and win the 'rating wars'.

Children learn from media in the same way that they learn from the real world by, for example, imitating things they have seen, taking on attitudes that they have heard expressed and experiencing indirect reinforcement. In fact, very young children may be unable to distinguish between television and reality. They think the characters on television reside in the box.

# FOCUS ON...
# *television violence and aggression*

A most persistent question of recent times is the extent to which violence on television increases levels of aggression in people, particularly among children. Whenever an incomprehensible crime is committed, the media themselves turn to television and video as possible scapegoats for the increasing levels of aggression in our society. It is true that human aggression is largely learned, and so we might expect there to be a profound media influence. A recent survey conducted by Gunter and Harrison (1995) reports that violence only takes up one per cent of programme time, but that a third of all programmes carry some violence, and almost a fifth of the incidents happen in children's programmes.

How does such violence lead to aggressive behaviour? Research in this area is hampered by obvious ethical objections to deliberately exposing children to violence. Probably for this reason, one experiment stands out as a classic (classically informative and classically unethical). Bandura and his colleagues (1961, 1963) demonstrated that children could learn aggression indirectly, through vicarious reinforcement and modelling (social learning). His participants were children as young as three. The results indicated that exposure to an adult model who was shouting at and hitting a life size 'Bobo' doll increased levels of general aggressiveness in the children and also led them to imitate specific acts of violence (see Figure 10.1 overleaf). In later experiments, Bandura exposed children to filmed or cartoon models and found that they were influential, though less effective than live ones. He also found that the status of the model was important, and that certain

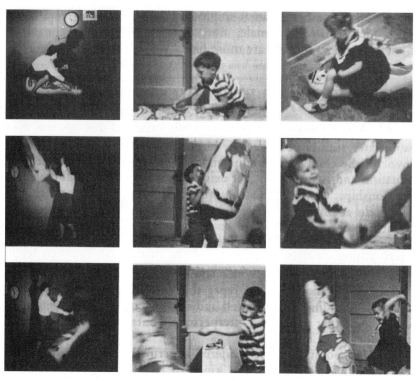

FIGURE 10.1 *Bandura et al. (1961) demonstrated how young children learn aggressive behaviour from watching an adult being aggressive with various toys, such as a life-style Bobo doll*

personality characteristics, such as low self-esteem, made observers more likely to imitate what they saw. Finally, a model who was punished was less likely to be imitated.

Further evidence for direct imitation comes from 'case studies' of copycat crimes. For example, in the James Bulger murder trial, it was suggested that the horrific behaviour of the boys was identical to things they might have seen in a horror video called *Child's Play* (Newson, 1994). More recently, a seventeen-year-old boy in America murdered his step-mother and half sister. Evidently, he was obsessed by the film *Natural Born Killers*, having seen it ten times, and was imitating what he had seen. It is clear that not everyone is affected by vicarious violence in this way, but that some children are.

Comstock (1991) reviewed nearly 200 studies,

concluding that the evidence does show a link between television violence and aggressive behaviour. Such correlations may be due to the fact that aggressive personalities watch more violence on television. A recent study by Wiegman et al. (1992) followed 400 Dutch secondary schools pupils over a period of three years. They found that positive correlations between watching television violence and aggressive behaviour disappeared if initial levels of aggression were taken into account. Some children might have higher levels of aggressive feelings, due to life frustrations, a coercive home environment or an innately more aggressive personality.

Certain programmes function as a trigger for the expression of aggression. An experimental study by Friedrich and Stein (1973) confirms this view. They observed children in a nursery school for three weeks to establish how aggressive they were. After this initial period of observation, the children were shown aggressive, prosocial, or neutral films. In the final two weeks, behaviour was again observed. Children who initially were above average in aggression were affected by the violent cartoons, whereas those who were neutral did not react to either type of programme. So, it might be suggested that an aggressive nature is a cause rather than an effect. It causes aggressive people to watch violent programmes, which then increases the likelihood that they will imitate what they have seen. Alternatively, it has been claimed that violent programmes can serve a useful cathartic purpose for people with aggressive natures.

However, there are reasons to suppose that watching violence affects all viewers, but that it affects less aggressive people less noticeably. First, the culture of the media establishes certain norms of behaviour, convincing us that such responses are acceptable. This may disinhibit our normal responses and increase our likelihood to respond aggressively. In America, the lawyer for a fifteen year old who shot his neighbour in the course of a burglary claimed that the boy's sense of reality had been distorted through excessive exposure to television. Gerbner and Gross (1976) found that people who watch a lot of television rate the outside world as being more dangerous and threatening than it actually is. This tendency, present in all of us, has been called *deviance amplification* or *moral panic*.

Second, violence on television may also *desensitise* children, by making them less emotionally upset by such acts and more able to tolerate them in real life. Drabman and Thomas (1975) demonstrated this in a number of experiments with primary-school children. In each experiment, the children were divided into groups and shown a film, either one which was violent or a non-violent but exciting one. The participants were then led to believe that they were responsible for monitoring the behaviour of two younger children viewed on a TV monitor and to summon help if any violence which occurred. The younger children at first played quietly but became progressively more destructive, finally hitting each other and the TV camera. The researchers found that the children who were exposed to the violent film were slower to respond, suggesting that the aggression they had viewed in the films made them more able to tolerate aggression in real life.

Third, watching violence may be arousing, which could increase the likelihood of aggressive behaviour. This will depend on what the child has learned about dealing with arousal and frustration through role models, especially their parents. It will also depend on the presence of environmental 'triggers'. Geen and Berkowitz (1967) demonstrated that frustrated participants will behave more aggressively. In their experiment, those participants who watched a violent rather than an exciting film behaved more aggressively, and these participants behaved most aggressively towards a person with the same name as someone in the film they watched.

Much of the violence in children's programmes is presented in rather unreal and stereotyped ways, as in cartoons. It is argued that this will have a less of an influence because of its lack of reality. Alternatively, Newson (1994) argues, when a victim is portrayed in sub-human ways, we do not develop any empathy for them and therefore feel that no one really gets hurt. One of the differences between current video material and traditional gruesome fairy tales is that the viewer is more able to identify with the aggressor rather than the victim. Therefore a child is more likely to imitate a figure seen on television and is less likely to empathise with the victim. Newson also argues that, because violence is viewed in the context of entertainment, we get the message that 'this is all

**133**

good fun', rather than any moral message.

Finally, it is important to distinguish between violent programmes as a *primary* cause of aggressive behaviour, which it probably isn't, and as a *contributory* cause. The fact that there is universal objection to experimentally exposing children to violent programmes suggests that we intuitively regard such violence as harmful. The issue is, in truth, not whether it is harmful but what kinds of violence are too harmful. Some answers have been suggested here, for example, when perpetrators receive little punishment or when we are not encouraged to feel empathy for victims. Too much exposure may also be critical because it limits the child's experience of the real world which would act as a counterbalance to fictional norms. Some exposure might actually be helpful, as in situations where children are shown how to deal with violence and how to respond to aggression from others or from within themselves.

# STEREOTYPES

All media need to communicate a great deal of information in a relatively short time, and so they use standard cultural stereotypes. While these may well reflect the true state of affairs, reality may be something that needs changing, and stereotypes are self-reinforcing. Moreover, stereotypes frequently don't reflect reality. For example, advertisements continue to present men and women in traditional roles: men as powerful, dominant, rational and interested in DIY, and women as mothers, housewives and consumers who are concerned with making decisions about what product to buy. This is not true of all advertisements but the majority still use gender stereotypes (Manstead and McCulloch, 1981). Such stereotypes appear on all programmes, including children's television. For example, Mulac et al. (1985) analysed the content of a number of children's programmes such as Mr. *Roger's Neighbourhood* and *Sesame Street*, and found strong gender differences: males were more dynamic and female characters had greater socio-intellectual status and aesthetic quality.

There are a wide variety of stereotypes used in the media, such as people with strange accents or handicaps (e.g. an eye patch) who play 'baddies'. Numerous other images abound: overweight people depicted as jolly, older people as forgetful, minority ethnic groups in positions of servitude and wolves as big, bad man-eaters. Various age groups and professions are presented in a stereotypical way, such as the 'naughty teenager' and the 'left-wing social worker'. Such use of stereotypes is not just limited to television, but used to be well known in children's literature. For example, fairy stories are renowned for the stereotypical wicked step-mother and the beautiful princess. Children's magazines also reinforce gender stereotypes, such as promoting the ideal of romantic love.

In a field study, Williams (1985) produced evidence of the effects of these television stereotypes. The residents of a Canadian town ('Notel') had previously been unable to watch television because the signal did not reach their valley. Williams designed his experiment to coincide with their first experience of television. He found that the children's aggressive behaviour increased, and their sex role attitudes became more traditional and sex-stereotyped after they had been exposed to americanised television culture.

Gunter (1986) found that people who watch a lot of television hold more stereotyped beliefs, suggesting that the use of stereotypes on television does have an influence. Alternatively, people who have a more simplistic cognitive style may prefer to watch more television. This, of course, describes children exactly and we should expect them to be highly receptive to stereotyped information. Once a stereotype is learned, it will be highly resistant to change, especially because children will be unlikely to experience contradictory information. In addition, children, like adults, prefer material which fits in with their existing schema rather than experience dissonance arising from conflicting schema. This suggests that attempts to present counter-stereotypes will be ignored.

# COUNTER-STEREOTYPES

In recent years, there have been moves to counter inaccurate or undesirable racial, gender and other stereotypes by presenting people in more realistic ways. For example, children's books showing one-parent families, men washing up and women at work. There have also been efforts to deliberately present people in atypical roles, such as a black female judge, a movement which is designed to promote social change. However, the deliberate manipulation of stereotypes, for good or bad, is ethically questionable because it presumes that it is possible to objectively identify which stereotypes are preferable.

It does appear that changing stereotypes has had positive consequences. For example, Greenfield (1984) found that *Sesame Street's* use of ethnic and disabled minorities helped children from minority groups have a greater sense of cultural pride. Gorn et al. (1976) found that three- to five-year-old white children preferred playing with non-whites after watching a segment of *Sesame Street* featuring non-white children.

# DISPLACEMENT EFFECT

A media bias would be less harmful if it was sufficiently counterbalanced by experience of the real world. However, those children who spend a lot of time watching television or reading books have less time for real interactions. This is called a 'displacement' or 'reduction' effect. There are a variety of activities that children could be doing if they were not watching television, such as physical activity, social interaction and active fantasy play. However, Mutz et al. (1993) found that decreased television watching does not lead to increases in other activities. One reason for this may be that television provides instant rewards with little effort or input; the passive activity of watching television makes children lazy, and they then find it harder to engage in activities which require some self-generated activity, such as reading or inventing their own games. Gunter (1982) found evidence that 'heavy' television viewing at an early age did have a damaging effect on how well children learned to read and suggests this is because it affects their willingness to exert the mental effort necessary for reading. It has also been found that children who watch far more television than average perform less well at school (Keith et al., 1986). This might be because children with fewer intellectual resources prefer to watch television, in which case television is an effect rather than a cause of poor cognitive skills.

# SOCIAL DEPRIVATION

Watching television may displace social interactions, resulting in children who lack social skills. It is probably true that the advent of television in any household leads to changed patterns of family life, such as meals eaten in front of the television and/or altered bed times. Ideally, mothers or fathers should watch television programmes with their pre-school children and discuss questions which arise. Without this interaction, children are missing out on social contact and, perhaps more importantly, they are learning in a situation devoid of opportunity to question the material they receive (anyone familiar with a pre-school child knows how often they ask the question 'Why?'). Alternatively, constant interruptions of a programme prevent a child listening and practising attentiveness – it is easier to ask 'Why' than to listen to an explanation.

Children who are watching television also miss out on peer contacts and children's social games. This may not just be because of increased television watching, but might also be an effect of changing social patterns, such as the fact that families tend to be more self-contained and children have less freedom to play unsupervised in the streets or in playgrounds. The restrictions placed on children today may in part be due to the fact that their parents perceive the world as a dangerous place, a worldview fed to them by the media. As we have seen, this is called *deviance amplification*.

Another way in which television affects children's social interactions is by providing models of how to behave in social situations. Soap operas, a favourite of many primary-school children, present a particular form of conflict resolution which promotes a confrontational approach. Some teachers report that this is becoming increasingly common in classrooom interactions, and blame this on television models.

However, television viewing may not be universally harmful to social interactions. For example, Lyle and Hoffman (1972) found that popular children who are involved in extracurricular activities watch as much television as their less popular peers. Therefore, it may be more of a problem for children who already lack social skills. The same has been suggested for children who become obsessed with computers; withdrawn children who lack social skills may find that a computer offers the kind of company that they otherwise lack. This activity then prevents them from overcoming their social problems.

# STIMULATION HYPOTHESIS

It would be wrong to suggest that there are no positive benefits from the media. Many books and television programmes aim specifically to educate their audiences and enhance emotional and social development. An example of this is the programme *Sesame Street*, a product of the Children's Television Workshop, a US government-sponsored organisation. It is produced by a team of television writers and child development experts, and continually assessed by educational researchers. The childcare experts conduct seminars with the writers and suggest suitable topics for the programme's curriculum, such as counting strategies, map-reading skills, the reassessment of stereotypes and how to deal with emotional problems. Hayes and Schauble (1978) describe how the team worked on producing material which would help children overcome unproductive fears. The production team decided to adopt a cognitive approach which would teach children to recognise and re-label their fears. Hayes and Schauble advised that it was important to avoid all aggression and threat, and the producers should clearly demarcate the lines between reality and fantasy. After programme segments have been made, they are analysed for their effectiveness. The researchers also investigate what techniques produce most learning and what kind of message or characters have the greatest appeal (Lovelace, 1990). Earlier in this chapter, we cited research which supported the effectiveness of *Sesame Street*'s counter-stereotyping. This evidence is related to short-term effectiveness. For example, Bankart and Anderson (1979) found positive short-term effects on the prosocial behaviour of a group of pre-schoolers from exposure to *Sesame Street*.

There are many examples of educational children's television, especially those programmes used by schools as part of their classwork. Children also benefit from nature programmes, can 'visit' different parts of the world, gain valuable perspectives on our own culture, listen to stories, watch plays and see ballet. The value of television and all media is related to *what* you actually watch, read or listen to.

# IS TELEVISION A GOOD THING OR A BAD THING?

To what extent is the anti-television lobby a 'child of our times'? Many parents today had little experience of television when they were young, and therefore their opinions may be biased. It is possible that, before television was commonplace, the same conversations were taking place with regard to reading – too much reading is a bad thing, reading 'penny novels' is undesirable, a child should get out and play with others and get some physical exercise. Today, it is suggested that too much television may deter a child from learning to read. However, watching television also encourages the development of important cognitive skills such as attentiveness, being able to listen to instructions or explanations, making choices about what to watch, and has the potential for increasing children's knowledge and experience enormously.

In the same way that certain kinds of books are written for mass appeal and parents would prevent their children from reading them, the same can be said for television programmes designed to win mass audiences. This does not mean that the medium of television is necessarily a bad thing, providing exposure allows a child to develop other cognitive and social skills.

# SUMMARY

Many parents believe that the amount and kind of television and video that their children watch should be limited and censored. The evidence on this is equivocal. Television may well displace other important activities and create habits which are hard to break. It may present children with undesirable stereotypes and unrealistic world views. Conversely, children clearly can learn much from the television. In many ways, television is the ideal medium to present this kind of information, and it is a resource much used by schools.

Where violence and aggression are concerned, the media are a more contributory than primary cause. Parents might do better to consider their roles as models for aggressive behaviour rather than simply blaming the media.

# Atypical Development

# ABNORMALITY

Any discussion of childhood disorders is complicated by the fact that many abnormal behaviours are ones which were considered normal at an earlier age. For example, bedwetting might be acceptable in a four year old, but is a sign of disturbance in a ten year old; a score of 30 on an IQ test is average for a five year old, but not for an older child; avoiding the cracks in the pavement is common in children but a sign of obsessive-compulsive disorder in an adult. The fact that 'normal' development proceeds at different rates means that we cannot always be certain that a delay is pathological. Abnormal behaviour is not *qualitatively* different from normal. Rather, it is more persistent, severe and inappropriate for a person's age.

This suggests that disabled behaviour is *quantitatively* different from normal behaviour, but this approach means we must establish what we mean by normal. Some behaviours are statistically more frequent, such as divorce or depression, yet we would not want to regard them as normal. Various aspects of human potential, such as genius, are rare, but somehow don't seem to be 'abnormal'. Certain disabilities, such as blindness, seem in some sense to be normal because they occur within the common range of experience. For these reasons, normality is not a concept that can be objectively defined.

An alternative approach is to define behaviour in terms of its maladaptiveness, dysfunction or lack of mental health. A disability is a condition which impairs individuals or those around them and hinders some aspect of human performance. The term 'atypical' seems to express this better, meaning 'not having the characteristics of the group'.

*chapter eleven*

# PHYSICAL DISABILITIES

## CHAPTER OVERVIEW

In this chapter and the one which follows, various childhood disabilities will be described. Physical disabilities are physical deficits which hinder some aspect of human performance. They have a biological basis and may have a known biological cause. Recent research in genetics means that we can identify some disabilities before birth and possibly prevent them. The question of whether such genetic counselling is desirable will be discussed in this chapter, and we will also look at coping with disability.

## CAUSES OF DISABILITY

Childhood disabilities may be caused by inherited factors (e.g. Duchenne muscular dystrophy), genetic abnormalities (e.g. Down's syndrome), pre-natal or perinatal influences (e.g. anoxia), illness (e.g. polio) or experiential factors (e.g. head injury). The outcome may be sensory and/or physical deficit plus behavioural symptoms (either as a primary or secondary consequence). The severity of all disabilities is determined by an interaction between innate predispositions and life events; a mentally retarded child from an economically disadvantaged home will never achieve as much as a similar child from a middle-class home because of differences in cognitive stimulation. This is no different from any other aspect of human development (as described by the phrase 'reaction range', see page 5). We each possess certain potentials, but the degree to which we achieve them depends on our experiences.

# FOCUS ON...
# *a personal success story*

'When Audrey Wisbey was a child, no one believed she'd go far. "At nine, I had polio and doctors said I'd never walk again," she says... She practised the same painful exercises over and over until she could walk... At sixteen and recovering in hospital from one of many major operations, Audrey was told she was too ill to sit her O levels. She asked her parents to discharge her [from hospital], sat them – and passed all eight! "But in those days, you had to pass a medical to go to university ... you didn't need a medical for music. So I learned to play the piano in six months and the violin in three weeks. When I told the examiners, their mouths dropped. But I was accepted and got my degree in music education and psychology."' [From *Woman* magazine, 1995].

In 1984, Audrey set up a school for dyslexic children who had additional medical problems, she has written four books on dyslexia, and this year was voted *Woman/Encyclopaedia Britannica* Teacher of the Year. Her story serves to remind us that achievement is not fixed by inherent abilities. This was the same conclusion reached in relation to creative geniuses (see page 13); a burning passion to succeed is more important than innate talents.

# SENSORY IMPAIRMENT

## Hearing impairment and deafness

Approximately two children in every thousand have some hearing impairment; any such hearing loss deteriorates with age. Only one per cent of these children will be profoundly deaf. There are three main forms of hearing impairment, which may occur together. Nerve deafness is the result of damage to the inner ear or auditory nerve, resulting in the loss of a particular range of auditory frequencies, usually the high ones. Hearing aids can compensate for this loss. The damage may be due to inherited factors. Alternatively, it may have happened in pregnancy from rubella, or as a side-effect from some diseases, such as multiple sclerosis. It may even develop from prolonged exposure to loud noise. Conductive deafness occurs when the bones of the middle ear don't transmit noise properly. Such damage is usually caused by infection. Some hearing remains because the inner ear is still functional and sound is transmitted through the skull. It may be possible to correct this surgically. Finally, 'glue' or sticky ear (secretory otitis media) is a common problem in young children. It is caused by the build-up of catarrh in the middle ear and, with age, will drain naturally as the eustachian tubes (connecting the middle ear to the throat) get larger. However, the child may suffer some cognitive delay because of hearing loss during a critical period of their development, and so it is usually treated with surgically implaced grommets.

When a child has a profound hearing loss, many aspects of their development will be affected. Phelps and Branyan (1990) found that non-verbal IQ scores for pre-linguistically deaf children are consistently one standard deviation or more below normal. This is probably because linguistic deficits hamper learning. Conrad (1979) considers that deaf children inevitably suffer reading deficits because reading is taught through saying words out loud.

Early diagnosis is of obvious importance in providing compensatory education as well as providing the child with a hearing aid. However, this often does not happen because hearing loss is easily overlooked in a young child. In the past, 'dumb' children were often regarded as mentally retarded, and there is still a tendency to attribute a lack of response to stupidity rather than to hearing impairment.

Using sign language as a form of communication is becoming increasingly widespread. However, the deaf will always find social interactions difficult, and deaf children's emotional and social development will be hampered by this. These secondary problems of hearing impairment complicate the general picture. This, and the fact that deaf children often have other visual, mental or learning disorders, means that it is rarely possible to observe the effects of deafness in isolation.

## Visual impairment and blindness

Total blindness is rare, most so-called 'blind' people in fact have some degree of vision, if only for light and dark. Statutory blindness is defined in terms of acuity (discrimination of fine detail) and the width of a person's visual field. The effects of such impairment vary depending on the age of onset. If a child has had some experience of sight, this makes learning very much easier. Case studies of individuals blind from birth who later become able to see suggest that, after a certain age, it is not possible to develop visual perception (see page 24).

A young, visually impaired child may suffer emotionally and cognitively because smiling is important for attachment and eye gaze is a part of pre-speech. Lack of visual contact continues to handicap such children in social interactions. Blindness also restricts learning opportunities, leading to a developmental lag in motor, perceptual and cognitive capacities. For example, Tait (1990) found that blind children performed less well than same-age sighted children on Piagetian conservation tasks. Braille is a poor substitute for reading because it has a smaller visual field, places greater demand on short-term memory and is harder to learn and slower to process.

# GENETIC CONDITIONS

## Down's syndrome

Genetic abnormalities may be due to mutations or inheritance. Mutations occur during the formation of the egg or sperm cells, as in the case of Down's syndrome where an individual has three copies of chromosome 21 rather than the usual two. The incidence of such mutations increases with maternal age. For example, the incidence for Down's syndrome is 1:1500 live births for women in their twenties, and 1:40 for women over the age of forty. Recently it has been accepted that the cause may equally be due to paternal age, since the mutation can come from either parent. Down's syndrome babies have distinctive facial features which are similar to those of the Mongoloid racial group, which is why they used to be called 'Mongol children'. The syndrome is characterised by mental retardation and some physical defects, such as heart or gastrointestinal problems. Twenty-five per cent of Down's syndrome babies do not live beyond their first few years. Those who do survive into middle age invariably develop Alzheimer's disease (Rosenhan and Seligman, 1989). Behaviourally, such children are usually very friendly and affectionate. The expression of this chromosome 21 mutation varies enormously so that cognitive impairment may range from moderate to severe.

There are other, much less common genetic abnormalities involving either the absence or addition of certain genes or chromosomes. Klinefelter's syndrome occurs when an individual has XXY sex chromosomes. This results in a male who is sterile and lacks many male characteristics, such as facial hair.

## Fragile-X

Fragile-X syndrome occurs when an individual has a weak 'spot' on their X sex chromosome. This has a greater effect on a boy than a girl because there is no other X chromosome to compensate (boys have XY sex chromosomes whereas girls have XX). Boys with Fragile-X syndrome almost always experience developmental delays. They may also suffer severe mental impairment and behave autistically (see page 157). Girls with Fragile-X syndrome may experience some intellectual, social or emotional problems.

## DMD

Duchenne muscular dystrophy (DMD) is an example of an inherited genetic abnormality. It is caused by a gene on the X chromosome and results in an incurable muscular wasting disease that kills most affected boys by the time they are in their early twenties (greater susceptibility in boys is again due to the fact that they have only one X chromosome).

## Other inherited disorders

The condition achondroplasia, which leads to abnormally short limbs and short stature, is usually inherited, although it can also be caused by genetic mutation. Other genetic conditions include cystic fibrosis, haemophilia, mental illness (see page 161), and colour blindness.

For many inherited conditions, environmental factors or 'triggers' may modify the severity of the condition or may even determine whether a gene is expressed at all. This appears to be the case in some, if not all mental illnesses, and also cancers.

## PKU and hypothyroidism

Perhaps the most clear-cut case of the interaction between nature and nurture can be seen in metabolic disorders such as phenylketonuria (PKU) and hypothroidism. PKU occurs when a baby is born with an inherited inability to metabolise phenylalanine, a substance found in all proteins. Phenylalanine builds up and poisons the central nervous system, causing irreversible brain damage. If a baby has such a defect, it can be given a diet which controls the levels of phenylalanine, which avoids mental retardation. Another common metabolic disorder, hyperthyroidism, can be treated with synthetic thyroid hormones, thus avoiding the ill-effects of abnormal growth. In both cases, environmental adjustments prevent subsequent abnormality.

# FOCUS ON...
# *genetic counselling*

It is becoming increasingly possible to prevent the occurrence of many disabilities, either through vaccination programmes in early childhood or screening programmes carried out before birth or before conception. Such measures raise difficult ethical questions, which to some extent are matters of legislation, but are also questions which individuals have to decide for themselves.

The ongoing 'human genome project' aims to identify every gene and its effect on physical and psychological development. It will probably never be possible to predict behaviours which are influenced by a variety of genes (polygenetic), such as the intellectual or criminal potential of a child. However, for some time it has been possible to identify a variety of genetically caused disabilities, such as

Down's syndrome, Parkinson's disease, spina bifida and PKU.

Pre-natal genetic screening is done by taking cells from the developing embryo and culturing them so that the genetic material can be examined. The results indicate whether the embryo has a particular gene. However, what the test cannot tell is the extent to which the individual will be affected. As we have seen, for all disabilities there is a scale of severity. In the case of Down's syndrome, this may be irrelevant, as many parents feel that any disability of this sort is undesirable. There are other conditions, such as breast cancer, where the presence of the genetic marker does not mean the disease will definitely appear. A further consideration is that some conditions are clearly life-threatening and untreatable, such as Duchenne muscular dystrophy (DMD). Others, such as cancer, are treatable, and others 'merely' impair the child and its family's quality of life, as in the case of Down's syndrome.

Genetic tests may be used either before or after birth to forewarn parents of a potential disability so that they can cope better. This has been done for sickle cell anaemia, where babies who are given early treatment do fare better than those diagnosed later in childhood because such treatment avoids further complications of the disease. Testing is routinely done for PKU and congenital hyperthyroidism, without consent or objection, because the benefit to the child is overwhelming. The same may not be true for DMD. A child tested before or just after birth may benefit from some forewarning of the impending disease, but equally may suffer years of anxiety when, in the end, the disease is never manifested. When the US state of Pennsylvania introduced compulsory testing of all newborn boys for DMD, the tests had to be abandoned after many parents objected, saying that such knowledge was unwelcome (Vines, 1994).

A person who knows they carry a particular gene might feel 'genetically inferior' and experience negative prejudice. In the 1970s, there was a campaign to screen black Americans for the presence of a carrier gene for sickle cell anaemia. Those who were found to be carriers experienced widespread discrimination. For example, they were rejected from the army and charged higher insurance premiums, even though they would never have the illness themselves (Vines, 1994).

Some adults decide to be tested so that they can assess their risks as prospective parents. Huntington's chorea is a disease whose symptoms appear only in middle life. In Huntington's chorea, the brain tissue degenerates and ultimately this leads to death around the age of 50. A person whose mother or father is found to have the disease has a one in two chance of inheriting it themselves, and so do their children. People in this position often do not wish to know whether they have the gene because a positive result is a sentence of early death. They also don't want their unborn babies tested because this would tell them the same information. In fact, the uptake of this test is very low, with less than five per cent of those who have a parent with the disease taking the test (Harper and Houlihan, 1995).

The same gene that causes a disability may, at the same time, cause other *desirable* characteristics. Temple Grandin, an autistic woman, points out that 'if the genes that cause [autism, manic depression and schizophrenia] were eliminated, there might be a terrible price to pay. It is possible that persons with bits of these traits are more creative, or possibly even geniuses ... If science eliminated these genes, maybe the whole world would be taken over by accountants' (Sacks, 1995).

The logical extension of genetic testing and elimination is eugenics, the science of selective breeding. In 1995, the Chinese passed the

'Law on Maternal and Infant Health Care', which requires all doctors to perform pre-marital tests on couples. If a genetic disease is diagnosed, the couple can marry only if they agree to sterilisation or long-term contraception. This is partly due to the fact that all couples in China are limited to having only one child; if they give birth to a disabled child, they prefer to abandon it and try again. It would be preferable to prevent babies with disabilities being born in the first place. However, the result is eugenics, not dissimilar to the kind practised by the Nazis. We may be slipping into a eugenic system by default, while trying to offer better health care.

## Pre-natal screening

There is a distinction between genetic screening and other pre-natal tests used to detect abnormalities occurring during development. These are not a form of eugenics, but they do raise other ethical questions. Foremost is the question of abortion. If an abnormality is detected then the only remedial action is to terminate the pregnancy. Even those who are pro-abortion must be concerned with what is acceptable in

terms of age limits. This is partly because improved medical techniques enable younger foetuses to be kept alive outside the womb. In addition, recent research has demonstrated that even very young foetuses feel pain, as indicated by increased movement or heart rate when they are exposed to excessive noise or prodding by a needle during, for instance, the procedure for amniocentesis (Anand and Hickey, 1987).

Another method of screening is the use of ultrasound, which reveals things such as heart defects or multiple pregnancies. There are current developments which mean that an increasing variety of surgical procedures will be possible before birth in the womb. Being able to detect multiple pregnancies is important in relation to fertility treatments, where it is sometimes unavoidable and undesirable. All multiple pregnancies have associated risks for things such as prematurity and physical disabilities. Women receiving fertility treatment are sometimes offered 'embryo reduction' (i.e. selective abortion) to limit the number of embryos and maximise the development of those remaining. Should the same be offered to women with 'normal' multiple pregnancies?

# DISABILITIES WHICH DEVELOP PRE- OR PERINATALLY

Other disabilities may be present, though not necessarily apparent, at birth. The effects of various drugs, vitamins and diseases on the growing foetus were identified in Chapter 1 (see pages 10–11).

## Spina bifida

One condition, spina bifida, is due to faulty development of the neural tube during the first thirty days after conception; rather than being safely protected within the vertebrae, it remains open to the outside world. The extent of closure varies enormously. In serious cases, the infant will die. In some neonates, it is possible to surgically close the defect, but surviving children may have complete paraplegia and incontinence. There are mild cases of spina bifida in which a child may experience almost no ill-effects. One of the pre-natal screening procedures (the AFP, alpha-feto protein test) can detect this abnormality, and parents may elect to terminate such pregnancies. There is evidence that the risk of spina bifida can be greatly reduced if a woman increases her intake of folic acid before becoming pregnant and during early pregnancy.

## Cerebral palsy

Cerebral palsy is a motor disability where individuals have difficulty controlling the muscles of their arms, legs and/or head. These difficulties are due to brain cell death in the motor cortex, usually caused by a lack of oxygen (anoxia). This may happen before or during birth, or it can happen later in infancy. Other areas of the brain may also be affected, such as the visual or auditory cortex, so that palsied children often have multiple disabilities. Mild anoxia may have no long-term consequences, though it may cause minimal brain damage, which goes undiagnosed, and the child is simply regarded as clumsy and intellectually below average.

# CHRONIC PROBLEMS WITH ONSET DURING CHILDHOOD

The way that nature and nurture interact can be seen in a range of chronic childhood conditions such as diabetes, epilepsy, asthma, eczema and kidney disease. There are probably inherited susceptibilities to these disabilities, but the condition may never be manifested unless triggered by appropriate environmental factors.

## Diabetes

Diabetes affects about five per cent of the population, with most cases appearing after childhood. It occurs when the pancreas stops producing sufficient insulin. This results in too much glucose in the blood, which will ultimately cause death. The kind of diabetes that appears in childhood is usually of the insulin-dependent kind. Its treatment involves daily injections of insulin, glucose monitoring and a carefully regulated diet. In the other kind of diabetes (non-insulin-dependent diabetes), which is more common through the lifespan, the pancreas is usually still able to produce some insulin, and it is therefore possible regulate the condition through dietary control. Both forms of diabetes require major changes to the child's lifestyle and considerable psychological readjustment. Diabetes may be inherited. Alternatively, it is possible that complete loss of insulin production may be caused by virus infections of pancreas cells which, in susceptible individuals, leads to a loss of these cells. Less severe forms of diabetes may be caused by overeating in vulnerable individuals. Both viral infections and overeating are examples of environmental triggers.

# Asthma

Asthma is a respiratory disorder caused by an allergic reaction to, for example, pollen, dust, soap powders or specific foods. The tendency to develop asthma appears to be passed on by a cluster of genes that are associated with eczema and hay fever, both of which are allergic reactions. Attacks may be aggravated by infections, weather, exercise, pollution, smoking (active or passive) or psychosocial factors, such as stress. The main symptom is difficulty with breathing, which can be very frightening and is, in fact, life-threatening; in the UK, 2,000 asthmatics die every year, especially those who are elderly. Treatment involves learning behavioural techniques and counselling to help the patient understand what causes the problem and how to relax during an attack. Sufferers are also given inhalers which dilate the bronchia and ease breathing, or are given inhaled steroids which reduce the inflammation in the lungs. Asthma is particularly common in children, especially boys. About one in seven children is affected and one in twenty adults. In most cases, asthma appears before the age of five and the symptoms will disappear by the time the child reaches adulthood.

# Eczema

Eczema is a similar condition which is common in young children and which may disappear before school age. Like asthma, the cause may be allergic, but may also be stress-related and/or innate. It has been suggested that formula milk or other foods given too early in life may precipitate the condition. Some treatments involve the exclusion of certain foods (such as milk products) from a sufferer's diet.

# Epilepsy

An epileptic attack is a sudden seizure caused by electrical discharges in the cerebral cortex. Similar attacks can occur in 'normal' children due to a high temperature, in which case the attack is called a febrile convulsion. Epileptics are people who experience repeated attacks. The two most common forms of attack are *grand mal* (loss of consciousness and severe muscle contortions) or *petit mal* (a person stares blankly ahead and may twitch). An epileptic can be treated with anticonvulsant drugs, though these are not totally effective and have undesirable side-effects, such as drowsiness and possible long-term cognitive impairments. Some epileptics can be helped with biofeedback techniques which teach them to control the electrical activity in their brain. Epilepsy may be caused by inherited factors or may be the result of a head injury, anoxia or an infectious disease, such as meningitis. A tendency for febrile convulsions may also be inherited in so far as some children have a lower threshold for convulsions.

# FOCUS ON...
# *coping with disability*

## The public image of the disabled

In general, public attitudes towards handicap have become more positive. Shakespeare (1975) reported that about a half of the people interviewed in research expressed negative attitudes, though this outlook was changing. For example, from 1949 to 1964, the number of people believing that epilepsy was a form of insanity decreased from sixty-five per cent to twenty-six per cent, and those who believed epileptics should be employed in the same manner as everyone else increased from forty-five per cent to seventy-five per cent.

How can such attitude change be encouraged? The answer to this question is the same as the answer to decreasing prejudice generally. Increased contact may decrease the 'illusion of outgroup homogeneity'. In other words, one learns that the 'visually impaired' or 'dyslexics' are not very different from anyone else, aside from their particular disability. Classic research by Sherif et al. (1961) and, later, Aronson et al. (1978) showed that simply increasing contact does little and may even increase prejudice. Involving everyone in cooperative activity, in

particular working on superordinate goals, is much more likely to be successful. In the case of disabled persons, contact may arouse feelings of fear, and therefore it is important to ensure that any contact is positive and involves working together, not just being together.

Such increased contact may be achieved through legislation, such as enabling children with special educational needs (SEN) to receive mainstream education. The value of such integration is mainly social rather than cognitive, and more likely to benefit SEN children (Maras, 1995). Disabled children may develop higher self-esteem from their inclusion in normal life, but equally they may experience a greater sense of what they cannot do.

Increasing contact is a means of encouraging a more positive image of the disabled. Alternatively, there can be direct attempts to change stereotypes, such as the use of advertisements. It is possible that media images of disabled persons which elicit pity tend to reinforce outdated stereotypes, and the 'charity ethic' directly contradicts the 'independent living ethic'. This latter ethic suggests that it is better to portray the disabled as persons who are as 'in control' and on a par with others, rather than needing our help.

# Personal problems stemming from disability

When a child is ill or disabled, both the sufferer and their immediate family experience a series of adjustments. The degree of difficulty experienced is associated with an individual's personality and coping skills, the extent of financial and social support available, the nature of the disability and the amount of impact it has on daily life.

The child's developing self-image will be seriously affected by the negative reactions of others, and they learn to dislike themselves. Thomas (1995) reports that negative stereotyping begins at birth because the newborn baby picks up non-verbal signals of sadness and disaffection.

Disabled children have far less access to role models with whom they can identify. For some disabled, it's not clear whether they belong to the 'handicapped' or the 'normal' population, and this further confuses their sense of identity. Cowen and Bobrove (1966) found that the totally disabled were better adjusted than those who had partial disabilities, presumably because their group identity was clearer. In this way, labelling can act as a positive influence (see page 154).

Often, disabled people have considerable difficulty with communication, particularly language and non-verbal behaviour, which affects their ability to interact socially. They may also experience a loss of privacy, due to things such as nursing care or people having to dress them. These persistent invasions of personal space create stress and may exacerbate ill-health.

In some families, certain disabilities are more of a problem. For example, a sport-oriented family would find it more difficult to adjust to a child with physical disabilities, in the same way as an academic family might find a mentally retarded child more difficult. Similarly, disabilities are more of a disadvantage in fast-moving, urban settings than in a rural community.

# Recommendations

Reducing the problem is in everyone's interest because the disabled person becomes less of a financial and psychological burden to society. Disabled children can be helped by giving them clear information about their condition and how to improve it. The disabled person may assume 'the sick role': expecting to be looked after, being absolved of responsibility and relinquishing control for major decisions. This is a form of learned helplessness (see page 90). Over-protection probably only encourages the sick role and prolongs recovery and/or adjustment. If disabled persons are given, and take, greater control, this may lead to improvements in their self-image. Such control should start in childhood. Self-help groups are a means of sharing experiences and gaining emotional support.

A disabled child must learn to cope with the responses of friends and strangers. The disabled and their families have expertise which they can pass on to assist the general public in their responses to disability.

# CHILDHOOD ILLNESS AND INJURY

Long-term physical disabilities, including deafness and paralysis, may result from events during childhood, such as head and spinal injuries, infectious diseases (e.g. polio, tuberculosis and meningitis) and childhood cancers (e.g. leukaemia).

Different children respond differently to exposure to an infectious disease. Not everyone exposed will become infected, and even among those who are, the consequences vary considerably because of such things as the medical care which is available, and the child's constitution and personality. Many diseases which were once a problem are no longer so because of improved living conditions and continually improving schemes of immunisation. Smallpox has been eradicated world-wide, and similar schemes exist for other childhood diseases, such as polio, TB, whooping cough, measles, mumps and rubella. For example, in 1951, there were over 600,000 reported cases of measles, a notifiable disease. By 1988, annual cases had dropped to 50,000 due to the vaccination programme and improved methods of treatment. In 1940, 1,000 children died from measles; by 1990 there were no deaths and there were less than 1,000 cases.

In the case of the whooping cough vaccine, the uptake rate was initially more than eighty per cent until public concern was roused over the possibility that the vaccine led to brain damage. The vaccination rate dropped to thirty per cent, and cases of whooping cough increased, leading in some cases to death or permanent disability. The uptake is now nearly ninety per cent and in 1991, there were no related deaths. In some cases, a child is not actually fully protected by a vaccine. However, if the child develops the disease, it is usually less severe. They are also less likely to develop it because their peers will be immune and will not pass on the disease.

# SUMMARY

All physical disabilities are expressed along a continuum, which varies according to environmental influences and personal motivation. Those children suffering from moderate losses may escape detection and suffer as a result. Disabilities generally incur secondary problems, such as difficulty with social interactions and limited learning opportunities. An important means of coping with disability is to take a position of greater control (the 'independent living' ethic). Increased contact between normal and disabled populations can help if the contact involves co-operative activity.

# *chapter twelve*

## CHAPTER OVERVIEW

Psychological disabilities are distinguished from physical ones because they are expressed chiefly in terms of a psychological deficit. They may have a known or suspected biological basis and associated physical symptoms. This chapter will look at the descriptions and causes of the most familiar psychological disabilities of childhood, as well as some kinds of remedial action. The advantages and disadvantages of labelling such deficits will also be discussed.

## DEVELOPMENTAL DISORDERS

Childhood psychological disabilities are classified along with other psychological disorders in both the current American diagnostic scheme, DSM IV, and the British version, ICD 10.

**Box 12.1**  Major categories of psychological disorders

| | |
|---|---|
| Development disorders | Mental retardation, learning disorders, autistic disorder |
| Disruptive behaviour disorders | Attention-deficit hyperactivity disorder, conduct disorder (delinquency), oppositional defiant disorder. |
| Emotional disorders | Separation anxiety disorder, avoidant disorder (shyness), overanxious disorder, childhood depression, phobias. |
| Habit and eating disorders | Elimination disorders (e.g. bedwetting, soiling), speech disorders (e.g. stuttering), anorexia nervosa, bulimia nervosa. |

# Mental retardation

About three per cent of children, and more boys than girls, suffer some degree of mental retardation. Mental retardation is defined by the American Association on Mental Deficiency as an IQ of less than 70, a deficit which appears before the age of eighteen. Sub-average general intellectual functioning can be further subdivided into mild (55–69 IQ), moderate (40–54), severe (25–39), and profound (below 25). The condition may be caused by intrinsic factors, such as genetic abnormalities (Fragile X or Down's syndrome, see page 143), or it may be caused by extrinsic factors, such as trauma (anoxia or head injury), disease, absence of essential vitamins/proteins or the presence of harmful substances (such as cadmium, lead or other pollutants). In all of these, retardation is worsened by an unstimulating or impoverished home environment. Various factors associated with low social class may cause or exacerbate the problem. These include foetal alcohol syndrome, smoking in pregnancy, low birth-weight, malnourishment and poor health. For most retarded persons there is no clear injury or disease, in which case it is assumed to be the result of innately low intelligence combined with an environmental deficit.

Children with such difficulties may be helped by language training and special education programmes in school. There is a continuing argument over whether they are better served in separate schools or within mainstream education. For social reasons, children who can function in a normal classroom probably should be placed there, because it helps them adjust to normal life and helps other children to better understand the problems of subnormality and hold less stereotyped views of retardation.

# Specific learning disabilities

Where intellectual deficit is global, it is termed mental retardation; it is termed a specific learning disability when a child has a specific psychological disruption or delay in perceptual or cognitive functioning that is independent of any other disorder. In practice, this is diagnosed when the delay is of a magnitude of at least two years and the child's IQ and background indicate that the child should be functioning at the expected level. Such disabilities are believed to be neurologically rather than psychologically caused. The best-known example is dyslexia, whose symptoms are difficulties with reading, spelling and writing. This is sometimes called 'developmental dyslexia' to distinguish it from 'acquired dyslexia' which results from either accidental injury or brain disease. Even within the category 'developmental dyslexia', there are distinctions. One group of dyslexics tend to have general language disorders in addition to their reading difficulties, such as problems with language acquisition and speech disorders. A second broad group have problems generally with visual perception and memory, for example reversals of the letters 'b' and 'd'.

There are other disorders, such as developmental arithmetic disorder and developmental articulation disorder. Diagnosis of such disabilities may be helpful in providing remedial help before secondary problems, such as low self-esteem and disruptive behaviour in school, compound the problem. Conversely, diagnosing and then labelling a child may ultimately be self-fulfilling.

# FOCUS ON...
## *labelling*

A label is a word or phrase representing a number of other characteristics; labels are the result of diagnoses. The problem is that many labels conjure up a negative stereotype and lead to lower expectations for an individual which inevitably shape that individual's self-image and have a self-fulfilling effect. In this way, the stereotype acts as an additional disadvantage. For this reason, many disabilities are given new labels which, for some time at least, have neutral stereotypes: 'hearing impairment' rather than 'deafness', 'economically disadvantaged' instead of 'lower class', 'conduct disorder' instead of 'delinquency', and perhaps most importantly, 'disabled' rather than 'invalid' or 'handicapped'. Words such as 'idiot', 'moron' and 'spastic' were once official labels, but they became derogatory terms.

It can be argued that a label is useful for providing a disabled child with appropriate education. However, for many conditions there are no cures, and remedial schemes are not always successful because many problems remain outside the clinic or educational setting. In fact, such schemes may be ultimately counterproductive. Ringness (1961) found that the expectations of forty mentally retarded children showed greater disparity with reality than groups of average- and high-intelligence children. He suggested that this was probably because the mentally retarded children's accepting and encouraging educational environment created unrealistic attitudes, and these attitudes eventually caused difficulties.

A label may not only be unhelpful, but may even be disadvantageous. Rosenhan and Seligman (1989) give the example of Nelson Rockefeller, a former American vice-president. Throughout his life he had severe reading difficulties. Rosenhan and Seligman pose the question, 'would his life have been any easier if those difficulties had been described as a severe psychological disorder of childhood? Indeed, could he have been elected to high office if he had been so diagnosed?'

The use of a label suggests that disabilities are discrete entities with clearly recognisable symptoms. This concept of discrete entities with distinct symptoms is referred to as the 'medical model' of illness. When illnesses have a known physical cause, such as in the case of measles, no two people have identical symptoms because of the interaction between nature and nurture. This leads us to question whether such a model is appropriate for psychological problems which are even more affected by environmental factors.

Labels can, however, have a positive effect.

For example, one mother of an autistic child expressed the feeling that having her child labelled autistic was preferable to the child being just seen as naughty or disturbed (*The Independent on Sunday*, 8 January 1995). Labels may lead to greater understanding and elicit greater help. Atypical behaviour has the effect of making a person seem odd, whereas, once the condition is explained in terms of causes, the individual is easier to accept by both strangers and family. We are unsure how to respond when we see a person stumbling along the road, but when we see a white cane we are ready to help (Piliavin et al., 1969). It is also true that, with-

out diagnoses, we have no statistics to represent the extent of a problem, and this restricts the amount of political and financial resources made available. Finally, we should recognise that the process of stereotyping is an inevitable aspect of human cognitive processes and, without any 'official' labels, people will probably make up their own.

What is the best solution? Labels are stigmatising and self-fulfilling, but can also be helpful. Perhaps, if everyone increases the amount of contact they have with disabled persons, this will increase their knowledge and promote positive stereotypes.

# Autism

Infantile autism is a pathological condition first recognised as a distinct syndrome by Kanner (1943). Autism literally means 'self-orientation' and is also used to denote a range of normal inwardly directed activities, such as autistic thought. This pathological condition occurs in about three children per 10,000, and boys outnumber girls by three to one. It is more common in high socio-economic families, though this may be because it goes unrecognised elsewhere or is labelled differently. It is apparent very early in life and is almost always diagnosed before school age.

The most characteristic behaviour is the autistic's aloneness and aversion to contact with other people. Autistics are socially impaired, use language abnormally, have few facial expressions and lack empathy and emotion. Autistics often exhibit bizarre, stereotyped behaviours and insist on routines. This may be because of difficulty in coping with change. Some autistics have heightened sensitivity, such as feeling overstimulated by crowds of people, whereas other autistics are less sensitive than normal. For example, they may feel little pain. Autistics generally perform poorly on verbal intelligence tests, but have 'islands' of intelligence, such as talents in rote memory, music or drawing. Some autistics are very successful, for example, Temple Grandin is an autistic with a Ph.D. who runs her own business.

Some autistics have a range of other problems, including epileptic seizures or problems of co-ordination. It is difficult to know which of these symptoms are primary and which are secondary. For example, a lack of sociability may be directly due to innate differences or may result from linguistic deficits in turn caused by cognitive impairments.

Autism may be due to genetic, biological or experiential factors. A neurological basis is suggested by the fact that many autistics are also epileptic, have abnormal brain waves and altered sensitivities. The neurological view is additionally supported by the fact that many of the typical autistic behaviours, such as repetitive movements, tics, rocking, finger play, are also seen in people who have experienced some brain damage. Furthermore, patchy intelligence and linguistic deficits are also consistent with some brain damage. Such damage might be the result of viral infections. For example, in the 1960s, an epidemic of rubella resulted in many babies being affected prenatally, and some of them later developed autism.

Autism could also be a consequence of genetic abnormalities, which is presumed to be the case where Fragile-X and autism co-occur (see page 143). Another suggestion is that some individuals lack a 'personal intelligence'. This is Gardner's (1983) term for the ability to perceive one's own and other people's state of mind. Research by Hobson (1986) found that autistic children were far less able to match pictures of facial expressions to an emotion, which suggests that they might have difficulty right from the start in distinguishing people from objects and attributing emotional states to other people. This would explain their lack of pretend play and other social deficits.

It is possible that vulnerable individuals only become autistic when they are exposed to what Kanner described as emotional refrigeration, that is, parents who are introverted, distant, intellectual and meticulous. Bettleheim (1967) suggested their behaviour was similar to that of children in concentration camps who withdrew psychologically from their hostile surroundings. However, it is unlikely that parents are the primary cause of autism. It may be the consequence of a poor 'fit' between parents and an emotionally difficult child.

There are actually two types of autism: classic infantile autism (as described by Kanner) and Asperger's syndrome (described by Hans Asperger). There are many similarities between the two types, such as their characteristic aloneness and insistence on sameness. However, Kanner-type children tend to be retarded, have seizures and other neurological symptoms such as language problems, repetitive movements, lack of pain perception and co-ordination difficulties. Asperger-type children are often of normal or even superior intelligence and have few neurological problems.

Ways of treating the condition include behaviour therapy, structured education and play therapy, as vividly described by Axline (1971).

# DISRUPTIVE BEHAVIOUR DISORDERS

## Attention-deficit hyperactivity disorder

Many young children are overactive and, perhaps mistakenly, called 'hyperactive'. They find it hard to sit still and concentrate for any length of time, but usually this disappears as their attention span increases with age. Attention-deficit hyperactivity disorder (ADHD) is characterised by inappropriate inattention, impulsiveness and motor hyperactivity for the child's age. Again, it affects more boys than girls, and tends to appear early. The cause is thought to lie with the brain's arousal mechanism, either because of over-arousal, which leads to continual switching of attention, or, conversely, because of under-arousal, the inability to maintain attention. This latter view is supported by the fact that stimulants appear to reduce hyperactivity. Arousal problems may be caused by innate neurological differences or environmental factors, such as diet. There has been considerable research into dietary factors including artificial food colourings and flavourings, as well as specific food allergies to things like milk, chocolate and wheat. Many parents hope that ADHD could be treated by eliminating such substances from the child's diet, but this has not been supported by research (e.g. Mattes and Gittelman, 1981). Varley (1984) suggests that families latch on to the idea of dietary control because it gives them something concrete to do, but that any behavioural change is probably due to a placebo effect.

Other methods of treatment include the use of drugs such as Ritalin. This has become widespread in America, but is far from desirable when dealing with children because of side-effects. Another possibility is to use behaviour modification, which aims to teach parents how to give the child attention for positive rather than negative reasons, the 'time out' method as we described in Chapter 7 (see page 93).

## Conduct disorder (delinquency)

Conduct disorder is another kind of disruptive behaviour which involves transgressing important rules of conduct. Like hyperactivity, this is to some extent present in all children's behaviour, but is atypical when a child persistently engages in such behaviour. Such a child may be labelled 'delinquent' because he (or she) habitually commits non-serious crimes, for example stealing, lying or fighting. This is not generally seen as pathological behaviour, though extreme individuals may be suffering from antisocial personality disorder (a psychopath or sociopath, see page 96). Certain parenting styles are associated with aggressiveness and a lack of social responsibility (see Chapter 7). It may be that the form of discipline is too lax or too severe, nonexistent or inconsistent. More importantly, the child may have failed to develop important attachment bonds and, as a result, has no ability to empathise with others and will commit antisocial crimes. This, of course, was Bowlby's view, which we described in Chapter 3.

Delinquency is also associated with economic and social deprivation, such as frustration from poor living conditions and poor prospects. There is some evidence of a genetic link. For example, Mednick and Hutchings (1978) found that adopted sons were more likely to become criminals if their biological parents were criminals, even if their adoptive parents were law abiding. At the extreme end of the scale, sociopaths appear to be unable to experience high emotional arousal and therefore are less responsive to praise and punishment, so that they fail to develop a proper sense of right and wrong. The basis of such a condition would be biological and innate.

Traditional methods of treatment involve punishment – the short sharp shock. More recently, there have been attempts to develop different approaches. For example, the Achievement Place, a special children's home started in the US, was run by foster parents looking after between six and eight delinquent children sent there by the courts. The regime in this home can best be described as social skills training, which has had some success although it is undermined by children having to return to troubled homes. The final cost is significantly less than a state institution, despite the public impression that such schemes are expensive to run.

# Bullying

Bullying can be physical (hitting, pushing, taking money) or emotional (telling tales, teasing, social exclusion). Surveys suggest that between five and ten per cent of pupils have experienced being bullied (e.g. Yates and Smith, 1989). At minimum, it is distressing, and at worst has led to suicide. Children who are bullied may permanently suffer from loss of self-esteem. Gillmartin (1987) found a link between later relationship difficulties and having been bullied as a child. It is possible that children lacking in social skills are the ones that are bullied. Children who bully may also experience permanent consequences, perhaps because their bullying tactics are positively reinforced. Olweus (1989), for example, found that former school bullies were four times more likely to have three or more court convictions by the age of twenty-four. It is often said that bullies become bullies because they have been bullied. They have learned at home that aggression and control are successful methods of social interaction. Schools may be able to manage the problem by enlisting the support of all children by, for example, setting up 'bully courts' where children arbitrate on bullying incidents, or conducting lessons where role play shows children ways of coping and teaches bullies more co-operative ways of behaving.

# EMOTIONAL DISORDERS

The greatest emotional problem for children is distress. This occurs within the normal range of experience. For example, almost all children experience separation anxiety and have fears of such things as spiders, loud noises or water. Research indicates that nearly half of all children aged between six and twelve suffer from at least seven fears or worries at any one time (LaPouse and Monk, 1959). Pre-school children tend to be afraid of tangible objects, such as animals or insects. As they grow older, they become afraid of imaginary creatures, disastrous events and the dark. A fear becomes a phobia when it is out of all proportion to the reality of the danger. Girls are more likely to develop phobias than boys. Becoming phobic may represent the existence of other underlying problems which are displaced onto the feared object.

Separation anxiety may also be exhibited in an excessive and maladaptive way, called extreme separation anxiety disorder. Children suffering from this remain anxious about being separated from their family for a period of weeks or months. They may follow their mother about the house and have nightmares about being left and panic whenever there is any separation. School phobia may be a result of such anxiety. In such cases, the phobia is the fear that, by leaving home, they may lose their family. Other school phobics may have school-related rather than personal problems. These children are often previously good pupils who perhaps have unrealistically high levels of aspiration, or they may have been bullied at school. Remedial action for anxiety includes the use of anti-depressants or, preferably, behavioural techniques such as systematic desensitisation where a child is gradually taught to cope with separation and school.

Extreme shyness is another emotional disorder which becomes apparent during early years at school. Social skills training may help a child overcome their social problems. Other emotional problems include chronic sadness, over-attachment, social withdrawal and feelings of inferiority.

# FOCUS ON...
## *therapeutic techniques*

## Somatic treatments

The use of drugs often alleviates symptoms which prevent normal functioning and thus may allow a child to continue their social and cognitive development. While drugs do not cure a problem, they may give a child sufficient respite to overcome secondary problems, and thus promote coping. However, there can be undesirable side-effects of drugs, for example, they may affect growth or become addictive.

## Psychotherapy

Most psychotherapies rely on linguistic competence and therefore are unsuitable for children. Play therapy (see page 128) is based on the principles of both psychoanalysis and counselling. It aims to allow children to express and deal with their emotions through play.

## Behavioural techniques

Behaviourists suggest that maladaptive behaviour occurs as a result of inappropriate learning. Treatment involves unlearning through conditioning and does not require any understanding of underlying causes. Examples include aversion therapy (e.g. the bell and pad method for bedwetting, see below), systematic desensitisation (e.g. to treat phobias), token economies (giving rewards for good behaviour) and social skills training (e.g. for unpopular children).

# HABIT AND EATING DISORDERS

Habit and eating problems, like all other psychological disorders, are behaviours which may be normal at some ages and/or in some situations.

## Bedwetting

Some degree of enuresis (bedwetting) is normal through childhood. However, it is regarded as a problem if, after school age, it occurs more than once a month (Rosenhan and Seligman, 1989). The cause may be physical, but it more usually related to anxiety. There is a tendency for it to run in families, suggesting an inherited predisposition. It is also about twice as common in boys, possibly because they develop motor skills later than girls. Treatment includes behaviour modification methods, such as using a pad which, when wet, causes a bell to ring (the bell and pad method). The dry-bed procedure is more effective but also more time-consuming. It involves rousing the child hourly through the night and taking them to the toilet to train the habit of waking and going to toilet.

## Stuttering

Stuttering is yet another problem which is more common in boys, with four times as many boys than girls experiencing problems. Sufferers are often teased by peers, and teachers avoid asking them questions in class. The social difficulties and continuing stutter lead to increased tension which only exacerbates the problem. Behavioural training may reduce the difficulty. For example, stutterers can be taught to pace their speech using a metronome or they can be given delayed auditory feedback which distracts them from monitoring what they are saying.

## Obesity

Obesity often starts during childhood, although strictly speaking it is not a psychological disorder. It is a combination of genetic tendency and formation of habit. Short-term treatments have had reasonable success, but over the long term, the most successful methods have de-emphasised weight loss as the main goal and focused on self-control more generally.

## Anorexia and bulimia

Anorexia nervosa and bulimia nervosa are life-threatening eating problems mainly occurring in adolescence, though the problem is beginning to appear in much younger children. Riley (1995) reported that about fifteen per cent of children aged between five and seven are dieting, and even claim that they want to be thinner. The symptoms of anorexia are a deliberate restriction of calorie intake and considerable weight loss. Anorexics see themselves as being overweight and resist food. In about fifteen to twenty per cent of all cases, this leads to death. Almost all sufferers are female, and it may be that it is largely created by pressure to conform to feminine stereotypes. Anorexics are often somewhat obsessive personalities, who are low in self-esteem and simultaneously desire and fear their own autonomy. Dieting may be a way of exerting some control over themselves against the pressure of their parents and other adults. Therapy may help to increase self-esteem and autonomy; other methods of treatment include behaviour management and hospitalisation.

# MENTAL ILLNESS

Mental illness is rarely exhibited in childhood. However, experiences during childhood are undoubtedly critical to psychiatric problems in adulthood. For example, one view of schizophrenia suggests that the condition emerges as a result of mutually exclusive (double-bind) demands being made on the child (Bateson et al., 1956). It may also be an inherited condition. Evidence from studies of twins and adopted children suggests that, of those with an innate predisposition, only those exposed to environmental stresses will develop the condition (Kendler, 1983; Wender et al., 1974). An example of an environmental stressor could be a pathological family.

People who are prone to incapacitating depression later in life may have learned this pattern of response in childhood. It is essentially a form of learned helplessness, where the person feels an inability to take control (see page 90). Some very young children do experience clinical depression. In the

US, about 200 children under the age of fourteen commit suicide each year, and some of these are pre-schoolers (Rosenhan and Seligman, 1989).

# SPECIAL TALENTS

Any discussion of abnormal or exceptional behaviour should also include children at the other end of the scale, those with above average abilities, because they are equally as exceptional as any of the others mentioned. Their precociousness often excludes them from normal peer group relations. Children who become movie stars or musical prodigies can and do suffer later emotional problems due to having missed out on the formative experiences of a normal childhood. In this sense, their characteristics are a kind of disability.

FIGURE 12.1 *Drew Barrymore, star of Steven Spielberg's ET, had an exceptional childhood due to the stardom she experienced at a young age. This may have contributed to problems she experienced later in life, including drug dependency in adolescence*

# SUMMARY

Most psychological disorders are exaggerations of the normal spectrum of childhood experiences and behaviours. They are considered disabilities when they are exhibited at an inappropriate age or in an unsuitable situation, and when they hinder normal social and cognitive development. Treatment is only possible when a condition is diagnosed, or 'labelled'. Such labelling may have negative consequences due to, for example, associated self-fulfilling stereotypes, or may be helpful in avoiding other explanations, such as laziness. Behavioural techniques are often the most successful means of treating these disabilities. If a problem is left untreated, secondary symptoms may compound the original difficulty.

# *chapter thirteen*

## PRIVATION

# CHAPTER OVERVIEW

This chapter looks at a fortunately rare and atypical occurrence, that of a child failing to form any bonds of attachment during their early years, and the effects this has on subsequent development. As we saw in Chapter 8, separation from a main caregiver does not *per se* cause emotional maladjustment, but extreme privation may. The two lines of evidence which will be examined are studies of institutionalised children and case studies of children reared in extreme isolation. The effects described will include attachment disorder and under-development, plus some kinds of child abuse.

# DEPRIVATION AND PRIVATION

In Chapter 8, the distinction was drawn between deprivation and privation, that is the difference between having formed attachments, but then experiencing their temporary or permanent loss (deprivation) and forming no attachments at all during a critical period of childhood (privation). Such a clear distinction does not exist in the literature on deprivation, where the term is rather universally applied to all kinds of separation, both loss and lack. For example, the term 'deprived children' is used to refer to cases of children reared in isolation, though it is probably truer to say that they have experienced privation.

# INSTITUTIONAL CARE

Bowlby's early views were that a bad home was preferable to any institution. In part, this may be because poor institutional care involves more than emotional privation; institutionalised children also lack social and mental stimulation (see page 27). There are still institutions, perhaps not in this country, where infants are imprisoned in their cribs and given nothing to play with and almost no social contact. Observation of such children shows that, for the first three to six months, they continue to behave like normal infants, crying for attention, smiling, babbling and holding out their arms to be picked up. By the second half of their first year, their behaviour changes. They become depressed, lack interest in social contact and their language skills are grossly retarded. A classic study by Goldfarb (1943) compared children who left an institution during their first year with those who spent another two years there before finally being fostered. He conducted a follow-up study of these children at age twelve and found that those who had remained longer in the institution lagged behind the others on every measure that was taken. Thus, they had lower IQs, poor language skills, were socially immature, very dependent on adults and had behaviour problems such as hyperactivity and aggressiveness. Goldfarb attributed their poorer development to a lack of attachments during their early years.

Two further studies illustrated how increased stimulation, social contact and emotional care could change this. Skeels and Dye (1939) observed how two apparently retarded children changed when they were transferred from their orphanage to a women's ward in an institution for the mentally retarded. The children were given much more attention, particularly from some of the older inmates, and, within fifteen months, their cognitive development was at a normal level. On the basis of this case study, Skodak and Skeels (1949) conducted some more research. They transferred thirteen mentally retarded infants from their orphanage to an institution for the mentally retarded when they were aged between eleven and twenty-one months. At that time, the orphaned children's mean IQ was 64. After nineteen months in the new institution, their mean IQ had increased to 92, whereas a control group who had stayed in the orphanage showed a decrease in IQ from 87 to 61 over the same period. When the children were assessed twenty years later, it appeared that the differences between the groups remained (Skeels, 1966). One criticism should be considered: the children may have been responding to the researcher's expectations, and it was this, rather than the increased stimulation, which led to their intellectual improvements.

A more specific test of Bowlby's hypothesis was started in the early 1970s by Barbara Tizard (Tizard and Rees, 1975; Tizard and Hodges, 1978, Hodges and Tizard, 1989), following a group of sixty-five children who had been placed in an institution before the age of four months, and assessing them again at age eight and sixteen. There was an explicit policy in the institution against staff forming strong attachments with the children, and before the age of four, an average of fifty different caretakers had looked after the children for a period of at least a week. So we may reasonably conclude that these children experienced privation.

By the age of four, twenty-four of the children were adopted and fifteen had returned home, often to single parents. The rest remained in the institution. There was also a control group of children raised by their natural parents.

Both the adopted and control children did best in terms of intellectual and social development, though the adopted children were described as over-friendly and more attention-seeking. Those children restored to their natural homes did less well on almost every measure taken. This may be because families who had needed temporary fostering for their children continued to have major problems. The fact that the adopted children were able to thrive suggests that attachment can take place later than Bowlby suggested, and the finding that the natural homes weren't the best contradicts Bowlby's views that institutions are necessarily undesirable.

FIGURE 13.1 *Institutions such as this Rumanian orphanage used to be more commonplace. Psychological research has shown that long-term institutional care with no parental contact is associated with permanent emotional and cognitive deficits*

Pringle and Bossio (1960) also studied a group of institutionalised children, in this case to determine whether the long-term ill-effects of institutionalisation were due to early separation or prolonged privation. They assessed 188 children who were living in large children's homes, using the Bristol Social Adjustment Scale, a personality test, and clinical observations by the investigators. A group of eleven of the most severely maladjusted children were selected for further study, plus a control group of five of the most 'notably stable' children. The most marked difference between the two groups was the amount of contact maintained with parents or parent substitutes. All the stable children had a lasting relationship, whereas this was true for only one of the maladjusted group. Pringle and Bossio also observed that those children who were maladjusted seemed unable to make stable relationships with other children or adults. Pringle and Bossio concluded that early physical separation and institutionalisation do not necessarily lead to maladjustment. However, privation, where a child is rejected and *remains* unwanted, is likely to lead to continued emotional and social problems.

In a similar way, a study by Kirk (1958) found that institutionalised children only recover if they are given a continuing experience of enrichment, warmth and stimulation. If they were given enrichment before entering school, the effects soon wore off. However, when enrichment continued throughout their school life, the changes were permanent.

# MANAGING INSTITUTIONAL CARE

The message for institutional care is clear: the provision of attachment figures who can give quality care is critical. A carer need not devote large amounts of time, but should be responsive to the child's emotions and needs. Since institutions invariably experience frequent staff changes, it is preferable to have many attachment figures rather than a single one, so that there is always some overlap.

# FOCUS ON...
# *effects of privation: attachment disorder*

## The children who hate to be loved

George was 18 months old when Lucy and Martin Lansdowne adopted him. They knew it was an act of faith. The couple, who already had two adopted children, had seen him advertised and heard that his mother had not wanted him, had scarcely touched him, and that already in his short life he had twice been fostered.

"The last family had him for five months, then, without warning, told social services that they couldn't handle him," Lucy says. "It's not difficult to imagine what three early rejections meant to

that baby's sense of trust, and we had no doubt that it might be hard going for a while."

But although they knew George would need a lot of dedicated care and affection to help him feel safe, the Lansdownes had not imagined that the following 10 years would, in Martin's words, be "almost unremitting hell and anguish".

Lucy is a sociable, motherly woman, strongly built, with a broad knowledge of child development and psychology. She had always wanted a large family and, unable to have her own, was happy to adopt – including, after George, a handicapped child.

But she shudders when she describes how

pathetic little George, who walked around for several years as if in shock – his pale, staring face never smiling, never crying – turned into a demon.

As he progressed through the primary school years "he began sending us death threats", she says. "He would hide knives, take things and break them. He broke all the glass panels in our front door. He swore and reacted with wild rages to anything that displeased him. It seemed the whole day was geared around trying not to rile George.

"I realised I was intimidated by him. I also realised he was in terrible turmoil. He had dreadful fears and seemed to be full of dark terrors, but there was no way we could get close to him."

excerpt from *The Independent*, 29 July 1994

There are a number of adopted children who behave in the same way as George. In the US, this has for some time been recognised as a syndrome called attachment disorder.

Children like George have invariably been adopted after the age of six months, subsequently experiencing multiple foster homes or care institutions. This means that they have little or no early experience of attachments. When they are offered the chance to develop a relationship, it comes too late. Attachment disorder children appear to have no conscience, which may be due to the fact that they have been unable to identify with any parent figure. This accords with the psychoanalytic account of moral development (see page 94).

The Evergreen Attachment Centre in Colorado offers intensive treatment for such children and their adoptive parents. It involves working one-to-one with the child, taking them back through their lives to help them see that their behaviour is not their fault and allow them the opportunity to express their anger towards those who have deserted them.

# CHILDREN REARED IN ISOLATION

Another line of evidence regarding the effects of privation comes from a sad collection of personal tragedies. These are situations where a family has severely restricted a child's social and cognitive experiences. The list includes Isabelle (Mason, 1942) and Anna (Davis, 1947), but perhaps the best known are the 'Koluchova' twins and Curtiss' study of Genie, mentioned in Chapter 4.

Koluchova (1972, 1976, 1991) studied the Czech twins, P.M. and J.M., whose own mother died when they were born. They spent the next eighteen months mostly in care and then went to live with their father and a stepmother. They were kept apart from the rest of the family, never went out, lacked proper food, exercise and any social or intellectual stimulation. When they were rescued, aged seven, they looked like three-year-olds, and their speech was very limited. They soon made remarkable gains and were adopted by two sisters who gave them a loving home environment. By the age of fourteen, they were socially well-adjusted and had IQs just below 100. They were said to functioning at a level about one and a half years below their chronological age.

The case of Genie had a less successful outcome (Rymer, 1993). She was older, aged thirteen when discovered, and had experienced a more lonesome childhood. Her father, Clark, had never wanted children, and in fact two older children had died, one in somewhat suspicious circumstances. Clark kept her locked up in a bedroom because he thought she was retarded and therefore vulnerable. By day, she was tied to a potty seat and at night she was moved to a cot covered with wire mesh and tied into a sleeping bag. If Genie tried to attract attention, she was beaten. She was occasionally given a few items to play with, but generally lacked any visual, auditory or tactile stimulation. She was fed baby foods, in a hurry, and if she choked, she would have her face rubbed in it.

When Genie was first seen by the social services department they thought she was only six or seven, since she weighed just over four stone and was four and a half feet tall. She was incontinent, could not focus beyond twelve feet, salivated constantly and spat indiscriminately. She could not hop, skip, climb or fully extend her limbs, showed no perception of heat or cold and could not talk.

Genie spent the next few years being cared for by a number of different people, ultimately being placed in a foster home, where she was abused once again. At this point, what language she had developed disappeared altogether. Even before this, it appeared unlikely that she would ever become socially or intellectually normal. For example, one psychologist observed Genie's distant demeanour with people. She didn't ignore or reject them, she just treated them in the same way that she did the walls or the furniture.

Both of these case histories have similarities with the histories of abused and deprived children generally. What they don't tell us is the extent to which the different factors contribute to the eventual outcome. For example, all the children suffered both emotional *and* cognitive privation, and there is no way of knowing whether the children were cognitively retarded from the beginning. It can only be surmised that their lack of progress was due to lack of adult attachments and social interaction. In any case, most of the evidence is unreliable because it was retrospectively collected and subjective. What these sad stories do appear to suggest is that, first of all, children who are rescued early enough (perhaps before the age of eight) can recover and, second, that where a child has had some social contact (in other words they are deprived rather than privated) the effects are ameliorated. The Czech twins had each other, whereas Genie had a life of deprivation *and* privation.

# PHYSICAL UNDER-DEVELOPMENT

In such cases of extreme isolation, the children are invariably described by their rescuers as being extremely small for their age, unable to walk or talk, and both cognitively and socially immature. Dennis (1960) made similar observations in a study of institutionalised orphans in Iran. He found that only about half of all the infants aged between one and two were able to sit. None of this age group could walk at all, and only fifteen per cent of those aged between three and four could walk unaided. This under-development has been called *deprivation dwarfism*. How can we be certain that it is due to emotional rather than nutritional starvation? Some evidence comes from a study by Widdowson (1951) of orphanage children whose physical development was very retarded. It was first thought that this was due to a lack of vitamins and so they were given dietary supplements. However, they remained under-developed. Later, after a harsh and unsympathetic supervisor left the institution and was replaced by a more caring one, their weight improved.

Such an association between emotion and under-development can also be seen in anorexia nervosa (see page 161). At a physiological level, this can be understood in terms of the fact that stress has been found to lead to the production of certain hormones, such as adrenalin, and these affect growth and physical health (see research by Kiecolt-Glaser et al., (1984), page 107).

# FOCUS ON...
# *effects of privation: child abuse*

## What is child abuse?

For some children, childhood is blighted by the physical and emotional effects of being abused. Gross child abuse is easy to define and identify, but the boundary between inadequate parenting and minor abuse is problematic. Suggestions include 'any maltreatment of children which prevents attainment of the child's full potential' or 'misuse of parental power'. Any definition which is too broad is impractical, not least because it would result in unmanageable case loads. The term 'abuse' covers a wide range of ill-treatment: sexual abuse, physical injury, inadequate supervision, encouraging delinquency, emotional mistreatment, educational neglect, moral danger because of parental sexual mores and parental substance abuse.

In March 1994, there were 34,500 children on the Child Protection Register in England, which is about 12,000 less than were on the register in 1992. This figure is out of a total of about ten million children aged under seventeen. It is difficult to estimate the number of non-accidental injuries there are each year; the NSPCC put the annual figure for England and Wales at approximately 6,400 children, including 650 who are killed or seriously harmed.

## Characterising abusive parents

Abusive parents tend to belong to low socio-economic groups. The same childcare difficulties occur in the higher social classes, but probably are hidden behind, for example, a front of respectability, better use of health services and money for alternative care. Persons of low socio-economic status tend to possess a cluster of other characteristics which are related to abuse, such as being young parents, being unemployed, having a criminal record, a history of mental illness, large families, poor housing conditions and greater incidence of premature births or birth complications. These factors, rather than low socio-economic status *per se*, are more relevant. They result in frustration, lack of adequate resources and/or poor mother-infant attachment.

Other characteristics are less related to socio-economic status. Abusers tend to have certain personality characteristics, such as being impulsive, having a rigid approach to discipline, distorted perceptions of a child's behaviour, ignorance of normal child development and physical or mental handicap. Crittenden (1988) interviewed 124 abusing mothers in the US and found that they tended to represent relationships in terms of power struggles, were controlling and hostile with their anxiously attached children and had angry, unstable adult relationships. Other abusing mothers were emotionally empty, unresponsive to their children and had stable but affectionless relationships.

Affectionless parents or ones who are rigid disciplinarians may have learned this in their own childhood. Abusers are often people who were abused themselves. But not all abused children go on to be abusers. This may partly be because potential abusers only erupt when their own life conditions reach intolerable levels. A study by Egeland et al. (1988) found that high-risk parents were only likely to become abusive if they were suffering other social or environmental stress.

One must be careful about making generalisations and stereotyping abusers. The typical characteristics of abusers may help to explain why some parents behave as they do, but these characteristics have little predictive value, because many families or individuals with the same characteristics are not abusive.

# Characterising the victims of abuse

It has been suggested that certain children 'invite' abusive interactions. It is true that boys are more at risk than girls, which may be because boys tend to give a more aggressive response to their parents. In adolescence, the reverse is true, perhaps because parents feel they have to be more protective towards teenage girls, which may lead to excessive restrictions and punishment. It is also the case that the youngest child is the most likely to be abused, possibly because a younger child is inevitably part of a larger family, which is more stressful for parents. A child born with a difficult temperament or one who has had a difficult birth may immediately present its parents with relationship problems. A study by Egeland and Sroufe (1981) found that emotionally unresponsive, hyperactive or ill infants are more likely to be abused than infants who are easy to care for. This view does emphasise the fact that abuse is an interactive problem, though parents ultimately have all the power.

# Lack of bonding

There is a particular type of child abuser, a 'primary rejecter', who is a woman who has had a difficult pregnancy or an unwanted baby. The mother rejects the child from the time of its birth. Unlike other child abusers, such mothers are usually middle-class and have close relationships with their other children. The child is physically well cared for, but has no emotional relationship with the mother, who may inflict injury when 'provoked' by the child (Jones et al., 1987). The reason may lie in a lack of early bonding. In fact, a similar lack of bonding may underlie most cases of abuse. When the early history of abused children is examined, it is often found that there were neo-natal separations due to illness or the infant started life in a special care unit. The mother and infant failed to develop an emotional relationship after this bad start, which may lead the mother to feel guilty and to lack empathy for the child. Later in infancy or childhood, any period of stress or seemingly naughty behaviour results in excessive discipline, at which time the abuse becomes apparent to outsiders. Lynch and Roberts (1982) concluded that lack of attachment was a key feature of all abusive interactions, though it is not the only factor.

One means of preventing problems of abuse with vulnerable individuals is to encourage early bonding. It should be emphasised that separation alone does not *cause* abuse, but if the mother and infant are *not* separated, this may help prevent later problems. This approach is equally important with 'marginal' fathers who are known to have problems. If the father is excluded and isolated, this only increases his feelings of jealousy and disrupts the development of a healthy father-child relationship. Jones et al. (1987) describe one case involving subnormal parents, where the mother was given intensive support during her stay in hospital and also at home. Nevertheless, within a few weeks of the baby's birth, the infant arrived back at hospital with several broken bones inflicted by the father, whose interests had been overlooked. Had he been given support as well, the situation might have been avoided.

# Managing child abuse

Ideally, it would be desirable to prevent abuse by identifying high-risk families and improving their parenting skills. Schinke et al. (1986) conducted one such intervention programme, working with single teenage mothers and trying to create higher levels of confidence and competence through teaching relaxation and problem-solving techniques. It might also be possible to provide special maternity units for high-risk mothers to encourage bonding and teach them necessary skills. This could be followed up with 'outpatient' care at special day centres.

In dealing with cases where an offence has already been committed, it is preferable to treat the problem rather than removing the child from the home, because this will cause the child further emotional suffering, and the parents may go on to have other children who experience abuse. In such cases, the family is usually given help in the form of a family social worker to monitor the situation and provide support. The family may be offered therapy and financial assistance. Social services cannot provide perfect assistance, partly because it is hard to strike the right balance between too much and too little care, and partly because of staff turnover. Hill (1980) found that over seventy-five per cent of families had a least one change of social worker in the first year, making it hard for a trusting relationship to develop.

Families may seek help themselves, through self-help groups, such as Parents Anonymous, or 'hotlines' like Childline, which offer support to parents who feel in danger of injuring their children. Parents are encouraged to seek such help through media campaigns against child abuse and the threat that their child may be taken into care or that they may be prosecuted.

# SUMMARY

Privation, unlike deprivation, does appear to have permanent consequences, regardless of the quality of care that may be subsequently offered. The effects include under-development, social and cognitive deficits, emotional flatness and difficulties in forming personal relationships. Child abuse leads to an emotional privation in abused children. It may be possible to help parents who are perceived to be at risk by encouraging good early bonding with their infant and giving education in parenting skills.

# References

Aboud, F. (1988) *Children and Prejudice*. Oxford: Basil Blackwell.

Adorno, T.W., Frenkel-Brunswick, E., Levinson, D. and Sanford, N. (1950) *The Authoritarian Personality*. New York: Harper.

Ainsworth, M.D.S. (1967) *Infancy in Uganda: Childcare and the Growth of Love*. Baltimore: John Hopkins University Press.

Ainsworth, M.D.S. (1972) The effects of maternal deprivation: a review of findings and controversy in the context of research strategy. In *Deprivation of Maternal Care: A Reassessment of its Effects*. Geneva: World Health Organisation.

Ainsworth, M.D.S., Blehar, M.C., Waters, E. and Wall, S. (1978) *Patterns of Attachment: A Psychological Study of the Strange Situation*. Hillsdale, N.J.: Lawrence Erlbaum.

Amato, P.R. (1993) Children's adjustment to divorce: theories, hypotheses and empirical support. *Journal of Marriage and the Family*, 55, 23–38.

Anand, K.J.S. and Hickey, P.R. (1987) Pain and its effects on the human neonate and fetus. *New England Journal of Medicine*, 317, 1321–9.

Anastasi , A. (1990) *Psychological Testing* (6th edition). London: Macmillan.

Argyle, M. (1978) *The Psychology of Interpersonal Behaviour* (3rd edition). Harmondsworth, Middlesex: Penguin.

Aronson, E., Bridgeman, D.L. and Geffner, R. (1978) The effects of a co-operative classroom structure on student behaviour and attitudes. In Bar-Tal, D. and Saxe, L. (eds) *Social Psychology of Education*. New York: Wiley.

Aronson, E. and Rosenbloom, S. (1971) Space perception within a common auditory-visual space. *Science*, 172, 1161–3.

Axline, V. (1971) *Dibs: In Search of Self*. Harmondsworth: Penguin.

Bandura, A., Ross, D. and Ross, S.A. (1961) Transmission of aggression through imitation of aggressive models. *Journal of Abnormal and Social Psychology*, 63, 575–582.

Bandura, A., Ross, D. and Ross, S.A. (1963) Imitation of film-mediated aggressive models. *Journal of Abnormal and Social Psychology*, 66, 3–11.

Bankart, C. and Anderson, C.C. (1979) Short-term effects of prosocial television viewing on play of pre-school boys and girls. *Psychological Reports*, 44 (3, Pt 1), 935–941.

Banks, M.S., Aslin, R.N. and Weiskopf, S. (1975) Sensitive period for the development of human binocular vision. *Science*, 190, 675–677.

Banyard, P. (1996) *Applying Psychology to Health*. London: Hodder & Stoughton Educational.

Barker, D.J.P. (1992) *Foetal and Infant Origins of Adult Disease*. London: British Medical Journal Publishing Group.

Bateson, G., Jackson, D.D., Haley, J. and Weakland, J. (1956) Toward a theory of schizophrenia. *Behavioural Science*, 1, 251–264.

Baumrind, D. (1971) Current patterns of parental authority. *Developmental Psychology Monographs*, 4 (1, 2)

Beddard, P. (1995) Children of the 90s. *New Generation*, September, 6–7.

Bell, A.P., Weinberg, M.S. and Hammersmith, S.K. (1981) *Sexual Preference: Its Development in Men and Women*. Bloomington: Indiana University Press.

Bem, S.L. (1974) The measurement of psychological androgyny. *Journal of Consulting and Clinical Psychology*, 42, 155–162.

Bem, S.L. (1983) Gender schema theory and its implications for child development: raising children in a gender-aschematic society. *Signs: Journal of Women in Culture and Society*, 8, 598–616.

Benton, D. and Cook, R. (1991) Vitamin and mineral supplements improve intelligence scores and concentration. *Personality and Individual Differences*, 12 (11), 1151–1158.

Berko, J. (1958) The child's learning of English morphology. *Word*, 14, 150–177.

Bernstein, B. (1961) Social class and linguistic development. In Halsey, A.H., Flaud, J. and Anderson, C.A. (eds) *Education, Economy and Society*. London: Collier-Macmillan Ltd.

Berryman, J.C., Hargreaves, D., Herbert, M. and Taylor, A. (1994) *Developmental Psychology and You*. Leicester: BPS Books.

Bettleheim, B. (1967) *The Empty Fortress*. New York: The Free Press.

Bifulco, A., Harris, T. and Brown, G.W.

(1992) Mourning or early inadequate care? Re-examining the relationship of maternal loss in childhood with adult depression and anxiety. *Development and Psychopathology*, 4, 433–449.

Blakemore, C. and Cooper, G.F. (1970) Development of the brain depends on the visual environment. *Nature*, 228, 477–478.

Bouchard, T.J. Jr., Lykken, D.T., McGue, M., Segal, N.L. and Tellegen, A. (1990) Sources of human psychological differences: the Minnesota study of twins reared apart. *Science*, 250, 223–228.

Bower, G. and Hilgard, E. (1981) *Theories of Learning*. New Jersey: Prentice-Hall.

Bower, T.G.R. (1966) The visual world of infants. *Scientific American*, 215, 80–92.

Bower, T.G.R. (1981) Cognitive development. In Roberts, M. and Tamburrini, J. (eds) *Child Development 0–5*. Edinburgh: Holmes McDougall.

Bower, T.G.R. (1982) *Development in Infancy*. New York: W.H. Freeman.

Bower, T.G.R., Broughton, J.M. and Moore, M.K. (1970) Infant responses to approaching objects: an indicator of response to distal variables. *Perception and Psychophysics*, 9, 193–196.

Bowlby, J. (1946) *Forty-four Juvenile Thieves*. London: Balliere, Tindall and Cox.

Bowlby, J. (1951) *Maternal Care and Mental Health*. Geneva: World Health Organisation.

Bowlby, J. (1969) *Attachment and Loss, Vol. 1: Attachment*. London: Hogarth Press.

Bowlby, J. (1973) *Attachment and Loss, Vol. 2: Separation, Anxiety and Anger*. London: Hogarth Press.

Bowlby, J. (1980) *Attachment and Loss, Vol. 3: Loss, Sadness and Depression*. London: Hogarth Press.

Bowlby, J., Ainsworth, M., Boston, M. and Rosenbluth, D. (1956) The effects of mother-child separation: a follow-up study. *British Journal of Medical Psychology*, 29, 211.

Brackbill, Y., McManus, K. and Woodward, L. (1985) *Medication in Maternity: Infant Exposure and Maternal Information*. Ann Arbor: University of Michigan Press.

Bradley, L.E. and Bryant, P. (1983) Categorizing sounds and learning to read: a causal connection. *Nature*, 301, 419–421.

Braine, M.D.S. (1963) The ontogeny of English phrase structures: the first phase. *Language*, 39, 1–13.

Brazelton, T.B., Tronick, E., Adamson, L., Als, H. and Wise, S. (1975) Early mother-infant reciprocity. *Parent-Infant Interaction Ciba Foundation Symposium*, 33, 137–154.

Brown, G.L., Goodwin, F.K., Ballenger, J.C., Goyer, P.F. and Major, L.F. (1979) Aggression in human correlates with cerebrospinal fluid amine metabolites. *Psychiatry Research*, 1, 131–139.

Brown, G.W. and Harris, T.O. (1978) *Social Origins of Depression: A Study of Psychiatric Disorder in Women*. London: Tavistock Publications.

Brown, R. (1973) *A First Language: the Early Stages*. Cambridge, Mass.: Harvard University Press.

Bruner, J.S. (1966) *Toward a Theory of Instruction*. Cambridge, Mass.: Harvard University Press.

Bruner, J.S. (1973) The organisation of early skilled activity. *Child Development*, 44, 1–11.

Bruner, J.S. (1983) *Child's Talk*. New York: Norton.

Bryant, B., Harris, M. and Newton, D. (1980) *Children and Minders*. London: Grant McIntyre.

Bryant, P.E. and Trabasso, T. (1971) Transitive inferences and memory in young children. *Nature*, 232, 456–458.

Burchinal, M., Lee, M. and Ramey, C. (1989) Type of day-care and pre-school intellectual development in disadvantaged children. *Child Development*, 60, 128–137.

Busch, F., Nagera, H., McKnight, J. and Pezzarossi, G. (1973) Primary transitional objects. *Journal of the American Academy of Child Psychiatry*, 12, 193–214.

Butterfield, E.C. and Siperstein, G.N. (1972) Influence of contingent auditory stimulation on non-nutritional suckle. In Bosma, J.F. (ed.) *Third Symposium on Oral Sensation and Perception: the Mouth of the Infant*. Springfield, Ill.: Charles C. Thomas.

Carmichael, L., Hogan, P. and Walter, A. (1932) An experimental study of the effect of language on the reproduction of visually perceived forms. *Journal of Experimental Psychology*, 15, 73–86

Chomsky, N. (1959) Review of Skinner's Verbal Behaviour. *Language*, 35, 26–58.

Chomsky, N. (1965) *Aspects of a Theory of Syntax*. Cambridge, Mass: MIT Press.

Clarke, A.M. and Clarke, A.D.B. (1976) *Early Experience: Myth and Evidence*. New York: Free Press.

Cockett, M. and Tripp, J. (1994) Children living in disordered families. *Social Policy Research Findings*, No. 45, Joseph Rowntree Foundation.

Cohen, D. (1993) *The Development of Play* (2nd edition). London: Routledge.

Cohen, K.N. and Clark, J.A. (1984) Transitional object attachments in early childhood and personality characteristics in later life. *Journal of Personality and Social Psychology*, 46, 106–111.

Colby, A., Kohlberg, L., Gibbs, J. and Lieberman, M. (1983) A longitudinal study of moral judgement. *Monographs of the Society for Research in Child Development*, 48, nos. 1–2.

Comstock, G. (1991) *TV and the American Child*. London: Academic Press.

Connolly, J.A. and Doyle, A.B. (1984) Relation of social fantasy play to social competence in pre-schoolers. *Developmental Psychology*, 20, 797–806.

Connor, S. (1995) Do your genes make you a criminal? *The Independent on Sunday*, 12 February.

Conrad, R. (1979) *The Deaf School Child*. London: Harper & Row.

Cooley, C.H. (1902) *Human Nature and the Social Order*. New York: Scribner.

Coopersmith, S. (1968) Studies in self-esteem. *Scientific American*, 218 (2), 96–106.

Cowen, E.L. and Bobrove, P.H. (1966) Marginality of disability and adjustment. *Perceptual and Motor Skills*, 23, 869–870.

Cowen, E.L., Pederson, A., Babigian, H., Izzo, L.D. and Trost, M.A. (1973) Long-term follow-up of early detected vulnerable children. *Journal of Consulting and Clinical Psychology*, 41, 438–446.

Crittenden, P.M. (1988) Distorted patterns of relationship in maltreating families: the role of internal representation models. *Journal of Reproductive and Infant Psychology*, 6, 183–199.

Curry, N.E. and Arnaud, S. (1984) Play in pre-school settings. In Yawkey, T. and Pellegrini, A. (eds) *Child's Play, Developmental and Applied*. London: Lawrence Erlbaum.

Curtiss, S. (1977) *Genie: A Psycholinguistic Study of a Modern-day 'Wild Child'*, London: Academic Press.

Davenport, G.C. (1991) *An Introduction to Child Development*. London: Collins Educational.

Davis, K. (1947) Final note on a case of extreme isolation. *American Journal of Sociology*, 52, 432–437.

DeCasper, A.J. and Spence, M.J. (1986) Pre-natal maternal speech influences newborns' perception of speech sounds. *Infant Behaviour and Development*, 9, 133–150.

Dennis, W. (1960) Causes of retardation amongst institutional children: Iran. *Journal of Genetic Psychology*, 96, 47–59.

Dodge, K.A., Schlundt, D.C., Shocken, I. and Delugach, J.D. (1983) Social competence and children's sociometric status: the role of peer group entry strategies. *Merrill-Palmer Quarterly*, 29, 309–336.

Donaldson, M. (1978) *Children's Minds*. London: Fontana.

Doss, S.H. (1980) A study of maladjustment in relation to birth order. *Journal of Psychological Researches*, 24 (3), 156–159.

Douglas, J.W.B. (1975) Early hospital admissions and later disturbances of behaviour and learning. *Developmental Medical Child Neurology*, 17, 456–480.

Drabman, R.S. and Thomas, M.H. (1975) Does TV violence breed indifference? *Journal of Communication*, 25 (4), 86–89.

Duck, S.W. (1991) *Friends for Life*. Hemel Hempstead: Harvester-Wheatsheaf.

Duck, S.W. (1992) *Human Relationships*. London: Sage.

Dunn, J. (1984) *Sisters and Brothers*. Glasgow: Fontana/Open Books.

Dunn, J. and Kendrick, C. (1982) *Siblings: Love, Envy and Understanding*. Cambridge, Mass: Harvard University Press.

Eder, R.A. (1990) Uncovering young children's psychological selves: individual and developmental differences. *Child Development*, 61, 849–863.

Egeland, B., Gerhard, D.S., Pauls, D.L., Sussex, J.N., Kidd, K.K., Allen, C.R., Hostetter, A.M. and Housman, D.E. (1987) Bipolar affective disorders linked to DNA markers on chromosome 11. *Nature*, 325, 783–787.

Egeland, B., Jacobitz, D. and Sroufe, L.A. (1988) Breaking the cycle of abuse. *Child Development*, 59, 1080–1088.

Egeland, B. and Sroufe, L.A. (1981) Attachment and early maltreatment. *Child Development*, 52, 44–52.

Erikson, E.H. (1963) *Childhood and Society* (2nd edition). New York: Norton.

Erikson, E.H. (1972) *Play and Development*. New

York: Norton.

Exploring Parenthood (1994) in Sainsbury's *The Magazine*, May.

Fantz, R.L. (1961) The origin of form perception. *Scientific American*, 204 (5), 66–72.

Farquharson, J., Cockburn, F., Patrick, W.A., Jamieson, E.C. and Logan, R.W. (1992) Infant cerebral cortex phospholipid fatty acid composition and diet. *Lancet*, 340, 810–813.

Feldman, D.H. (1986) *Nature's Gambit: Child Prodigies and the Development of Human Potential*. New York: Basic Books.

Fergusson, D.M., Beautrais, A.L. and Silva, P.A. (1982) Breastfeeding and cognitive development in the first seven years of life. *Social Science and Medicine*, 16 (19), 1705–1708.

Field, T.M., Sandberg, D., Garcia, R., Nitza, V., Goldstein, S. and Guy, L. (1985) Pregnancy problems, postpartum depression, and early mother-infant interactions. *Developmental Psychology*, 21, 1152–1156.

Fischer, K.W. (1980) A theory of cognitive development: the control and construction of hierarchies of skills. *Psychological Review*, 87, 477–531.

Flanagan, G. (1996) *Beginning Life: The First Nine Months*. London: Dorling Kindersley.

Floody, O.R. (1968) Hormones and aggression in female animals. In Suare, B.B. (ed) *Hormones and Aggressive Behaviour*. New York: Plenum Press.

Fox, N. (1977) Attachment of Kibbutz infants to mother and metapelet. *Child Development*, 48, 1228–1239.

Frank, F. (1966) Perception and language in conservation. In Bruner, J.S. (ed) *Studies in Cognitive Growth*. New York: Wiley.

Freeman, N.H. and Janikoun, R. (1972) Intellectual realism in children's drawings of a familiar object with distinctive features. *Child Development*, 43, 1116–1121.

Freud, S. (1920) *Beyond the Pleasure Principle*, (1975 edition). New York: Norton.

Freud, S. (1935) *A General Introduction to Psychoanalysis*. New York: Washington Square Press.

Freund, L.S. (1990) Maternal regulation of children's problem-solving behaviour and its impact on children's performance. *Child Development*, 61, 113–126.

Friedrich, L.K. and Stein, A.H. (1973) Aggressive and prosocial television programmes and the natural behaviour of pre-school children. *Monographs of the Society for Research in Child Development*, 38 (no. 4).

Furman, W. and Buhrmester, D. (1985) Children's perceptions of the qualities of sibling relationships. *Child Development*, 56, 448–461.

Furth, H.G. (1966) *Thinking without Language*. New York: Free Press.

Gallup, G.G. (1977) Self-recognition in primates. *American Psychologist*, 32, 329–338.

Gardner, H. (1983) *Frames of Mind: The Theory of Multiple Intelligence*. New York: Basic Books.

Garvey, C. (1977) *Play*. London: Fontana.

Geen, R. and Berkowitz, L. (1967) Some conditions facilitating the occurrence of aggression after the observation of violence. *Journal of Personality*, 35, 666–676.

Gerbner, G. and Gross, L. (1976) The scary world of TV's heavy viewer. *Psychology Today*, 9, 41–45.

Gibson, E.J. (1987) Introductory essay: what does infant perception tell us about theories of perception? *Journal of Experimental Psychology: Human Perception and Performance*, 13, 515–523.

Gibson, E.J., Gibson, J.J., Pick, A.D. and Osser, H.A. (1962) A developmental study of the discrimination of letter-like forms. *Journal of Comparative and Physiological Psychology*, 55, 897–906.

Gibson, E.J. and Walk, R.D. (1960) The 'visual cliff'. *Scientific American*, 202 (4), 64–71.

Gibson, E.J. and Walker, A.S. (1984) Development of knowledge of visual-tactile affordances of substance. *Child Development*, 55, 453–460.

Gillmartin, B.G. (1987) Peer group antecedents of severe love-shyness in males. *Journal of Personality*, 55, 467–489.

Girodo, M. and Wood, D. (1979) Talking yourself out of pain: the importance of believing that you can. *Cognitive Therapy and Research*, 3, 23–33.

Goffman, E. (1959) *The Presentation of Self in Everyday Life*. Garden City, NY: Doubleday.

Goldberg, S. (1983) Parent-infant bonding: another look. *Child Development*, 54, 1355–1382.

Goldfarb, W. (1943) The effects of early institutional care on adolescent personality.

*Journal of Experimental Education*, 12, 106–129.

Goldwyn, E. (1979) The fight to be male. *Listener*, May 24, 709–712.

Gorn, G.J., Goldberg, M.E. and Kanungo, R.N. (1976) The role of educational television in changing the intergroup attitudes of children. *Child Development*, 47(1), 277–280.

Gottesman, I.I. (1963) Heritability of personality: a demonstration. *Psychological Monographs*, 77 (whole no. 572).

Greenfield, P.M. (1984) *Mind and Media: The Effect of Television, Video Games and Computers*. Aylesbury: Fontana.

Gregory, R.L. and Wallace, J. (1963) *Recovery from Early Blindness*. Cambridge: Heffer.

Gulerce, A. (1991) Transitional objects: a reconsideration of the phenomenon. *Journal of Social Behaviour and Personality*, 6 (6), 187–208.

Gunter, B. (1982) Does television interfere with reading development? *Bulletin of the British Psychological Society*, 35, 232–235.

Gunter, B. (1986) *Television and Sex-Role Stereotyping*. London: John Libbey & Co.

Gunter, B. and Harrison, J. (1995) *Violence on Television in the United Kingdom: A Content Analysis*. Summary report to the BBC and ITC (July).

Gyte, G. (1995) *Letter to New Generation*, September 29.

Halliday, M.A.K. (1975) *Learning How to Mean*. London: Edward Arnold.

Hamer, D.H., Hu, S., Magnuson, V., Hu, N. and Pattaucci, A.M. (1993) A linkage between DNA markers on the X chromosome and male sexual orientation. *Science*, 261, 321–327.

Harari, H. and McDavid, J.W. (1973) Teachers' expectations and name stereotypes. *Journal of Educational Psychology*, 65, 222–225.

Harlow, H.F. (1959) Love in infant monkeys. *Scientific American*, 200 (6), 68–74.

Harper, P.S. and Houlihan, G. (1995) Paper delivered at World Federation of Neurology Conference, Belgium.

Hartshorne, H. and May, M.A. (1928) *Studies in the Nature of Character: Studies in Deceit (Vol. 1); Studies in Self-Control (Vol. 2); Studies in the Organisation of Character (Vol. 3)*. New York: Macmillan.

Haslam, N. (1992) Temperament and the transitional object. *Child Psychiatry and Human Development*, 22 (4), 237–248.

Hayes, L. and Schauble, L. (1978) Nothing to fear but fear itself: experiences from Sesame Street. *Fernsehen und Bildung*, 12 (1–2), 58–71.

Heber, R., Garber, H., Harrington, S., Hoffman, C. and Falender, C. (1972) *Rehabilitation of Families at Risk for Mental Retardation: Progress Report*. University of Wisconsin: Rehabilitation Research and Training Centre in Mental Retardation.

Held, R. and Hein, A. (1963) Movement-produced stimulation in the development of visually guided behaviour. *Journal of Comparative and Physiological Psychology*, 56, 607–613.

Hembree, R. (1988) Correlates, causes, effects and treatment of test anxiety. *Review of Educational Research*, 58, 47–77.

Hepper, P.G. (1991) An examination of foetal learning before and after birth. *Irish Journal of Psychology*, 12, 95–107.

Hill, K.P. (1980) *Decision-Making in Child Abuse Cases: Retrospective Study of 200 Cases of Non-Accidental Injury to Children in Nottinghamshire*. Unpublished thesis, CCETSW: London.

Hinchcliffe, S.A., Van Velzen, D., Howard, O.V., Lynch, M.R. and Sargent, P.H. (1992) Effect of intra-uterine growth retardation on the development of renal nephrons. *British Journal of Obstetrics and Gynaecology*, 99, 296–301.

Hobson, R.P. (1986) The autistic child's appraisal of expressions of emotion. *Journal of Childhood Psychology and Psychiatry*, 27, 321–342.

Hodges, J. and Tizard, B. (1989) Social and family relationships of ex-institutional adolescents. *Journal of Child Psychology and Psychiatry*, 30 (1), 77–97.

Hoffman, L.W. (1989) Effects of maternal employment in the two-parent family. *American Psychologist*, 44, 283–292.

Hoffman, M.L. (1970) Moral development. In Mussen, P.H. (ed) *Carmichael's Manual of Child Psychology* (Vol. 2). New York: Wiley.

Horn, J.M. (1983) The Texas adoption project: adopted children and their intellectual resemblance to biological and adoptive parents. *Child Development*, 54, 268–275.

Hovland, C.I., Janis, I.L. and Kelley, H.H. (1953) *Communication and Persuasion*. New Haven: Yale University Press.

Howe, M.J.A. (1990) *Sense and Nonsense about Hothouse Children*. Leicester: BPS Books.

Howes, C. (1990) Can the age of entry into child care and the quality of child care predict adjustment in kindergarten? *Developmental Psychology*, 26, 292–303.

Hutt, C. (1966) Exploration and play in children. *Symposia of the Zoological Society of London*, 18, 61–81.

Hutt, C. and Bhavnani, R. (1972) Predictions from play. *Nature*, 237, 171–172.

Jacklin, C.N. and Maccoby, E.E. (1978) Social behaviour at thirty-three months in same-sex and mixed-sex dyads. *Child Development*, 49, 557–569.

Jahoda, G. (1954) A note on Ashanti names and their relationship to personality. *British Journal of Psychology*, 45, 192–195.

Jalongo, M.R. (1987) Do security blankets belong in pre-school? *Young Children*, 42 (3), 3–8.

James, W. (1890) *Principles of Psychology*. New York: Holt.

Janis, I.L. (1984) The patient as decision maker. In Gentry, W.D. (ed) *Handbook of Behavioural Medicine*. New York: Guilford.

Jensen, A.R. (1969) How much can we boost IQ and scholastic achievement? *Harvard Educational Review*, 39, 1–123.

Jiao, S., Guiping, J. and Jing, Q. (1986) Comparative study of behavioural qualities of only children and sibling children. *Child Development*, 57 (2), 357–361.

Johnson, M.B. and Torres, L. (1994) Bonding and contested parental rights termination: The New Jersey 'JC' case, part 1. *American Journal of Forensic Psychology*, 12 (2), 37–57.

Jones, D.N., Pickett, J., Oates, M.R. and Barbor, P. (1987) *Understanding Child Abuse* (2nd edition). London: Macmillan.

Julien, R.M. (1992) *A Primer of Drug Action* (6th edition). New York: W.H. Freeman & Co.

Kagan, J. (1972) Do infants think? *Scientific American*, 226, 74–82.

Kagan, J., Kearsley, R.B. and Zelazo, P.R. (1980) *Infancy: Its Place in Human Development*. Cambridge, Mass.: Harvard University Press.

Kallmann, F.J. (1952) Twin and sibship study of overt male homosexuality. *American Journal of Human Genetics*, 4, 136–146.

Kamarck, T.W., Manuck, S.B. and Jennings, J.R. (1990) Social support reduces cardiovascular reactivity to psychological challenge: a laboratory model. *Psychosomatic Medicine*, 52, 42–58.

Kanner, L. (1943) Autistic disturbances of affective contact. *Nervous Child*, 2, 217–250.

Keith, T.Z., Reimers, T.M., Fehrmann, P.G., Pottsbaum, S.M. and Aubey, L.W. (1986) Parental involvement, homework and TV time: direct and indirect effects on high school achievement. *Journal of Educational Psychology*, 78, 373–380.

Kendler, K.S. (1983) Overview: a current perspective on twin studies of schizophrenia. *American Journal of Psychiatry*, 140, 1413–1425.

Kiecolt-Glaser, J.K., Garner, W., Speicher, C.E., Penn, G.M., Holliday, J. and Glaser, R.(1984) Psychosocial modifiers of immunocompetence in medical students. *Psychosomatic Medicine*, 46, 7–14.

Kirk, S.A. (1958) *Early Education of the Mentally Retarded*. Urbana, Ill: University of Illinois Press.

Klaus, M.H. and Kennell, J.H. (1976) *Maternal-Infant Bonding*. St. Louis: Mosby.

Kohlberg, L. (1969) Stage and sequence: the cognitive-developmental approach to socialisation. In Goslin, D.A. (ed) *Handbook of Socialisation Theory and Practice*. Skokie, Ill: Rand McNally.

Koluchova, J. (1972) Severe deprivation in twins: a case study. *Journal of Child Psychology and Psychiatry*, 13, 107–114.

Koluchova, J. (1976) The further development of twins after severe and prolonged deprivation: a second report. *Journal of Child Psychology and Psychiatry*, 17, 181–188.

Koluchova, J. (1991) Severely deprived twins after twenty-two years' observation. *Studia Psychologica*, 33, 23–28.

Kuhn, H.H. (1960) Self attitudes by age, sex and professional training. *Sociological Quarterly*, 1, 39–55.

Kunkel, J.H. (1985) Vivaldi in Venice: a historical test of psychological propositions. *Psychological Record*, 35, 445–457.

Labov, W. (1970) The logic of non-standard English. In Williams, F. (ed) *Language and Poverty*. Chicago: Markham.

Ladd, G.W. (1990) Having friends, keeping friends, making friends and being liked by peers in the classroom: predictors of children's early school adjustment. *Child*

*Development*, 61, 1081–1100.

Lamb, M.E. (1981) The development of father-infant relationships. In Lamb, M.E. (ed) *The Role of the Father in Child Development*. New York: Wiley.

Lamb, M.E. and Roopnarine, J.L. (1979) Peer influences on sex-role development in pre-schoolers. *Child Development*, 50, 1219–1222.

Langlois, J.H., Roggman, L.A. and Rieser-Danner, L.A. (1990) Infants' differential social responses to attractive and unattractive faces. *Developmental Psychology*, 27, 79–84.

LaPouse, R. and Monk, M. (1959) Fears and worries in a representative sample of children. *American Journal of Orthopsychiatry*, 29, 803–818.

Lazar, I. and Darlington, R. (1982) Lasting effects of early education: a report from the Consortium for Longitudinal Studies. *Monographs of the Society for Research in Child Development*, 47, nos. 2–3.

LeFrançois, G.L. (1983) *Of Children* (4th edition). Belmont, Calif: Wadsworth.

Lenneberg, E.H. (1967) *The Biological Foundations of Language*. New York: Wiley.

Lepper, M.R., Greene, D. and Nisbett, R.E. (1973) Undermining children's intrinsic interest with extrinsic reward: a test of the overjustification hypothesis. *Journal of Personality and Social Psychology*, 28, 129–137.

LeVay, S. (1991) A difference in hypothalamic structure between heterosexual and homosexual men. *Science*, 254, 1034–1037.

Lewis, M. and Brooks-Gunn, J. (1979) *Social Cognition and the Acquisition of Self*. New York: Plenum.

Litt, C. (1986) Theories of transitional object attachment: an overview. *International Journal of Behavioural Development*, 9, 383–399.

Logan , B. (1987) Teaching the unborn: precept and practice. *Pre- and Peri-Natal Psychology Journal*, 2(1), 9–24.

Lorenz, K. (1935) Der Kumpan in der Umwelt des Vogels. *Journal of Ornithology*, 83, 137-213. Published in English (1937) The companion in the bird's world. *Auk*, 54, 245–73.

Lorenz, K.Z. (1952) *King Solomon's Ring: New Light on Animal Ways*. New York: Thomas Y. Crowell.

Lorenz, K.Z. (1966) *On Aggression*. New York:

Harcourt, Brace & World.

Lovelace, V. (1990) Sesame Street as a continuing experiment. Special Issue: children's learning from television: research and development at the Children's Television Workshop. *Educational Technology Research and Development*, 38 (4), 17–24.

Lyle, J. and Hoffman, H.R. (1972) Children's use of television and other media. In Rubenstein, E.H., Comstock, G.A. and Murray, J.P. (eds) *Television in Day-to-Day Life: Patterns of Use*, Washington, DC: US Government Printing Office.

Lynch, M. and Roberts, J. (1982) *Consequences of Child Abuse*. London: Academic Press.

Lynn, R. (1986) The rise of national intelligence: evidence from Britain, Japan and the USA. *Personality and Individual Differences*, 7 (1), 23–32

Maccoby, E.E. and Jacklin, C.N. (1974) *The Psychology of Sex Differences*. Stanford, Calif: Stanford University Press.

MacFarlane, A. (1975) Olfaction in the development of social preferences in the human neonate. *Parent-Infant Interaction Ciba Foundation Symposium*, 33, New York: Elsevier.

MacFarlane, A. (1977) *The Psychology of Childbirth*. Cambridge, Mass: Harvard University Press.

Manstead, A.R. and McCulloch, C. (1981) Sex-role stereotyping in British television adverts. *British Journal of Social Psychology*, 20, 171–180.

Maras, P. (1995) 'What's 'e doing here, then?' *The Psychologist*, 8 (9), 410–411

Mason, M.K. (1942) Learning to speak after six and one-half years silence. *Journal of Speech Disorders*, 7, 295–304.

Mattes, J.A. and Gittelman, R. (1981) Effects of artificial food colorings in children with hyperactive symptoms: a critical review and results of a controlled study. *Archives of General Psychiatry*, 38 (6), 714–718.

Mayall, B. and Petrie, P. (1983) *Childminding and Day Nurseries: What Kind of Care?* London: Heinemann Educational Books.

McFadyen, A. (1994) *Special-Care Babies and their Developing Relationships*. London: Routledge.

McGarrigle, J. and Donaldson, M. (1974) Conservation accidents. *Cognition*, 3, 341–350.

McIlveen, R., Long, M. and Curtis, A. (1994) *Talking Points in Psychology*. London: Hodder & Stoughton.

McKeachie, W.J. (1984) Does anxiety disrupt poor information processing or does poor information processing lead to anxiety? *International Review of Applied Psychology*, 33,187–203.

Mead, M. (1935) *Sex and Temperament in Three Primitive Societies*. New York: Morrow.

Mead, M. (1972) *Blackberry Winter*. New York: William Morrow.

Mednick, S.A. & Hutchings, B. (1978) Genetic and psychophysiological factors in asocial behaviour. *Journal of the American Academy of Child Psychiatry*, 17, 209.

Miller, N. and Maruyama, G. (1976) Ordinal position and peer popularity. *Journal of Personality and Social Psychology*, 33, 123-31.

Minde, K., Goldberg, S., Perrotta, M., Washington, J., Lojkasek, M., Carter, C. and Parker, K. (1989) Continuities and discontinuities in the development of sixty-four very small premature infants to four years of age. *Journal of Child Psychology and Psychiatry*, 30, 391–404.

Mitchell, D.E., Freeman, R.D., Millodot, M. and Haegerstrom, G. (1973) Meridional amblyopia: evidence for modification of the human visual system by early visual experience. *Vision Research*, 13, 535–558.

Money, J. and Ehrhardt, A.A. (1972) *Man and Woman, Boy and Girl*. Baltimore, Md: Johns Hopkins University Press.

Mulac, A., Bradoc, J.J. and Mann, S.K. Male/female language differences and attributional consequences in children's television. *Human Communication Research*, 11 (4), 481–506.

Mussen, P.H., Conger, J.J., Kagan, J. and Huston, A.C. (1984) *Child Development and Personality*. New York: Harper & Row.

Mutz, D., Roberts, D.F. and Van Vuuren, D.P. (1993) Reconsidering the displacement hypothesis: television's influence on children's time use. *Communication Research*, 20 (1), 51–75.

Nelson, J. and Aboud, F.E. (1985) The resolution of social conflict among friends. *Child Development*, 56, 1009–1017.

Nelson, K. (1973) Structure and strategy in learning to talk. *Monographs for the Society for Research in Child Development*, 38 (serial no. 149).

Newman, F. and Holzman, L. (1993) *Lev Vygotsky*. London: Routledge.

Newport, E. (1990) Maturational constraints on language learning, *Cognitive Science*, 14, 11–28.

Newson, E. (1994) Video violence and the protection of children. *The Psychologist*, 7(6), 272–274.

Newson, J. and Newson, E. (1970) Four years old in an urban community, Harmondsworth: Penguin.

Nobles, W.W. (1976) Extended self: rethinking the so-called Negro self-concept. *Journal of Black Psychology*, 2, 99–105.

Oden, S. and Asher, S.R. (1977) Coaching children in social skills for friendship making. *Child Development*, 48, 495–506.

Olweus, D. (1989) Bully/victim problems among schoolchildren: basic facts and effects of a school-based intervention program. In Rubin, K. and. Pepler, D (eds) *The Development and Treatment of Childhood Aggression*. Hillsdale, N.J.: Erlbaum.

OPCS (1992) *Infant Feeding*. London: HMSO.

OPCS (1995) Infant and perinatal mortality social and biological factors, 1993. OPCS Monitor, DH3 95/1.

Padilla, M.L. and Landreth, G.L. (1989) Latchkey children: a review of the literature. *Child Welfare*, 68 (4), 445–454.

Parten, M.B. (1932) Social participation among pre-school children. *Journal of Abnormal and Social Psychology*, 27, 243–267.

Patterson, G.R., Stoolmiller, M. and Skinner, M.L. (1991) Family, school and behavioural antecedents to early adolescent involvement with antisocial peers. *Developmental Psychology*, 27, 172–180.

Pedersen, N.L., Plomin, R., Nesselroade, J.R. and McClearn, G.E. (1992) A quantitative genetic analysis of cognitive abilities during the second half of the life span. *Psychological Science*, 3, 347–353.

Pennebaker, J.W., Hendler, C.S., Durrett, M.E. and Richards, P. (1981) Social factors influencing absenteeism due to illness in nursery school children. *Child Development*, 52, 692–700.

Phelps, L. and Branyan, J. (1990) Academic achievement and non-verbal intelligence in public school hearing-impaired children. *Psychology in the Schools*, 27, 210–217.

Piaget, J. (1926) *The Language and Thought of the Child*. New York: Harcourt Brace Jovanovich.

Piaget, J. (1932) *The Moral Judgement of the Child.* Harmondsworth: Penguin.

Piaget, J. (1950) *The Psychology of Intelligence.* San Diego: Harcourt Brace Jovanovich.

Piaget, J. (1951) *Play, Dreams and Imitation in Childhood.* London: Routledge & Kegan Paul.

Piaget, J. (1954) *The Construction of Reality in the Child.* New York: Basic Books.

Piaget, J. (1970) Piaget's theory. In Mussen, P.H. (ed) *Carmichael's Manual of Child Psychology.* (Vol. 1). New York: Wiley.

Piliavin, I.M., Rodin, J. and Piliavin, J.A. (1969) Good Samaritanism: an underground phenomenon. *Journal of Personality and Social Psychology*, 13, 1200–1213.

Pinker, S. (1994) *The Language Instinct.* New York: William Morrow and Co., Inc.

Polit, D.F. and Falbo, T. (1988) The intellectual achievement of only children. *Journal of Biosocial Science*, 20 (3), 275–285.

Porter, R.H., Cernoch, J.M. and McLaughlin, F.H. (1983) Maternal recognition of neonates through olfactory cues. *Physiology and Behaviour*, 30, 151–154.

Pringle, M.L.K. and Bossio, V. (1960) Early prolonged separations and emotional adjustment. *Journal of Child Psychology and Psychiatry*, 1, 37–48.

Readdick, C.A. (1987) Schools for the American nanny: training in-home child-care specialists. *Young Children*, 42 (4), 72–79.

Resnick, M.B., Stralka, K., Carter, R.L., Ariet, M., Bucciarelli, R.L., Furlough, R.B., Evans, J.H., Cuman, J.S. and Ausbon, W.W. (1990) Effects of birth-weight and sociodemographic factors on mental development of neonate intensive-care survivors. *American Journal of Obstetrics and Gynaecology*, 162, 374–378.

Richards, M. (1995) Family relations. *The Psychologist*, 8 (2), 70–72.

Riley, A. (1995) Infant anorexia. *Independent on Sunday*, 8 October.

Ringness, T.A. (1961) Self-concept of children of low, average and high intelligence. *American Journal of Mental Deficiency*, 65, 453–461.

Robertson, J. and Robertson, J. (1968) Young children in brief separation: a fresh look. *Psychoanalytic Study of the Child*, 26, 264–315.

Rogan, W.J. and Gladen, B.C. (1993) Breastfeeding and cognitive development.

*Early Human Development*, 31 (3),181–193.

Rogers, C.R. (1961) *On Becoming a Person.* Boston: Houghton Mifflin.

Rosch, E. (1978) Principles of categorization. In Rosch, E. and Lloyd, B. (eds) *Cognition and Categorization*, Hillsdale, NJ: Erlbaum.

Rose, S.A. and Blank, M. (1974) The potency of context in childrens' cognition: an illustration through conservation. *Child Development*, 45, 499–502.

Rosenhan, D.L. (1970) The natural socialisation of altruistic autonomy. In Macaulay, J.L. and Berkowitz, L. (eds) *Altruism and Helping Behaviour.* New York: Academic Press.

Rosenhan, D.L. and Seligman, M.E.P. (1989) *Abnormal Psychology* (2nd edition). London: Norton.

Rosenstock, I.M. (1966) Why people use health services. *Millbank Memorial Fund Quarterly*, 44, 94–127.

Rutter, M. (1981) *Maternal Deprivation Reassessed* (2nd edition). Harmondsworth, Middlesex: Penguin.

Rymer, R. (1993) *Genie: Escape from a Silent Childhood.* London: Michael Joseph.

Sachs, J., Bard, B. and Johnson, M.L. (1981) Language learning with restricted input: case studies of two hearing children of deaf parents. *Applied Psycholinguistics*, 2, 33–54.

Sacks, O. (1995) *An Anthropologist in Mars.* Basingstoke, Hants: Pan Macmillan.

Sameroff, A.J., Seifer, R., Baldwin, A. and Baldwin, C. (1993) Stability of intelligence from pre-school to adolescence: the influence of social and family risk factors. *Child Development*, 64, 80–97.

Sameroff, A.J., Seifer, R., Barocas, R., Zax, M. and Greenspan, S. (1987) Intelligence quotient scores of four-year-old children: social-environmental risk factors. *Paediatrics*, 79, 343–350.

Samuel, J. and Bryant, P. (1984) Asking only one question in the conservation experiment. *Journal of Child Psychology and Psychiatry*, 25 (2), 315–318.

Savage-Rumbaugh, E.S. (1991) Language learning in the bonobo: how and why they learn. In Krasnegor, N.A., Rumbaugh, D.M., Schiefelbusch, R.L. and Studdert-Kennedy, M. (eds) *Biological and Behavioural Determinants of Language Development.* Hillsdale, N.J.: Lawrence Erlbaum Associates, Inc.

Schachter, S. (1959) *The Psychology of Affiliation.* Stanford, Calif: Stanford University Press.

Schaffer, H.R. and Emerson, P.E. (1964) The development of social attachments in infancy. *Monographs of the Society for Research in Child Development,* 29 (3, Serial No. 94).

Schinke, S.P., Schilling, R.F. II, Barth, R.P., Gilchrist, L.D. and Maxwell, J.S. (1986) Stress-management intervention to prevent family violence. *Journal of Family Violence,* 1, 13–26.

Schwarz , H.B., Albino, J.E. and Tedesco, L.A. (1983) Effects of psychological preparation on children hospitalised for dental operations. *Journal of Paediatrics,* 102 (4), 634–638.

Seligman, M.E.P. (1975) *Helplessness: On Depression, Development and Death.* San Francisco: W.H. Freeman.

Selman, R.L. (1980) *The Growth of Interpersonal Understanding.* Orlando, Fl: Academic Press.

Shaffer, D.R. (1993) *Developmental Psychology* (3rd edition). Pacific Grove, Calif: Brooks/Cole Publishing Co.

Shakespeare, R. (1975) *The Psychology of Handicap.* London: Methuen.

Shaw, M. (1986) Substitute parenting. In. Sluckin, W. and Herbert, M. (eds) *Parental Behaviour.* Oxford: Basil Blackwell.

Shea, J.D.C. (1981) Changes in interpersonal distances and categories of play behaviour in the early weeks of pre-school. *Developmental Psychology,* 17, 417–425.

Sherif, M., Harvey, O.J., White, B.J., Hood, W.R. and Sherif, C.W. (1961) *Intergroup Co-operation and Conflict: The Robbers Cave Experiment.* Norman, Oklahoma: University of Oklahoma Press.

Sherrington, R., Brynjolfsson, J., Petursson, H., Potter, M. Dudleston, K. Barraclough, B., Wasmuth J., Dobbs M. and Gurlung, H. (1988) Localisation of a susceptibility locus for schizophrenia on chromosome 5. *Nature,* 336, 164–167.

Shields, J. (1962) *Monozygotic Twins Brought up Apart and Brought up Together.* London: Oxford University Press.

Sinclair-de-Zwart, H. (1969) Developmental psycholinguistics. In Elkind, D. and Flavell, J. (eds) *Studies in Cognitive Development.* New York: Oxford University Press.

Singer, L.M., Brodzinsky, D.M., Ramsay, D., Steir, M. and Waters, E. (1985) Mother-infant attachments in adoptive families. *Child Development,* 56, 1543–1551.

Singleton, J. and Newport, E. (1993) *When Learners Surpass their Models: The Acquisition of Sign Language from Impoverished Input.* Unpublished manuscript, Department of Psychology, University of Rochester.

Skeels, H. (1966) Adult status of children with contrasting early life experiences: a follow-up study. *Monographs of Society for Research of Child Development,* 31 (3), whole issue.

Skeels, H. and Dye, H.B. (1939) A study of the effects of differential stimulation on mentally retarded children. *Proceedings and Addresses of the American Association on Mental Deficiency,* 44, 114–36.

Skinner, B.F. (1948) *Walden Two.* New York: Macmillan.

Skinner, B.F. (1957) *Verbal Behaviour.* New York: Appleton Century Crofts.

Skodak, M. and Skeels, H. (1949) A final follow-up study of 100 adopted children. *Journal of Genetic Psychology,* 75, 85–125.

Slade, A. (1987) A longitudinal study of maternal involvement and symbolic play during the toddler period. *Child Development,* 58, 367–375.

Smilansky, S. (1968) *The Effects of Sociodramatic Play on Disadvantaged Schoolchildren.* New York: Wiley.

Smith, C. and Lloyd, B. (1978) Maternal behaviour and perceived sex of infant: revisited. *Child Development,* 49, 1263–1265.

Smith, P.K. and Connolly, K.J. (1980) *The Ecology of Pre-school Behaviour.* Cambridge and New York: Cambridge University Press.

Smith, P.K. and Cowie, H. (1991) *Understanding Children's Development.* Oxford: Blackwell.

Smith, P.K. and Daglish, L. (1977) Sex differences in parent and infant behaviour in the home. *Child Development,* 48, 1250–1254.

Spencer, H. (1873) *Principles of Psychology.* New York: Appleton.

Spitz, R.A. and Wolf, K.M. (1946) Anaclitic depression. *Psychoanalytic Study of the Child,* 2, 313–342.

Stewart, R.B. (1983) Sibling attachment relationships: child-infant interactions in the Strange Situation. *Developmental Psychology,* 19, 192–199.

Tait, P.E. (1990) The attainment of conservation by Chinese and Indian children. *Journal of Visual Impairment and*

Blindness, 84, 380–382.

Takahashi, K. (1990) Are the key assumptions of the Strange Situation procedure universal? A view from Japanese research. *Human Development*, 33, 23–30.

Teti, D.M. and Ablard, K.E. (1989) Security of attachment and infant-sibling relationships: a laboratory study. *Child Development*, 60, 1519–1528.

Thomas, A. and Chess, S. (1986) The New York Longitudinal study: from infancy to early life. In Plomin, R. and Dunn, J. (eds) *The Study of Temperament: Changes, Continuities and Challenges*. Hillsdale, N.J.: Erlbaum.

Thomas, A, Chess, S. and Birch, H.G. (1970) The origin of personality. *Scientific American*, 223, 102–109.

Thomas, C. (1995) Social context and human development. *The Psychologist*, 8 (9), 407–409.

Tinbergen, N. (1952) The curious behaviour of the stickleback. *Scientific American*, 187 (6), 22–26.

Tinsley, B.J. and Parke, R.D. (1984) Grandparents as support and socialisation agents. In Lewis, M. (ed) *Beyond the Dyad*. New York: Plenum.

Tizard, B. (1979) Language at home and at school. In Cazden, C.B. and Harvey, D. (eds) *Language in Early Childhood Education*. Washington, DC: National Association for the Education of Young Children.

Tizard, B. and Hodges, J. (1978) The effect of early institutional rearing on the development of eight-year-old children. *Journal of Child Psychology and Psychiatry*, 19, 99–118.

Tizard, B. and Rees, J. (1975) A comparison of the effects of adoption, restoration to the natural mother and continued institutionalisation on the cognitive development of four-year-old children. *Child Development*, 45, 92–99.

Topping, K. and Wolfendale, S. (eds) (1985) *Parental Involvement in Children's Reading*. London: Croom Helm.

Trehub, S.E. (1985) Auditory pattern perception in infancy. In Trehub, S.E. and Schneider, B. (eds) *Advances in the Study of Communication and Affect Vol. 10, Auditory Development in Infancy*. New York: Plenum.

US Surgeon General's Report, United States Department of Health and Human Services (1986) *The Health Consequences of Involuntary Smoking: A Report of the Surgeon General* (publication no. CDC 87–8398). Washington, DC: US Government Printing Office.

Vandell, D.L. and Ramanan, J. (1991) Children of the National Longitudinal Survey of Youth: Choices in after-school care and child development. *Developmental Psychology*, 27 (4), 637–643.

Varley, C. (1984) Diet and the behavior of children with attention-deficit disorder. *Journal of the American Academy of Child Psychiatry*, 23 (2), 182–185.

Vines, G. (1992) Obscure origins of desire. *New Scientist*, 28 November (supplement), 2–8.

Vines, G. (1994) Gene tests: the parents' dilemma. *New Scientist*, 12 November, 40–44.

Vygotsky, L.S. (1987) The development of scientific concepts in childhood. In Rieber, R.W. and Carton, A.S. (eds) *The Collected Works of L.S. Vygotsky*, Vol. 1. New York: Plenum Press.

Wallman, J. (1992) *Aping Language*. Cambridge: Cambridge University Press.

Warren, J. (1995) *Supporting Breastfeeding in your Primary Health Care Team*. Edinburgh: The Scottish Office.

Weatherly, D. (1961) Anti-Semitism and expression of fantasy aggression. *Journal of Abnormal and Social Psychology*, 62, 454–457.

Weinberg, R.S., Gould, D. and Jackson, A. (1979) Expectations and performance: an empirical test of Bandura's self-efficacy theory. *Journal of Sport Psychology*, 1, 320–331.

Wender, P.H., Kety, S.S., Rosenthal, D., Schulsinger, F., Ortmann, J. and Lunde, I (1974) Psychiatric disorders in the biological and adoptive families of adopted individuals with affective disorders. *Archives of General Psychiatry*, 30, 121–728.

White, B.L. and Held, R. (1966) Plasticity of sensorimotor development. In Rosenblith, J.F. and Allensmith, W. (eds) *The Causes of Behaviour* (2nd edition). Boston: Allyn & Bacon.

Whorf, B.L. (1956) *Language, Thought and Reality*. Cambridge, Mass.: MIT Press.

Widdowson, E.M. (1951) Mental contentment and physical growth. *Lancet*, 1, 1316–1318,

Wiegman, O., Kuttschreuter, M. and Baarda, B. (1992) A longitudinal study of the effects of television viewing on aggressive and prosocial behaviours. *British Journal of Social Psychology*, 31, 147–164.

Williams, J.H. (1987) *Psychology of Women* (3rd edition). London: Norton & Co.

Williams, T.M. (1985) Implications of a natural experiment in the developed world for research on television in the developing world. Special Issue: television in the developing world. *Journal of Cross-Cultural Psychology*, 16(3), 263–287.

Winnicott, D.W. (1953) Transitional objects and transitional phenomena. *International Journal of Psychoanalysis*, 34, 89–97.

Yates, C. and Smith, P.K. (1989) Bullying in two English comprehensive schools. In Roland, E. and Munthe, E. (eds) *Bullying: an International Perspective*. London: David Fulton.

Zajonc, R.B. and Markus, G.B. (1975) Birth order and intellectual development. *Psychological Review*, 82, 74–88.

Zigler, E. and Muenchow, S. (1992) *Head Start: the inside story of America's most successful educational experiment*. New York: Basic Books.

# Index

# Picture credits

The author and publisher would like to thank the following copyright holders for their permission to use material in this book:

**Associated Press/Topham** for Figure 13.1 (p. 166); **BabyPlus UK Limited** for Figure 1.4 (p. 14); **Bubbles/L.J. Thurston** for Figure 6.1 (p. 83) and **Bubbles/P. Sylent** for Figure 9.1 (p. 122); **The Department of Health** for Figure 1.1 (p. 7); **Harcourt, Brace and Company Limited** for Figure 1.2 (p. 9) from Becker, M.H. and Rosenstock, I.M. (1984) 'Compliance with medical advice', Steptoe, A. and Matthews, A. (eds) *Health Care and Human Behaviour*; **The Health Education Authority** for Figure 1.3 (p. 12); **ParentLink** for Figure 7.1 (p. 101); **The Independent** for extract (pp 167–8) from 'The Children Who Hate to be Loved' by Angela Neustatter; **Joseph Rountree Foundation** for Figure 8.2 (p. 113); **Scientific American**, for Figure 2.1 from Robert L. Fantz, 'The origin of form perception', *Scientific American*, 204(5), May 1961, copyright © Scientific American; **Topham Picture Source** for Figure 12.1 (p. 162); **United Media International Syndicate** for Figure 3.1 (p. 38) PEANUTS © 1996 United Features Syndicate, Inc, reprinted by permission.

Every effort has been made to obtain necessary permission with reference to copyright material. The publishers apologise if inadvertently any sources remain unacknowledged and will be glad to make the necessary arrangements at the earliest opportunity.

**Further titles in the *Applying Psychology to...* series are available from Hodder & Stoughton.**

0 340 64756 6 **Applying Psychology to Health** by Philip Banyard £6.99
0 340 64392 7 **Applying Psychology to Early Child Development** £6.99
0 340 64758 2 **Applying Psychology to Organisations** by Sheila Hayward £5.99
0 340 64329 3 **Applying Psychology to Education** by Martyn Long £5.99

For full details of this series, please call Dan Addelman at Hodder & Stoughton on 0171 873 6272. Look out for forthcoming *Applying Psychology to...* titles, including Sport, the Environment and the Legal World.

*All Hodder & Stoughton books are available from your local bookshop or can be ordered direct from the publisher. Just tick the titles you want and fill in the form below. Prices and availability subject to change without notice.*

To: Hodder & Stoughton Ltd, Cash Sales Department, Bookpoint, 39 Milton Park, Abingdon, Oxon, OX14 4TD. If you have a credit card you may order by telephone - 01235 400471.

Please enclose a cheque or postal order made payable to Bookpoint Ltd to the value of the cover price and allow the following for postage and packing:
UK and BFPO: £1.00 for the first book, 50p for the second book and 30p for each additional book ordered up to a maximum charge of £3.00.
OVERSEAS & EIRE: £2.00 for the first book, £1.00 for the second book and 50p for each additional book.

Name: _____

Address: _____

_____

If you would prefer to pay by credit card, please complete:

Please debit my Visa/Mastercard/Diner's Card/ American Express (delete as appropriate)

card no: ☐☐☐☐ ☐☐☐☐ ☐☐☐☐ ☐☐☐☐

Signature _____ Expiry date _____ / _____